IN DEFENSE OF THE ALIEN

Volume XIX

*Critical Analysis of Practical Implications of
Newly Proposed Legislation – Welfare Reform:
What Benefits for Immigrants? – Redefining the Roles of
Local and State Government in Immigration Policy –
Refugee Resettlement and Asylum Reform*

IN DEFENSE OF THE ALIEN

Volume XIX

Critical Analysis of Practical Implications of
Newly Proposed Legislation – Welfare Reform:
What Benefits for Immigrants? – Redefining the Roles of
Local and State Government in Immigration Policy –
Refugee Resettlement and Asylum Reform

Proceedings of the 1996 Annual National Legal Conference
on Immigration and Refugee Policy

Edited by Lydio F. Tomasi

1997
Center for Migration Studies
New York

CMS is an educational nonprofit institute founded in New York in 1964 committed to encourage and facilitate the study of sociodemographic, economic, historical, political, legislative and pastoral aspects of human migration and refugee movements. CMS organizes an annual national legal conference on immigration and refugee policy, the proceedings of which are published in a volume series entitled **IN DEFENSE OF THE ALIEN**. This text represents the Nineteenth Volume of that series.

IN DEFENSE OF THE ALIEN
VOLUME XIX

*Critical Analysis of Practical Implications of Newly Proposed Legislation –
Welfare Reform: What Benefits for Immigrants? – Redefining the Roles of Local and
State Government in Immigration Policy – Refugee Resettlement and Asylum Reform*

First Edition

Copyright © 1997 by

The Center for Migration Studies of New York, Inc.
209 Flagg Place
Staten Island, New York 10304-1199

ISSN 0275-634X; v. 19
ISBN 0-934733-95-3

Printed in the United States of America

CONTENTS

Introduction

The 1996 National Legal Conference on Immigration and Refugee Policy was held at the time when Washington, DC, was the place of many gatherings dealing with immigration issues and the Senate Judiciary Committee was completing its mark-up of the Immigration Reform bill.

Both restrictionists and free-market-oriented individuals had been marshalling statistics to support their positions on border control, displacement of American workers, public assistance, and family reunification. These and other issues were still muddied as the congressional and public debates on immigration reform showed. The best hope for the *Wall Street Journal* that week was that the Lamar and Simpson bills would fall of their own weight and that the issue could be taken up by another Congress where cooler heads would prevail. Michael Teitalbaum, a member of the U.S. Commission on Immigration and Reform, lamented in *The New York Times* that same week that there were too many engineers and too few jobs, while A. M. Rosenthal stated that intellectually, idealistically and spiritually, the legislation would be for America an agent of desiccation. Insidious liquid metaphors for immigration, noted Timothy Christenfeld, are consistently used in the United States. Thus, for example, immigration is a flow, a flood, a tide, a wave, an influx, a stream, or, after restriction, a trickle; immigrants are drained from their homelands, they wash up like "wretched refuse" on the shores; the country is inundated, swamped, submerged, engulfed, awash. Metaphors of pollution and disease, instead, prevail in Europe.

Indeed, much is still unknown about immigration. Following its nineteen-year scholarly tradition, the CMS Conference presented a critical analysis of practical implications of newly proposed legislation, inventoried major shifts in redefining the roles of local and state government in immigration policy, and assessed the effects of reduced refugee resettlement in the United States and of proposed changes in asylum reform. Also, the Conference panelists did not neglect that the heart of the immigration debate is not about facts but about values, echoing Michael J. Sanders' concern about the public philosophy by which we live and the conception of citizenship that informs our political debates.

The first part of the Conference proceedings focuses on major legislative initiatives on immigration that were then pending in both Houses of Congress, including bills sponsored by Representative Lamar Smith (H.R. 2162) and Senator Alan Simpson (S. 1394). They provide an insider's view of content, likely scenarios on reconciling differences, and timing of action on the legislation. Presentations by an interdisciplinary group of experts assess the effects of the likely danger in immigration law on four areas of continued interest and contention: family-based immigration; employment-related immigration and nonimmigrant admission for employment; due process concerns; and employer sanctions and verification systems.

The United States was at a historic juncture in immigration policy in 1996. Of the two bills debated in the House of Representatives and the Senate – and representing the most significant immigration legislation since 1965 when the national origins quota system was abolished – one was control of illegal migration and the other was reform of the legal immigration system. Because the threshold issue was whether these two subjects are integrally related or should be considered separately, proponents of generous legal immigration sought separation of the issues into two bills. The Senate Judiciary Committee voted by a 12–6 vote to separate the two issues and to have two bills. As expected, later the House voted in favor of separating legal and illegal immigration. Of course, the concern was that the desire to address illegal migration would cast the negative view on a fair and balanced deliberation of legal migration. The debates were accompanied by intensive lobbying – the traditional groups, ethnic organizations, voluntary agencies, religious organizations, civil libertarians. They were joined by new allies comprised of some of the new emerging ethnic organizations which have really coalesced in the last ten years of so: conservative libertarians, family values organizations and, in 1996, really remarkably potent efforts by the American business community and the high technology research-based companies.

The debate on *illegal* migration focused on enforcement, increased border patrol, increased emphasis on employer sanctions. Although interesting issues were raised particularly in regard to employer verification in terms of the enforcement area, perhaps the most significant issue has been the limitation of benefits, such as schooling for illegal migrants and other basic social benefits, *e.g.*, health care, and the imposition of harsh penalties on illegal aliens.

On the side of *legal* immigration reform, the driving concerns were reducing overall levels of immigration, limiting benefits to permanent residents, and protecting U.S. workers from foreign competition. The debate has been complicated by insufficient and conflicting economic data and immigrants' impact on the U.S. job market and the national economy.

Looking back at the history of immigration legislation, observed Austin T. Fragomen, it is kind of curious because each time immigration legislation is proposed the sponsor starts out thinking it is going to be fairly straightforward, that the problems are obvious, and that they are going to be addressed in a politically acceptable manner. Then, of course, the debate heats up and virtually every issue becomes controversial. In the final analysis the potential for politicians to antagonize groups greatly exceeds any potential to please groups.

Immigration issues loom large in attempts to alter the role and costs of the federal government in American life. These include welfare reform, medical care, government grants for education and research, and legal services.

In many of the proposals on these and similar social programs, the thrust is to limit participation by legal residents, including those with immigrant (permanent resident) status, migrant farmworkers, and undocumented immigrants. The second part of the proceedings reviews major proposals to change the scope, participation, and costs of social programs.

The passage of Proposition 187 in California and the move to greater use of block grants and state/local initiative on federally financed programs underscore the redefinition of the role of state and local government in immigration policy and programs.

Charles B. Keely noted that it was not very long ago that state and local governments had very little interest, or at least no clear discernable interest, in the issue of international migration. That changed, to a very large extent, with the institutionalization of state refugee coordinators and with their further obligations under the 1986 Immigration Act dealing with the SLIAG monies. Since then, there has been tremendous interest on the part of states concerning immigration, particularly concerning state-federal relations and the question of unfunded mandates and decisions, made at the federal level, with local impacts. It has come more recently in the issue of the states wishing to be reimbursed for costs connected with undocumented aliens and others because of federal policies – everything from the cost of incarceration to the excess cost of providing medical care. Part III inventories the major shifts that have taken place and that are being proposed for state/local government initiative and decision, as well as the implications for immigrants and for local populations generally.

The first section of Part IV focuses on the issue of refugee resettlement in the United States in the post-cold war era. Legislative proposals would reduce the authorized resettlement numbers. The implications of this for NGO resettlement agencies, state/local governments, and the refugees will be reviewed.

Part IV also includes an assessment of the effect of reduced resettlement on U.S. support for international refugee activities, including burden sharing and maintaining first asylum practices. The thorny issue of how to choose candidates for resettlement if the total is severely reduced is addressed, together with the future role of Temporary Protection.

The issue of refugee admission has been central in the immigration debate of 1996. The decision made just before the Conference to strike the cap on refugee admissions demonstrates – according to Elizabeth Ferris – the broad constituency that refugee resettlement has in this country rooted in the grass-roots and communities throughout the nation. She thinks that there has been a mobilization of effort by people working at the grassroots level to say, "Refugees have been good for our country." Part of the reason for this broad constituency has to do with decades of work in this area with a unique private/public partnership between voluntary agencies, community groups, government agencies and so on. As we look toward the future, in Elizabeth Ferris' opinion, the first challenge we face is how to insure that our resettlement program meets the humanitarian needs of millions of refugees, internally displaced people, and other victims of violence and conflict that we see in every region of the world. To what extent is our policy responding to the international needs? And to what extent is our policy on resettlement contributing to long-term durable solutions and, indeed, to an international refugee regime which is both humanitarian and based on the reality that resettlement will always serve only a very few people?

Related to this is the question of how we can work more effectively with the U.N. High Commissioner for Refugees in setting priorities, determining needs and looking at the cases of individuals who have no other solution but to be served by resettlement.

A third challenge we face is on the domestic level. According to Elizabeth Ferris, it is time we start looking very seriously at how we can make our structures and procedures more flexible to be able to better respond to immediate needs of different groups, more diverse groups, people with particular problems who have needs that may not always fit so conveniently into the way in which we have become accustomed to working. A challenge facing all of us is to think more creatively about how we can get out of our bureaucratic mindset, look at the needs of refugees, and see to what extent we can develop ways of meeting those needs more effectively.

Connected with refugee resettlement but having a separate dynamic is the topic of asylum reform. Like many Western democracies, the United States has experienced an upsurge in asylum applications and has reasonable concern about the possibilities of mass asylum flows, for which the government has been engaged in planning. Steps have already been taken to streamline asylum adjudication and to enter agreements about deciding which country should review asylum applications. Here, pointed out Sandra Lief Garrett, we shift our focus from "are immigrants good for America" to "what is the depth of our generosity and compassion as a nation to offer safety to a particular group of immigrants – those seeking asylum." According to Sandra Lief Garrett, in today's environment – reinvent and reform – the issue of asylum is now most often viewed as how do we stop abuses in the asylum system.

The second section of Part IV reviews these changes and proposed changes, noting similarities with analogous initiatives in industrial countries generally and taking stock of important issues like due process and the maintenance of asylum as an integral aspect of global stability.

We are most grateful to the more than 30 outstanding panelists who participated in the Conference as well as to the authors who contributed essays for this volume of proceedings. Special thanks go to all members of the Conference Program and Advisory Committees. We are also grateful to New York State Education Department/SUNY; Migrant Health Program, DHHS; the USCC Migration and Refugee Services; Church World Service, Immigration and Refugee Program; the Lutheran Immigration and Refugee Service; and the New York Association for New Americans for their special assistance and support.

– *Lydio F. Tomasi*
Center for Migration Studies

PART I

CRITICAL ANALYSIS OF PRACTICAL IMPLICATIONS OF NEWLY PROPOSED LEGISLATION

1

Immigration Reform and U.S. System of Employment or Skills-Based Immigration

MARIA ECHAVESTE
U.S. Department of Labor

I appreciate the opportunity to represent Secretary of Labor Reich at this important conference.

This is a timely, exciting, and very busy time for this conference – with both Houses of the Congress dealing with immigration reform legislation, and so much public discussion of the many complex issues. I am sure that all of you recognize that some of the current discussion is very well informed, some less so, and too much is nearly hysterical. We should all hope that this conference will make some small contribution to increasing the former and dampening the latter. You will be hearing from many extremely knowledgeable and well-informed presenters during this meeting.

I am honored to open the session, but do not intend nor presume to try to encompass or summarize the scope of their knowledge and insight. Rather, I would like to briefly summarize the Administration's views on the broader issues – upon which I am sure others will elaborate – and then focus primarily, as I know Secretary Reich would do, on what we see as the principle issues relating to our system of employment- or skills-based immigration.

Let me start by stating unequivocally that this Administration supports and wants reform of our immigration system which addresses both illegal immigration control and legal immigration issues. We have consistently supported the principles and framework for immigration system reform presented so thoughtfully by the Commission on Immigration Reform, and we have been working closely and continuously with both Houses of Congress in an effort to achieve balanced, intelligent reform. We are hopeful that this goal can be accomplished despite recent and ongoing developments which must be regarded with great concern.

First, many of the provisions of immigration reform legislation pending in both Houses of Congress advance the Administration's four-part strategy to control illegal immigration.

This strategy calls for:

- regaining control of our borders;

- removing the job magnet through enhanced worksite enforcement – of both employer sanctions and the Nation's minimum labor standards;

- aggressively pursuing the removal of criminal and other illegal migrants;

- securing from Congress the resources necessary to assist states with the costs of illegal immigration.

The Administration also endorses a framework of legal immigration reform – largely outlined by the Jordan Commission – that respects this nation's proud and generous immigration tradition while achieving a moderate reduction in overall admissions numbers to promote economic opportunities for all Americans. The Administration seeks – and has vigorously advocated – legal immigration reform that:

- promotes family reunification;

- protects U.S. workers from unfair competition while providing the nation's employers with appropriate access to international labor markets to promote our global competitiveness, robust economic growth, the creation of more and better jobs for U.S. workers, and increasing incomes and standards of living for our families;

- promotes naturalization to encourage full participation in the national community.

With respect to reforms to better control illegal migration, the pending bills in many ways parallel the Administration's legislative proposal – the Immigration Enforcement Improvements Act of 1995 (H.R. 1929) introduced by Congressman Berman last June.

The House and Senate bills contain many provisions that are similar or identical to the Administration's legislative proposal, enforcement initiatives and overall strategy, and in this regard have our full support.

But there are some areas where we have registered concerns, and it looks like there may be several more coming. For example, it is our view that:

- changes to the employment eligibility verification system should contain necessary antidiscrimination and privacy protections and be pilot-tested before any nationwide implementation;

- labor standards and immigration law enforcement in the workplace should be increased and better coordinated;

- increased penalties for and enforcement of employer sanctions should be paralleled by similar increases in the enforcement of and penalties for laws against immigration-related employment discrimination;

- any "intent" standard in the antidiscrimination provisions of the law will severely undermine discrimination protections and enforcement.

Turning to reform of our legal immigration system, let me briefly address family reunification and humanitarian immigration before focusing on issues relating to employment-based immigration.

As I said, the Administration has endorsed a framework of legal immigration reform that respects our immigration tradition while moderately reducing overall admissions to promote economic opportunities. Achieving these fundamental goals does not require many of the draconian, in some cases punitive, measures that are currently being considered.

The Administration believes that family-sponsored visas for adult children of U.S. citizens and unlimited visas for mothers and fathers of U.S. citizens must be maintained to protect our cherished principle of family reunification.

Similarly, we support an appropriate and equitable process to address the extensive waiting list of persons in the fourth preference backlog (brothers and sisters of U.S. citizens) that is consistent with our overall framework, priorities, and principles.

The Administration has presented a plan that reduces the overall level of legal immigration while preserving the ability of U.S. citizens to reunite with their family members.

Legal immigration reform legislation

- should not set artificial time limits on asylum application nor inflexible, statutory numerical limits on refugee admissions;

- should not limit immigration of U.S. citizens' parents based on their age or the families' financial ability to secure long-term care health insurance;
- should not call into question the full participation of any child in public elementary or secondary education, including preschool and school lunch programs;
- should not impose new eligibility and deeming provisions on current recipients of benefits, including the disabled who are exempted under current law, and to programs, such as Medicaid, where it could adversely affect public health and welfare;
- deeming provisions for benefit eligibility should not create an un-precedented, unconstitutional second class citizenship by extending beyond naturalization.

These are some of the important principles that we are advocating as the immigration reform debate unfolds – but there are others, equally important, that apply in the area of employment-based immigration, which is the Labor Department's principal concern.

Employment-based immigration to the United States is premised on two fundamental and complementary principles. Immigration for employment purposes should:

1) benefit the economy and our domestic workforce by enhancing the nation's global competitiveness, expanding the economy, and creating more and better job opportunities for U.S. workers; and

2) not disadvantage U.S. workers by denying employment opportunities, undermining – or restraining improvements in – wages or working conditions, or discouraging efforts to train and develop the skills of the domestic workforce.

Our immigration policy should provide a safety valve of access to foreign labor markets to meet skill demands to which the U.S. workforce cannot adequately respond in the short term. But our primary public policy response to skills mismatches due to changing technologies and economic restructuring must be made to prepare the U.S. workforce to meet new skill demands, thereby assuring opportunities to get and keep better jobs.

If we can accept these fundamental premises – and recognize that only a few years ago (in 1990) our immigration law was changed to nearly triple the number of employment-based immigrants admissible each year (from 54,000 to 140,000 including immediate family members) and tilt heavily toward favoring higher skilled immigrants (and nonimmigrants) – then we believe that the goal of reforming the current system of employment-based immigration –

both permanent and temporary – should be to give U.S. workers the fair opportunity they deserve to get and keep high-wage, high-skill jobs.

We believe that four principles are essential to achieving that goal:

1) protecting U.S. workers who already have high-wage/high-skill jobs from being replaced by foreign workers;

2) recruiting U.S. workers who have the skills for high-wage/high-skill jobs;

3) training U.S. workers who want high-wage/high-skill jobs;

4) giving U.S. workers a better shot at getting high-wage/high-skill jobs.

At the same time, our immigration policy should give U.S. employers appropriate access to the international labor market to satisfy skill demands that the domestic workforce cannot meet in sufficient supply or with sufficient speed.

It currently appears, however, that the legal immigration reform that will be considered by the Congress will embrace the business community's goal of increased access to the global labor market by moving away from these four important principles – even retreating significantly from already inadequate U.S. worker protections in current law.

Some critics of the Senate bill – which went a long way towards encompassing these four principles – have contended that the changes it would make in our immigration system would seriously impede business access to the "best and the brightest" in the international labor market and, thus, adversely affect U.S. global competitiveness, economic growth, and domestic job creation. Like the dire warnings of impending critical skill shortages that preceded the 1990 reform, we believe that these contentions are simply unfounded.

The Senate bill had already been modified to change certain provisions in earlier versions which gave some credence to such contentions – for example:

- eliminating the immigrant preference category for "outstanding professors and researchers" which has since been restored;

- raising the minimum experience required to qualify for various employment-based immigrant categories, since reduced to levels in current law;

- requiring that minimum experience requirements be satisfied through work outside the United States, since removed.

The Administration opposed the first and last of these original provisions, and urged the Senate to make these changes.

More importantly, the simple truth is that employers which use these employment-based immigrant programs to obtain access to uniquely-talented, very highly skilled foreign workers are, in fact, the "exception." They are competing for limited numbers of admissions with the large majority of employer-users which most commonly seek access to entry-level "professional" workers.

A common measure of skills, wage data for those jobs for which employers applied for employment-based immigrants in FY1994, show that, of the jobs requiring more than a four-year college degree, nearly three-quarters (71%) paid $40,000 or less in annual wages. On the other hand, only three percent of applications were for jobs paying more than $80,000.

Wage data from H-1B applications – for nonimmigrant temporary "professionals" – indicate that two-thirds (65%) involve positions paying $40,000 or less, and almost three-fourths (73.7%) involve jobs paying $50,000 or less.

If most businesses were truly hiring uniquely talented and qualified individuals for positions for which no U.S. workers possessed the requisite skills, one would surely expect the uniqueness of the skills and unusual demands of the position to be reflected in higher wages.

Employers' applications for physical and occupational therapists accounted for half (49.9%) of all H-1B jobs during FY1994, and computer-related occupations accounted for another quarter (23.9%) of the jobs. These data indicate that at least three out of four H-1B applications pertained to occupations that rarely require more formal education than a Master's degree and, in most cases, no more than a baccalaureate degree and minimal occupational experience.

Do not mistake me – these are good jobs, the kind that many U.S. workers would like and have, or could acquire, the skills to perform with excellence. But they are not the kinds of jobs that only foreign workers are equipped to fill.

Certainly, many employers use these immigration programs to hire the world's "best and brightest," a national interest that should be preserved and protected in law, but this is clearly the exception and not the rule.

We believe that the kinds of changes in employment-based immigration criteria and systems which the Administration has advocated could actually improve U.S. business access to the best and the brightest in the international labor market for several reasons.

First, the Administration supports implementing a recommendation of the Commission on Immigration Reform to substitute a market-based system for the selection of employment-based immigrants in place of the current bureaucratic "command and control" system that can take up to two years and thousands of dollars in lawyer's fees to navigate. The Commission's simple idea is to transfer these costs imposed on business from bureaucratic and legal expenditures to a truly useful and directly-related purpose – training U.S. workers for the kinds of jobs for which U.S. employers are seeking immigrant workers and, thus, reducing the need for foreign workers over the long term. The Administration strongly supports such reform that relies on market-based mechanisms.

The Administration endorses this training contribution idea, and the U.S. worker training fund which would be built from these contributions, as the principal mechanism for giving U.S. employers real incentive to undertake appropriate efforts to first recruit, retain, and retrain U.S. workers to meet their employment needs.

Employment-based immigration to fill skill shortages, as well as the temporary admission of skilled foreign workers, is sometimes unavoidable. But the Administration firmly believes that hiring foreign over domestic workers should be the rare exception, not the rule. And we believe that such exceptions should become even rarer and more tightly targeted on gaps in the domestic labor market than is often the case under current law.

If employers must turn to skilled foreign labor, this is a symptom signalling defects in our skill-building system. Our systems for giving access to global labor markets should be structured to remedy such defects, not acquiesce to them. Our immigration system should progressively diminish, not merely perpetuate, firms' dependence on the skills of foreign workers. As I said, our primary public policy response to skills mismatches must be to effectively prepare the U.S. workforce to meet new demands. Importing needed skills should be a short-term response to meet urgent needs while we actively adjust to quickly changing circumstances. This is why we support a shift towards an employment-based immigration system which relies more on market-type incentives to discourage employers from abandoning the domestic workforce for foreign labor while, at the same time, making it less necessary to do so.

A training contribution from employers sponsoring skill-based immigrants, with the proceeds dedicated to building the skills and enhancing the competitiveness of U.S. workers, forges an admirably direct and efficient link between the problem of skill shortages and the only valid long-term solution – investment in the U.S. workforce – while at the same time affording the needed safety valve of access to foreign labor markets.

Some contend that such a training contribution would impose additional costs because the employer would still face the same bureaucratic hurdles and legal obstacles that characterize the current system, and these additional costs are at the head of impeding access to the best and the brightest in the international labor market. But this should not be the case. New employment-based immigrant selection systems – which depend on a market-based mechanism as the central element – can facilitate elimination of certain aspects of the current bureaucratic "command and control" system that impose extra costs on U.S. employers.

This new selection structure can facilitate the development of a streamlined "audit and profiling" system for adjudication of employers' applications which would significantly speed up the application process and yield savings by reducing the number of processing steps by nearly 80 percent (from over 100 to under 30) and reducing overall processing time by nine to twelve months. Under the current labor certification system, employers can experience application processing times that take as long as 18 to 24 months.

Lengthy processing times and complicated application procedures impose real costs on employers. A significant reduction in processing time and complexity should translate into savings of major consequence for most employers.

Real savings would result from the fact that the application processing steps and time involved can be cut dramatically for all employers who use the system and cut even further for those employers which clearly use the system to meet needs for high-skill, uniquely talented individuals.

At the same time, the training contribution gives U.S. employers a real, market-based incentive to look first to the U.S. labor market to meet their skill needs – as the nation's immigration policy should certainly assure – while helping in the longer term to redress domestic labor market deficiencies that result in a need to tap the international labor market in the first place.

In addition, the Administration and the Commission on Immigration Reform support a level of 100,000 employment-based immigrant visas, which would allow about a 10 percent growth from current comparable usage.

The Administration also supports retaining the structure of current law which gives highest preference to the highest skilled in the international labor market, while maintaining "flow down" access to lower-skilled individuals with Baccalaureate degrees and even "skilled workers" without degrees. And we support eliminating employment-based immigration of unskilled workers and the current diversity program to make more admission numbers available for other categories more in the national interest.

The Administration also strongly advocates employment-based immigration reform – in both the immigrant and nonimmigrant programs – that requires U.S. employers seeking foreign workers to recruit in the domestic labor market for the job for which they seek a foreign worker and not use foreign workers to replace laid-off U.S. workers.

Some seriously contend that these are unwarranted impediments to business access to the global labor market. But are these requirements really unwarranted? Should a nation's immigration policy countenance any less of a commitment to its own working people?

The underlying principles of our employment-based immigration policy cannot be realized if employers can reach out to the international labor market without first making efforts to recruit at home. This is an essential requirement of current law for employers seeking access to permanent employment-based immigrants, and it needs to be retained. But recruitment in the domestic labor market is not required of employers who seek access to H-1B foreign temporary "professionals." Half the time, probably much more often, it is on behalf of foreign workers already employed temporarily under H-1B visas that employ-ers apply for permanent status.

This creates the anomalous, inexplicable, and ultimately frustrating situation where employers do not have to recruit in the U.S. labor market when first hiring a foreign worker (as a nonimmigrant), but then do have to recruit U.S. workers when they later seek to convert the worker they already employ from temporary to permanent status. This later recruitment most often results only in frustration for U.S. worker applicants as the employer pursues the recruit-ment process with a single goal in mind – continuing the employment of the foreign worker.

Recruitment in the domestic labor market should be – must be – an essential component of our employment-based immigration system at every stage. Our immigration policy betrays a necessary commitment to the U.S. workforce if domestic workers can be ignored or bypassed in its implementation.

The Administration has also strongly urged that, beyond requiring unsuc-cessful recruitment in the domestic labor market, additional worker protections be built into our employment-based immigration selection systems.

If employers are trying to find foreign workers to fill labor shortages caused by deficiencies or a breakdown in the nation's skill development system, there can be no legitimate justification for laying off or otherwise displacing U.S. workers or using immigrant workers as strike breakers.

In nearly all situations it is entirely unfair and unreasonable that – as a matter of public policy – an employer in this country not only does not have to test the domestic labor market for the availability of qualified U.S. workers before gaining access to foreign workers but is actually able to lay off U.S. workers to replace them with foreign temporary workers in their own employ or through contract. This is exactly what is happening; current law tolerates it, perhaps even encourages it, and our policy must change.

The Administration believes that employment-based immigration reform should, in fact, enhance U.S. employers' access to the best and the brightest in the international labor market – especially for the majority of employers who use this system to supplement their largely domestic workforce – to help promote U.S. competitiveness, economic growth, and the creation of more and better job opportunities for U.S. workers. At the same time, our policy must serve to curb situations allowed under current law which involve primarily workers at the lower-end of the skill scale and create the potential for unfair competition with fully qualified U.S. workers.

U.S. employers seeking access to the international labor market to met their needs for skilled workers – especially temporary workers – ought to be required to attempt to recruit U.S. workers for these jobs and be taking meaningful steps to develop U.S. workers to meet their long-term needs. U.S. employers seeking access to the international labor market for skilled workers ought to be precluded from laying off or otherwise displacing U.S. workers to replace them with foreign temporary workers. U.S. employers ought not be allowed, much less encouraged, to develop long-term dependencies on foreign temporary workers.

We firmly believe that these simple – some would say obvious – principles should be reflected in our immigration law.

Finally, let me address one other related issue of great concern to the Administration. Amendments are being offered, to the immigration reform bill in the House to include a new agricultural guestworker program through the Temporary Agricultural Worker Amendments of 1995, sponsored by Congressmen Pombo and Chambliss. The proposed new program – designated as H-2B – would not replace the existing temporary agricultural worker program, H-2A, but rather create yet another means by which agricultural employers may import foreign farmworkers.

A new guestworker program is unwarranted because it would:

- increase illegal immigration;

- reduce work opportunities for U.S. citizens and other legal residents;

- depress wages and work standards for U.S. farmworkers; and

- not be a sustainable solution to any agricultural labor shortage which might develop.

Such results are entirely incompatible with the Administration's strenuous efforts to improve illegal immigration control and the wages and working conditions of U.S. workers.

Congressman Lamar Smith, principal sponsor of the House bill and chair of the Immigration Subcommittee, agrees with this position. Referring to this guestworker amendment, he is quoted as saying, "This undercuts everything we are trying to achieve." Two congressionally-mandated, bipartisan commissions – the Commission on Immigration Reform and the Commission on Agricultural Workers – also agree.

The Jordan Commission has stated its unambiguous opposition to a new agricultural guestworker program:

> The Commission believes that an agriculture guestworker program . . . is not in the national interest and unanimously and strongly agrees that such a program would be a grievous mistake.

Independently, the Commission on Agricultural Workers concluded in its 1992 report that "despite an expanding perishable crop industry, the national supply of agricultural labor has been more than adequate for the past several years." While acknowledging that in many localities a significant portion of the harvest workforce is unauthorized, the Commission went on to say that, to the extent that the agricultural labor supply needs to be supplemented, the existing H-2A program was sufficient.

Recent data from the Department of Labor's National Agricultural Worker Survey reveals a persistently high degree of underemployment among farmworkers at both the national and regional level. In fact, at any time during the year – including during the peak harvest season – at most 61 percent of U.S. farmworkers are engaged in farm work.

There is simply no evidence – nor even any assertion – of an agricultural labor shortage in this country. On the contrary, all of the available evidence indicates a continuing and structural agricultural labor surplus. For example:

- U.S. farmworkers average only 31 weeks of employment each year;

- at any time during the year at least 15 percent are not working while in the United States; and

- U.S. farmworkers' wages have stagnated – at about $6.00 per hour – for at least the last five years.

Advocates of a new agricultural guestworker program justify the purported need on fears of possible future shortages. This is no basis for a whole new guestworker program which poses such immense risks for U.S. farmworkers and our rural communities.

The burden must be squarely placed on the proponents of this new program to demonstrate that:

- there is, in fact, an agricultural labor shortage;

- should such shortages develop in the future, a foreign guestworker program is the best and only way to address it; and

- the existing temporary foreign agricultural worker (H-2A) program is incapable of responding to such a situation.

They have not – and cannot.

Further, nothing in the proposed guestworker program effectively addresses the many justified concerns that have been expressed by nearly all who have looked at it:

- the proposed program does not promote or protect job opportunities for U.S. workers; on the contrary, these amendments substantially weaken the statutory preference for and protections of U.S. workers currently in the H-2A program;

- the proposed program would largely negate current protections intended to ensure that wages and working conditions of U.S. farmworkers do not suffer from the presence of large numbers of guestworkers in the low wage, low-skill agricultural labor market;

- other provisions in the proposed program would simply eliminate many existing labor protections for U.S. and foreign workers, such as the employer's obligation to provide housing and transportation for migrant workers;

- the proposed new program could well increase the likelihood that guestworkers will not return to the sending countries upon completion of employment and will likely establish new illegal immigration networks.

The President has directed the Departments of Labor and Agriculture to work cooperatively to improve and enhance existing programs, including possibilities for streamlining the existing H-2A temporary agricultural worker program, to meet agricultural labor requirements consistent with our obligations to American workers if agricultural labor shortages should develop.

For all of these reasons, the creation of yet another agricultural guestworker program – or the gutting of the existing H-2A program – is entirely unjustified and would, in the words of the Commission on Immigration Reform, be a "grievous mistake."

I hope these remarks help outline some of the more important issues and clearly articulate positions of the Clinton Administration that will help shape your further discussions.

2

The Role of U.S. Commission on Immigration Reform in the Process of Legislative Development

ANDREW SCHOENHOLTZ
U.S. Commission on Immigration Reform

The Commission on Immigration Reform was mandated by the Immigration Act of 1990 to review and evaluate the impact of U.S. immigration policy and to transmit to the Congress its findings and recommendations for additional changes that should be made with respect to immigration into the United States. The Commission began holding hearings and consultations in January 1993. It has conducted fact-finding missions to many of the communities in which large numbers of immigrants settle as well as to selected countries of origin, such as Mexico, Cuba, and the Dominican Republic. It has heard testimony from elected officials and other community leaders and residents about the impact of immigration on their community's economy, services, education, community relations, and other issues.

The Commission analyzed the effects of the three major pieces of legislation adopted during the decade from 1980 to 1990 to govern immigration policy –

the Refugee Act of 1980, the Immigration Reform and Control Act of 1986, and the Immigration Act of 1990. Based on this analysis, the Commission found the broad framework established by these laws to be the appropriate one for the United States to continue into the next century: a legal immigration system that strives to serve the national interest in helping families reunify and employers obtain skills not available in the U.S. labor force; a refugee system that reflects both our humanitarian beliefs and international refugee law; and an enforcement system that seeks to deter unlawful immigration through employer sanctions and tighter border control. The Commission concluded, however, that more needs to be done to guarantee that the stated goals of our immigration policy are met.

The Commission has identified three broad areas deserving of policy attention: unauthorized entry and work, legal admissions, and the absorption and integration of newcomers. We have already made some recommendations to Congress and the Administration on the first two subjects. Let me highlight the key recommendations and then say a few words about where the Commission is heading in its final eighteen months.

So far, the Commission has found two major problems with the implementation of the stated goals of this framework. First, the enforcement system regarding entry and work is not functioning as well as is needed. When sizable numbers of people illegally enter, stay, or work in the United States, pubic support for the immigration system is seriously undermined. Unfortunately, that is precisely what has happened.

Second, our immigrant admissions system is out of whack. Currently we tell people that they are eligible to immigrate and then make them stand in line for five, ten, or twenty years. Such a system unnaturally separates close family members and encourages people to follow human nature and circumvent our laws. We've become complacent with backlogs – we shouldn't be.

How does the Commission propose to address these problems? First, the Commission believes that the rule of law must be enforced in order to have a credible immigration system. With respect to unauthorized entry, the Commission supports the strategy that emphasizes prevention at the border rather than apprehension following illegal entry. Prevention holds many advantages: it is more cost-effective than apprehension and removal; it eliminates the cycle of voluntary return and reentry that has characterized unlawful border crossings; and it reduces potentially violent confrontations on the border.

But better border management alone cannot address the real reason that people remain in the United States in unauthorized status – employment opportunities. Without a comprehensive strategy that includes the worksite, unauthorized immigration cannot be contained.

The Commission found that the employer sanctions law as currently implemented leaves too much up to the employer and the unauthorized worker.

Today the employer decides, based on certain documents, whether someone is eligible to work. Such a system can lead to increased discrimination against foreign-looking or foreign-sounding authorized workers. The current system is also too susceptible to fraud, particularly through the counterfeiting of work documents. The Commission recommended pilot testing a system that will not require employers to decide anything about an individual's citizenship or immigration status, but instead just asks for what all employees provide to employers today – their Social Security numbers. The Commission believes that such information can form the basis for a secure, nondiscriminatory verification system. The Kennedy-Simpson Amendment on verification exemplifies the pilot programs that the Commission recommended, with adequate protections regarding privacy and discrimination.

In examining legal immigration, the Commission found a system based on waiting. Families wait for incredibly long periods of time before their spouses, children, and/or siblings are admitted as permanent residents. Employers wait for certification from the Labor Department that no U.S. worker is available for a position that the employer cannot wait to fill. There are 3.5 million family members waiting in line right now. That simply does not make sense, so the Commission tried to find a way to create a new system able to admit immigrants in a timely fashion. Since the Commission did not find sufficient evidence indicating the need to increase or decrease current levels of immigration, we concluded that priorities should drive the numbers, not the other way around.

With respect to family immigration, the Commission proposed a system based on family priorities: the closest family members should be admitted first. Separating spouses or parents and children cannot be the basis of a rational immigration policy. The Commission would like to see a significant clearance of the 1.1 million backlog of spouses and minor children over the next few years. To do so means using numbers otherwise available to other family relationships.

In terms of skill-based immigration, we now have a labor certification process that requires employers to recruit for a position they have already recruited for. The process can take as long as two years, even though employers want the worker immediately. The Commissioners heard from employers all around the country about the problems of this system. The Commission proposed replacing the labor certification procedure with market forces: normal recruitment – the employer hires the best qualified person, whether citizen or alien – plus a fee, which would be invested in private initiatives to increase the competitiveness of U.S. workers. This would result in a more timely and effective labor market test.

The Commission made one other recommendation regarding legal admissions that I would like to emphasize. Our system needs to be as flexible as possible. Congress should regularly review admissions levels every few years.

This enables changes in the law to address unforeseen problems before they get out of hand. It also permits a highly political process to go forward in times when emotion and rhetoric do not run high.

Let me now turn to the Commission's current activities and then a word on our future ones. The Commissioners have been studying the so-called nonimmigrant system for some time and are nearing completion of that work. This is a very complex area, parts of which are closely led to the permanent skill-based system. The Commission's view, in fact, is that sound policies in the nonimmigrant area cannot be made in a vacuum – they must be made in relation to the immigrant system. So far, the Commission has made one major recommendation in this area – against an agricultural guestworker program. Proponents of such a program have failed to demonstrate that a labor shortage is about to occur or that there are no means other than a guestworker program available to agricultural producers to obtain sufficient employees in their industry.

The Commission has also been examining refugee policy for some time, focusing on three major areas: resettlement, asylum, and emergencies. The Commission made limited initial recommendations on the overseas admission program and is focusing now on the criteria and procedures used to admit refugees for resettlement as well as the domestic assistance programs designed to help refugees integrate into our society. With respect to asylum, the Commission is studying the effects of the asylum reforms initiated in January 1995. The report that emerges from these studies will also include recommendations on emergencies.

The Commission's final report in 1997 will concentrate on a neglected area of immigration policy – the absorption and integration of newcomers into U.S. society and the economy. Policymakers spend almost all of their time on issues of admissions and enforcement; we need to consider policies that ensure the successful integration of immigrants into our civic culture. This final report will also analyze the impact of immigrants on all sectors of life in the United States.

Finally, the Commission will also undertake an examination of the organizational roles and relationships of the federal agencies responsible for the implementation of immigration policy. Logically, this study can only come once the Commission has articulated a comprehensive set of policies regarding admission, enforcement, and integration. At that point the Commission will report to Congress on the strengths and weaknesses of the current system, as well as make recommendations to improve management of immigration-related activities.

I close by quoting Barbara Jordan on the subject of immigration reform: "We are a nation of immigrants, dedicated to the rule of law. That is our history – and it is our challenge to ourselves. . . .We cannot evade the responsibility to make the necessary choices to reform immigration. It is literally a matter of who we are as a nation, and who we become as a people."

3

Recent Immigration Reform: Using Commissions for Agenda Setting

MICHAEL LEMAY
California State University, San Bernardino

As this is being written the United States Congress is considering yet another major attempt at immigration reform – H.R. 2202 is the proposal before the Conference Committee which will attempt to rectify the two slightly different versions passed in each house. On March 21, 1996, the U.S. House of Representatives passed, by a vote of 333–87, its bill that would: set up a five-state program to check IDs of every worker, allow states to ban illegal immigrant children from their schools, deny welfare benefits to illegal immigrants, and double the number of Border Control agents to 10,000 by the year 2,000 (Davidson, 1996:C-10; Puente, 1996). The Senate, on May 2, 1996, passed its own version of the bill. President Clinton has indicated a willingness to sign into law the Senate version of the bill. These bills represent the latest efforts by the U.S. Congress to grapple with immigration reform.Their passage illustrates, moreover, what seems to be an important development in the manner in which Congress brings immigration policy proposals to its agenda.

The policy process has been conveniently described as consisting of six stages: problem formation, policy agenda setting, policy formulation, policy adoption, policy implementation, and policy evaluation (Anderson, 1984:5–10). Increasingly, and for many public policy areas, the initiative for policymaking has shifted from the legislative branch to the executive branch (*see* Cochrane and Malone, 1995:43; Berry, 1990:239–269; Dye, 1995:21–23). Immigration policymaking seems to be an area running counter to that trend. For it, Congress retained primacy in initiating legislation. In recent years Congress passed three major reforms of immigration policy: the Immigration Reform and Control Act of 1986 (IRCA), the Immigration Act of 1990 (IMMACT), and the 1986 bills cited above. Interestingly, in all three of these major efforts at immigration reform, a key element in setting the agenda of the effort was a special commission established to study the problem and develop proposals. While the use of the commission is neither new nor unique to immigration policy, these commissions had a profound impact on the policy process. This article discusses the use of the commission to set the agenda for recent immigration reform.

SCIRP AND IRCA

When President Reagan signed IRCA into law on November 6, 1986, he did so stating that its purpose was "to establish a reasonable, fair, orderly, and secure system of immigration into this country and not to discriminate against particular nations or peoples" (Montweiler, 1987:22). IRCA sought to resolve the illegal immigrant problem by attacking the primary "pull" factor – the U.S. economy. By enacting employer sanctions, IRCA intended to "demagnetize" the pull of the comparatively prosperous U.S. economy (LeMay, 1994:27). Congress, erroneously as it turns out, felt that IRCA had solved the illegal immigration problem (Mehlman, 1994:25).

The ending of the bracero program in 1964 and passage of the 1965 Immigration Act resulted in a shift in the immigration flow from Northwest Europe to Latin America and Asia, as well as a trend towards the growing influx of undocumented aliens.

A consequence of the growing influx and changing composition of the immigration flow, both legal and illegal, was a public sense of crisis in control of the border. The underfunded and understaffed INS simply could not keep up with the number of immigrants. Problems of corruption flowed naturally from the great pressures for immigration coupled with restrictions on legal immigration and the inefficiency of the INS. A lack of resources combined with the sense of lost control led the INS to engage in more secondary enforcement activities to locate illegal aliens: stopping traffic at checkpoints; watching air, bus and train terminal passengers; checking ranches and other areas of employment known to have a tradition of high levels of illegal workers; and following up on specific leads (LeMay, 1994:25–26).

The influx of illegal Hispanic immigrants also gave rise to social concerns among U.S. citizens: bilingualism, assimilation, and who would be entitled to benefits from social programs. Many U.S. citizens feared the perceived slow assimilation process of Hispanic immigrants would hurt U.S. cultural processes, perhaps even leading to a separatist political movement akin to the French-speaking separatist political party in Canada.

The growing anxiety over an apparent flood of illegal aliens entering the United States annually prompted the Congress, by the end of the 1970s, to establish a special commission to study refugee and illegal alien problems (LeMay, 1987:115).

The Select Commission on Immigration and Refugee Policy (SCIRP) was composed of members of Congress, the executive branch and the public. From Congress were Senators Charles Mathias (D., Md.), Alan Simpson (R., Wyo.), Edward Kennedy (D., Mass.), and Dennis DeConcini (D., Ariz.) and from the House, Peter Rodino (D., N.J.), Elizabeth Holtzman (D., N.Y.), Robert McClory (R., Ill.), and Hamilton Fish (R., N.Y.). The executive branch was represented by Secretary of State Cyrus Vance; Attorney General Benjamin Civiletti; Secretary of Labor Ray Marshall, and Secretary of Health, Education and Welfare Patricia Harris. Members of the public included Joaquin Otero of the Brotherhood of Railway and Airline Clerks, Judge Cruz Reynoso of the California Court of Appeals, Rose Ochi of the Office of the Mayor of Los Angeles, and by the time of its deliberations, its chairman was the Rev. Theodore Hesburgh, then President of Notre Dame University and former chairman of the Civil Rights Commission. Selected as staff director was Professor Lawrence Fuchs, of Brandeis University, an acknowledged ethnic and immigration scholar.

SCIRP issued its first report in January 1981, calling for "immediate action" on immigration reform. Its recommendations were a mixture of contradictory solutions and uneasy compromises that characterized IRCA as well. It recommended "closing the back door" to undocumented immigration while opening slightly the front door to allow more legal immigration (LeMay, 1994:35). It stated that:

> it is not the time for large-scale expansion of legal immigration, for resident aliens or temporary workers, because the first order of priority is bringing undocumented or illegal immigration under control, while setting up a rational system of legal immigration, [and it recommended] a modest increase in legal immigration sufficient to expedite the clearance of backlogs mainly to reunite families. (LeMay, 1994:35–36)

The focus of the SCIRP report, however, stressed enforcement of existing immigration laws, the imposition of employer sanctions, increased law enforcement, an amnesty program, and a restructuring of legal immigration. The importance of the work of the commission was the way in which all these proposals were linked. The United States could not hope to be successful in solving the problem of illegal immigration by employing one or two of the approaches at a time, it had to combine all of them for optimal results.

The Commission set the agenda for all subsequent discussions of and proposals to reform immigration law. Its prestige gave weight to proposals and ideas that before had been stymied in the congressional committee system. Another important contribution of SCIRP was the information it gave to the various parties about each other's positions. It spotlighted joint benefits that could be gained and underscored where the major compromises would take place. The power to influence the issue was seen as balanced between the labor and agricultural factions. Its clear stress on undocumented immigration as "the most pressing problem" shaped and limited the focus of debate over immigration policy reform for more than a decade. It issued a clear message: "Most U.S. citizens believe that the half-open door of undocumented/illegal migration should be closed" (SCIRP, 1981:35). Finally, it was from the Commission's congressional membership that many of the prime movers of congressional leadership on all subsequent immigration reform emerged. Its research was seminal for the work of the Simpson and Mazzoli staffs. Its procedures illustrated the methods by which the conflict might be resolved (Perrotti, 1989:104).

IMMACT

IRCA's focus on undocumented immigration required follow-up efforts at reforming legal immigration. Moreover, by early 1988 it became increasingly clear that problems in the implementation of IRCA necessitated some further changes in immigration law. By March of 1988, the Senate passed S-2104, more commonly known as the Kennedy-Simpson bill, by a vote of 88-4. It attempted to reform immigration law dealing with legal immigration as well as to address a few perceived flaws in IRCA. The bill followed the SCIRP recommendations in identifying separate tracks for family reunification and nonfamily immigrants. It likewise separated refugees from family-related immigrants. It followed the SCIRP recommendations for a substantial number of visas set aside for "second preference" family reunification by doubling the numbers for that preference. It also provided for a study of the permanent labor certification process and proposed changes in immigration and naturalization rules that would benefit U.S. workers, employers, and taxpayers (Tomasi, 1989:81–82). Conflict over the topic of the "ceiling" led to further debate over the issue (Bean, Vernez and Keely, 1989:105).

The Kennedy-Simpson-Simon bill was a slightly modified version of the one passed by the Senate in 1988. It more clearly addressed some problems associated with the implementation of IRCA, and it contained an amendment to end direct federal benefits to undocumented immigrants and a provision to grant stays of deportation to immediate relatives in the process of legalizing under IRCA. Its companion bill in the House was sponsored by Rep. Howard Berman (D., Cal.) – HR-67a. An important Moakley bill addressed the issue of measures against the deportation of Salvadorans and Nicaraguans. Chairman Rodino and Representative Mazzoli sponsored a bill that differed slightly from the Simpson-Kennedy-Simon bill in the Senate by imposing neither a ceiling on annual admissions of immediate relatives nor by offsetting them against other family-sponsored immigration, and it contained a provision that extended a section of IRCA permitting nationals of certain countries determined to have been adversely affected by the abolition of the national origins law to compete for 10,000 unrestricted visas (Tomasi, 1989:75–81). These various efforts to reform legal immigration culminated in the passage of the Immigration Act of 1990 (IMMACT). It contained elements of virtually all the ideas and bills discussed above. The bill passed on the last day of the session and then only after a last-minute flap that nearly killed the bill as patched together in the conference committee. The issue hinged on the Hispanic caucus's fears about establishing a "forgery-proof" driver's license – a step they held to be the first toward a national identification card. A concurrent resolution to strip the license provision from the conference report allowed the House vote on the adapted conference committee report, pegging it 264 to 118. It passed even more comfortably in the Senate, 89-8 (LeMay, 1994:147–148). For purposes of our discussion here, an important provision of IMMACT was its establishment of yet another commission to study immigration reform (Public Law 101-649).

THE JORDAN COMMISSION AND THE 1996 BILLS

IMMACT mandated creation of the U.S. Commission on Immigration Reform. The Commission was chaired by former Representative Barbara Jordan, the Lyndon B. Johnson Centennial Chair in National Policy at the School of Public Affairs, University of Texas-Austin. Its two vice-chairs were Lawrence Fuchs, Jaffe Professor of American Civilization and Politics at Brandeis University and formerly executive director of SCIRP, and Michael Teitelbaum, Program Officer at the Alfred P. Sloan Foundation. Other members included Richard Estrada, Associate Editor of the *Dallas Morning News*; Harold Ezell, President and Founder of the Ezell Group; Robert Charles Hill, a partner in the firm Jenkens and Gilchrist, P.C.; Warren Leiden, Executive Director of the American Immigration Lawyers Association; Nelson Merced, Chief Executive Officer of the Emergency Tenant Council, Inc.; and Bruce Morrison, partner in Morrison and Swains. Its Executive Director was Susan Martin. The Commission's Chair was appointed by the President, and two members each were appointed by the Speaker and the Minority Leader of the U.S. House of Representatives and the Majority and Minority Leaders of the U.S. Senate.

This Commission articulated what it saw as the challenges for immigration policy reform: that unlawful immigration is unacceptable and that current enforcement efforts had not been successful in deterring unlawful immigration. The failure to develop effective strategies to control unlawful immigration blurred public perception of the distinction between legal and illegal immigration. It saw the principal issue as how to so manage immigration that it will continue to be in the national interest. Especially:

- How do we ensure that immigration is based on and supports broad national economic, social and humanitarian interests rather than the interests of those who would abuse our laws?

- How do we gain effective control over our border while still encouraging international trade, investment, and tourism?

- How do we maintain a civic culture based on shared values while accommodating the large and diverse population admitted through immigration policy? (U.S. Commission on Immigration Reform: Executive Summary, ii–iii).

Like the SCIRP report, the Jordan Commission made a number of sweeping recommendations dealing with both legal and illegal immigration problems. By 1996, however, it became clear that in order to pass legislation the Congress would once again have to separate the issue of legal and illegal immigration reform. This section highlights the major recommendations which the Jordan Commission made that resulted in setting the agenda for the 1996 bills cited in the introduction.

The Commission supported a strategy emphasizing prevention of illegal entry at the border rather than apprehension after such entry. It recommend increased resources for prevention by adding staff to the Border Patrol, by enhancing their training, by the creation of a mobile, rapid response team to augment its capacity to react to changes in the sites of such illegal entry, by using fences to reduce border violence, and for systematic evaluation of any new border strategies. It recommended enhanced capacities to combat organized smuggling which included expanded enforcement authority of the RICO provisions, wiretap authority, expanded asset forfeiture for smuggling aliens, and enhanced intelligence gathering and diplomatic efforts to deter smuggling. It called for a better verification system of work authorization, with a focus on the computerized verification system in the five states with the highest levels of illegal immigration, as well as in several less affected states. It stressed measures to reduce the fraudulent access to so-called "breeder documents," particularly birth certificates that are being used to establish an identity in the United States. It recommended that illegal aliens not be eligible for any publicly-funded services or assistance except those made available on an emergency basis to protect public health and safety. It recommended defining comprehensive categories of aliens in the Immigration and Nationality Act to simplify determination of those eligible for public benefits, and it recommended the removal of criminal aliens from the United States in such ways that the potential for their return to the United States be minimized (U.S. Commission on Immigration Reform: Executive Summary, v–xxviii).

CONCLUSION

The decade of 1986–1996 saw the most significant reform of U.S. immigration law and policy since the 1965 law ending the quota system. Whereas in some policy areas the use of special commissions and similar "blue ribbon" study or task forces result largely in reports that sit on shelves gathering dust, the case of immigration policy shows the special commissions that largely set the agenda of policy reform and resulted in dramatic impacts on subsequent legislative debate, determining in no small measure the major provisions of those laws. The Select Commission on Immigration and Refugee Policy greatly influenced the 1986 and 1990 laws. It structured the debates of immigration reform efforts. It focused both congressional and public media attention on the problem. Its prestige gave weight to its recommendations. Its congressional members emerged as the leadership of a decade-long effort at immigration policy reform. Its research was seminal to subsequent studies of the issue. Its compromises became those reflected in the final passage of legislation.

The Jordan Commission, likewise, refocused attention on the issue and, like SCIRP, its prestige resulted in major recommendations that formed the base upon which additional reforms of the "illegal immigration" was addressed in the 1996 laws. And given its mandate for a 1997 Report and continued study of the issue, the Commission is likely to continue to be an important influence on subsequent legislative proposals well into the next decade.

REFERENCES

Anderson, J. *et al.*
1984   *Public Policy and Politics in America.* Monterey, CA: Brooks/Cole.

Bean, F., G. Vernez and C. B. Keely
1989   *Opening and Closing the Doors.* Santa Monica, CA and Washington, DC: The Rand Corporation and the Urban Institute.

Berry, J.
1990   "Subgovernments, Issue Networks, and Political Conflict." In *Remaking American Politics.* Ed. R. Harris and S. Milkis. Boulder, CO: Westview Press. Pp. 239–269.

Cochrane, C. E. and E. Malone
1995   *Public Policy: Perspectives and Choices.* New York: McGraw-Hill.

Davidson, J.
1996   "House Votes to Kill Attempts to Cut Legal Immigration," *The Wall Street Journal,*
            March 22, C-10.

Dye, T.
1995   *Understanding Public Policy.* 8th ed. Englewood Cliffs, NJ: Prentice-Hall.

LeMay, M.
1994   *Anatomy of a Public Policy.* Westport, CT: Praeger.

_____

1987   *From Open Door to Dutch Door.* New York: Praeger.

Mehlman, I.
1994   "Its Back," *National Review,* 46(6):25–26.

Montweiler, N. H.
1987   *The Immigration Reform Law of 1986.* Washington, DC: Bureau of National Affairs.

Perotti, R.
1989   "Beyond Logrolling: Integrative Bargaining in Congressional Policymaking."
            Political Science Association Meeting, August 31–September 3, Atlanta, GA.

Puente, M.
1996   "House Vote Curbs Illegal Immigration," *USA Today,* March 22, A-1.

Select Commission on Immigration and Refugee Policy (SCIRP)
1981   *U.S. Immigration Policy and the National Interest: Final Report.* Washington, DC:
            Government Printing Office.

Tomasi, L. F.
1989   *In Defense of the Alien,* Vol. XI. New York: Center for Migration Studies.

U.S. Commission on Immigration Reform
1994   *U.S. Immigration Policy: Restoring Credibility.* Washington, DC: Government Printing
            Office.

4

Immigration Legislation and Due Process: The Forgotten Issue[1]

LUCAS GUTTENTAG
American Civil Liberties Union National Immigrants' Rights Project

I am grateful for this opportunity to address some of the due process deprivations that the House and Senate are about to adopt in the pending immigration legislation. Due process is the forgotten issue in the current debate. It is forgotten, in part, because it has been subsumed within the "illegal immigration" shibboleth; in part because it is an issue for which the public typically shows little interest or support, and in part because all of us who care about this issue have failed to make it a higher priority.[2]

Yet, I fear we will live far longer with the pending legislation's denial of due process than with its threatened cuts to family or labor-based immigration or its impact on businesses or employers. When the passions of this era have cooled, as they eventually will after countless individuals have paid the price, I believe it will be far easier to persuade Congress to increase the number of immigrants admitted each year than to restore the procedural rights, the discretionary relief, and the right to judicial review that are about to be eviscerated.

In addition, the restrictions proposed in this legislation – particularly the prohibitions against federal courts exercising judicial review – have significance far beyond their immediate impact on those individuals who will be unjustly expelled and far beyond the realm of immigration law generally. These proposals constitute an attack on the historic role of the judiciary to enforce the Constitution, to give meaning to the fourteenth amendment and the Bill of Rights, and to prevent the political passions of the moment from trampling individual freedoms. As such, they also raise a fundamental question about the structure of our constitutional democracy: may Congress eliminate the role of the Judiciary by legislating away its jurisdiction?

The House and Senate bills take essentially the same three-step approach to undermine fundamental fairness and due process in our immigration laws. First, the bills dramatically reduce the discretionary defenses to which aliens are entitled and simultaneously increase the grounds for detention, the penalties for violating even the most minor immigration laws and the prohibitions against returning legally after a deportation.

Second, the bills adopt "summary exclusion" procedures for many and diminish the procedural rights for all by erecting new obstacles to the exercise of basic rights, including representation by counsel.

Third, as already noted, the bills radically restrict or completely eliminate judicial review of individual deportation orders and of INS practices, policies, and procedures.

LIMITATIONS ON RELIEF

I will not discuss in detail the many ways in which the proposed legislation reduces or eliminates discretionary relief for deportable aliens or the new penalties imposed on those who violate their status. However, let me identify just a few. For example, the House bill provides that any alien who is out of status for just twelve months in the aggregate is barred from admission for ten years (H.R. 2202, 104th Cong., 2d sess., 41–42, § 301). Both bills impose severe restrictions on eligibility for suspension of deportation. Under the House bill, suspension appears unavailable to anyone who was not inspected and admitted.[3] Both the House and the Senate impose new limits on the power of immigration judges to grant voluntary departure after exclusion or deportation proceedings have commenced (H.R. 2202 at 79, § 304 enacting § 204B(b); S. 269/1394, § 150 amending INA § 244(e)). That means aliens who assert their right to a deportation hearing must meet more restrictive criteria than those who relinquish that right. Finally, by floor amendment, the House bill imposes a permanent bar (subject to waiver) on the readmission of an alien who was deported or excluded and "had the intent to illegally enter," and the Senate bars any nonimmigrant who overstays a visa more than 60 days from receiving an immigrant or nonimmigrant visa for three years (H.R. 2202 § 301(c)(iii) enacting § 212(a)(6)(iii); S. 269/1394 § 143(b) enacting INA § 212(p)(1)).

Those are just a few of the new restrictions proposed by the pending legislation. They do not include such provisions outside the immigration system itself as restricting access by long-time legal resident immigrants to government programs and authorizing individual states to deny public education to school children based on their immigration status, in direct contravention to *Plyler v. Doe*, 457 U.S. 202 (1982) (H.R. 2202 § 616 enacting INA § 601 (Gallegly Amendment)).

DIMINISHED PROCEDURES AND PRACTICAL IMPEDIMENTS

Summary ("Special") Exclusion

Both the Senate and House bills establish unprecedented summary or "special" exclusion procedures. Under either bill, this new process would apply 1) to any person arrested at entry who is charged with possessing fraudulent documents or arrives with no documents;[4] also, 2) applicable under the Senate bill to any alien who is alleged to have entered without inspection (EWI) unless the alien can affirmatively demonstrate that she or he has been physically present in the United States for two years (S. 269/1394 § 141 enacting § 235(e)(1)(A)); 3) to any alien interdicted in U.S. territorial waters; and 4) to all arriving aliens without regard to their documentation or manner of arrival if the Attorney General declares a vaguely-defined "extraordinary migration situation" (S. 269/1394 §141 enacting § 235(e)(1)(B),(C)).

An individual subject to summary exclusion is not entitled to any hearing or decision by an immigration judge, is not afforded any administrative appeal, and is not allowed any meaningful judicial review. Instead, the determination of admissibility is made by an INS employee based solely on the information elicited at an on-the-spot interview.[5]

Refugees

The summary exclusion procedure poses a special threat to refugees fleeing persecution. They will not be entitled to present their claim to a neutral decisionmaker in an adversary hearing or to be represented by counsel. Instead, the inspecting INS officer will make a unilateral decision as to whether the arriving alien has demonstrated a "credible fear" of persecution.[6] If the INS officer makes a negative determination, the decision is final and no further review or appeal is permitted (except by a supervisory asylum officer) (H.R. 2202 at 46–47, § 302 enacting 235(b)(1)(B)(iii); S. 269/1394 § 141(a)(b)(6)).

The credible fear standard has no legal precedence in the INA and has no international definition under the Convention Relating to the Status of Refugees or the UNHCR Handbook. Summary exclusion would simply transplant the discredited Haitian interdiction program from the high seas to the territory of the United States by implementing it at every port of entry and land border.

Entry Without Inspection. Application of the summary exclusion procedures to persons who are alleged to have entered EWI and who cannot prove that they have been continuously physically present for two years eliminates rudimentary procedural protections for an entire category of immigrants, based on an arbitrary and inherently uncertain determination. The proposal seeks to eviscerate, if not wholly eliminate, constitutional rights through the artifice of a legislative definition. It dramatically expands the definition of "excludable" alien to include those who have, indisputably, made an entry but who did so illegally. If successful, Congress might well be tempted to undertake similar efforts to "define away" constitutional rights simply by categorizing other classes of aliens as "excludable" or otherwise outside the Constitution. Indeed, the House bill provides that any person "not admitted or paroled" into the United States shall be "inadmissible" (H.R. 2202 at 40, § 301 amending and enacting INA § 212(a)(9)). This new nomenclature appears designed to relegate into a permanent "excludable" alien category all aliens who were not admitted into the United States.

However, the Constitution does not permit Congress to determine the scope of its protections through legislative sleight-of-hands. Congress cannot "deconstitutionalize" aliens by changing their statutory status (*see, e.g., Landon v. Plasencia,* 459 U.S. 21, 1982; *Kwong Hai Chew v. Colding,* 344 U.S. 590, 1953; *Rafeedie v. INS,* 880 F.2d 506, D.C. Cir., 1989).

Extraordinary Migration Situation. The Senate provision allowing the Attorney General to designate, in her unreviewable discretion, that an "extraordinary migration situation" exists creates a similar risk of limitless application. Under the Senate bill the Attorney General may proclaim an extraordinary migration situation if "the arrival or imminent arrival in the United States . . . of aliens who by their numbers or circumstances substantially exceed the capacity of the inspection and examination of such aliens" (S. 269/1394 § 141 enacting § 235(e)(1)(C)(2)).

Invocation of this authority allows the Attorney General to suspend the operation of any immigration regulations regarding the inspection and exclusion of aliens.[7] Yet, judicial review of the Attorney General's finding of an extraordinary migration situation is prohibited, and the Attorney General's determination is "committed to [her] sole and exclusive discretion. . . ." (S. 269/1394 § 142 enacting § 106(f)(2)(A)(i)).

We should not assume that declaration of an immigration emergency will be deferred to some indefinite date in the future. I have little doubt that for many proponents the conditions justifying declaration of an extraordinary migration situation already exist.

Asylum Filing Time Limits

The House bill provides that an alien may apply for asylum only if she or he files the asylum application within 180 days of arrival.[8] Refugee advocates have unanimously stressed that such time limits are wholly unrealistic for persons unfamiliar with our legal system, possibly suffering from the trauma of persecution, unable to find an attorney to advise or represent them, and afraid to present themselves voluntarily to government authorities.

In addition to these practical impediments, we must consider this restriction in light of the very recent past when the INS systematically discriminated against many asylum applicants and arbitrarily denied their claims. For example, the INS pernicious discrimination against Salvadoran and Guatemalan refugees for reasons of U.S. foreign policy throughout the 1980s is no longer disputed (see American Baptist Churches v. Thornburgh, 760 F.Supp. 796, N.D. Cal. 1991; Orantes-Hernandez v. Meese, 685 F.Supp. 1488, C.D. Cal. 1988, aff'd, 919 F.2d 549, 9th Cir. 1990). Likewise, the discrimination against Haitian refugees in South Florida was revealed through litigation in the 1980's (see Haitian Refugee Center v. Smith, 676 F.2d 1023, 5th Cir. 1982). And, in Los Angeles, a federal court invalidated approximately 30,000 asylum interviews of all nationalities based on a showing that INS adjudicators were incompetent, biased, and hostile (Mendez v. Thornburgh, No. 88-04995-TJH, C.D. Cal. 1989). Under those circumstances, a refugee's delay in applying for asylum is not only understandable but appropriate.

Prohibit translation of OSC

The Senate bill amends INA § 242B(a)(3) to eliminate the current requirement that orders to show cause (OSC) commencing deportation proceedings be written in Spanish as well as English (S. 269/1394 § 146). This mean-spirited provision can only be attributed to a desire to deny individuals any realistic means of understanding the charges against them and of requesting a hearing to assert their legal rights. Countless individuals with claims to legal status, to asylum, to suspension of deportation, and to voluntary departure, as well as persons with legal defenses or claims of unlawful INS conduct, will lose their right to a hearing because they do not understand the INS charging document.

The proposal to eliminate Spanish translations of the OSC is directly contrary to a recent federal court ruling under the Due Process Clause that requires the

INS to translate into Spanish the INS document that charges individuals with violating INA § 274C (alleging civil document fraud). In that case, *Walters v. Reno*, No. C94-1204C, WD. Wash. (March 11, 1996), the court stated that "the use of English-only forms in a context in which it is uncontestable that most respondents speak primarily or only Spanish is simply unacceptable, particularly where, as here, the consequences are grave and [the multiplicity of forms confusing]. . . . Obviously, the one-time expense incurred in . . . translating the [form] is not great."

Impeding Legal Representation

Both the Senate and House bills also contain provisions that will severely impede, or practically deny, representation by counsel in those cases where an alien manages to request a hearing. The Senate bill mandates that the statutory right of an alien to be represented by counsel, which already provides that representation is permitted only if it is "at no expense to the government,"[9] be restricted to allow representation only so long as it does not "unreasonably delay" the proceedings (S. 269/1394 § 146 amending INA § 292).

The bills also amend the current statutory rule that deportation hearings cannot be scheduled sooner than fourteen days after an aliens' arrest (*see* INA § 242B(b)(1)). The Senate bill reduces that time to three days in the case of detained aliens, and the House bill reduces the time to ten days in all other cases (S. 269/1394 § 146 amending INA § 242B(b)(1); H.R. 2202 at 61, § 304 enacting § 239(b)(1)).

The restriction on the right to counsel and the authorization for accelerated hearing schedules are particularly prejudicial because of the increasing number of INS detention centers built in remote locations. The siting of detention facilities – whether operated by the INS, the federal Bureau of Prisons, or private contractors – far from urban centers drastically reduces the pool of lawyers who can be recruited to provide *pro bono* representation. By speeding up the process and seeking to deny respondents any adjournment to obtain counsel, the legislation will relegate ever greater numbers of respondents to being unrepresented.

Yet, immigration courts and the INS itself recognize the benefit of legal representation in deportation proceedings (*see* Amicus Curiae Brief of American Civil Liberties Union Immigrants' Rights Project et al., in Support of Petitioner, *Matter of Avila-Lituma*, No. A31 168 263, BIA, filed Jan. 31, 1996). Representation protects individual rights and alleviates the burden on immigration judges to ensure that legal claims are not inadvertently waived.[10] Respondents represented by counsel understand whether to contest deportability or seek discretionary relief and are more likely to agree to depart if counsel informs them that no relief is available. The INS has praised the operation of the private nonprofit Florence Representation Project, which provides legal counseling and representation to detainees at the INS Florence, Arizona, detention facility (GAO, 1992).

Rather than erecting new and higher hurdles to legal representation, Congress should facilitate the right to counsel by dismantling existing obstacles and by providing financial grants to independent nonprofit representation projects at other detention centers. More fundamentally, the right to appointed counsel for indigent aliens in deportation proceedings ought to be recognized as a mandate of due process (*see Escobar Ruiz v. INS*, 787 F.2d 1294 n. 3, 9th Cir. 1986).

Eliminating Deportation Stays Pending Judicial Review

The Senate bill was amended in the Senate Judiciary Committee to eliminate the current provision that the filing of a petition for review in the court of appeals automatically stays an order of deportation pending judicial review (INA § 106(a)(3)). Under the Senate's modification, "[s]ervice of the petition [for review] does not stay the deportation . . . unless the court orders otherwise" (S. 269/1394 § 142 amending INA § 106(a)(3)). This approach significantly increases the likelihood that aliens will be deported before a court can consider their legal claims. It also imposes significant additional burdens on INS district offices and on the federal courts, which must consider and adjudicate the stay requests before any hearing on the merits of the underlying appeal.

Secret Evidence for Alien "Terrorists" and Numerous Provisions Limiting Judicial Review and Other Rights of "Aggravated Felons"

The numerous provisions that deny adequate procedures and judicial review to aliens accused of "terrorism" and to those convicted of crimes are not the subject of this paper. It is significant, however, that the Antiterrorism and Effective Death Penalty Act (AEDPA), which the President is about to sign, would dramatically alter the existing law governing these cases.

ELIMINATING OR RESTRICTING JUDICIAL REVIEW

Elimination of Judicial Review for Discretionary Relief

The Senate bill prohibits any court from reviewing any claim that the Attorney General's discretionary judgment violated the law or constituted an abuse of discretion when an alien is denied any of the most important forms of relief from deportation. No matter how arbitrary or abusive an administrative decision may be, the courts could not review it. The forms of relief over which review would be eliminated are "suspension of deportation," "adjustment of status," "voluntary departure," and numerous waiver provisions (S. 269/1394 § 142 enacting § 106(b)(4)(B)).

Under current law, these discretionary decisions are reviewed upon an exceedingly deferential "abuse of discretion" standard. The total elimination of judicial review achieves the indefensible result of insulating the INS from judicial oversight for egregious errors, abuses of discretion, and manifestly illegal conduct.

No Review of Summary Exclusion

Both the Senate and House bills would virtually eliminate judicial review of decisions made under the proposed summary exclusion procedure. Specifically, the bills 1) prohibit any review other than through habeas corpus actions, and 2) expressly limit such habeas actions to three questions: a) whether the individual is an alien, b) whether he or she was ordered specially excluded; and c) whether he or she is a legal permanent resident.[11] This attempts to deny courts any authority to review whether a person was properly subjected to summary exclusion in the first place, whether he or she in fact had presented fraudulent documents or no documents, whether he or she is an arriving alien, whether (under the Senate bill) he or she has been in the United States for two years, and whether he or she was correctly found excludable. In addition, no court could determine whether INS complied with its obligations under the statute and provided even the minimal process required by law. The bill allows INS officers to make life-and-death determinations without any judicial oversight.

These legislative restrictions on habeas corpus raise fundamental constitutional questions. The power of the courts to review an order of deportation, especially under the constitutional Great Writ, has never been questioned. This legislation cannot survive constitutional scrutiny under the Due Process Clause, the separation of powers principles embodied in Article III, and the right to habeas corpus in Article I.

No Systemic Class Action Challenges

Summary Exclusion. The Senate and House bills impose broad new prohibitions on systemic challenges to INS policies and practices. The bills expressly provide that no court shall have jurisdiction to review any cause of action or claim arising from or relating to the implementation of the summary exclusion provision.[12] Presumably, this is intended to deny any class-action-type challenges to the general policies or practices applicable to INS operation of the summary exclusion process or to the constitutionality of the process itself. Systemic discrimination based on nationality or race, widespread incompetence by INS officers, and formal policies improperly defining fraudulent documents, entry, or other critical threshold matters would all be completely beyond judicial review even if they were contrary to law or the Constitution.

The bills would prohibit judicial review even to challenge INS violation of its own statutory obligations and duties, such as failure to apply the "credible fear" standard to a fleeing refugee, failure to use qualified asylum officers, or failure to provide for supervisory review. None of this is permissible under the Constitution.

*Inspection, Exclusion, and Deportation.*The House bill contains an even more sweeping provision that seeks to deny jurisdiction to any court (other than the Supreme Court) to issue an injunction against the operation of any of the provisions governing the new inspection, exclusion and deportation provisions proposed by the House bill (except by an individual alien with respect to his or her individual proceeding) (H.R. 2202 at 112, § 306 enacting § 242(g)). This is an attempt to completely prohibit class action litigation challenging systemic discrimination or illegal conduct by the INS and to immunize the INS from meaningful oversight.

The bill tries to prevent the only type of court cases that provide a meaningful remedy for INS policies, practices, and procedures that violate the law or the Constitution. In the last fifteen years, class action challenges brought an end to what is now broadly recognized as widespread INS illegalities. The major cases include: the Haitian litigation in South Florida of the 1970s and 1980s that successfully challenged systemic discrimination against Haitian nationals (*see, e.g., Haitian Refugee Center v. Smith*, 676 F.2d 1023, 5th Cir. 1982); the *American Baptist Churches* case that ended a decade of discrimination against Salvadorans and Guatemalan refugees for U.S. foreign policy reasons (*American Baptist Churches v. Thornburgh*, 760 F.Supp. 796, N.D. Cal. 1991);the *Orantes-Hernandez* case that enjoined coercive INS arrest and deportation practices aimed at Salvadorans (*Orantes-Hernandez v. Meese*, 685 F.Supp. 1488, C.D. Cal. 1988, aff'd 919. F.2d 549, 9th Cir. 1990); the Haitian litigation of 1992 that challenged high-seas interdiction and ordered the release of indefinitely detained Haitian refugees at Guantanemo (*Haitian Centers Council v. Sale*, 113 S.Ct. 2549, 1993; 823 F.Supp. 1028, E.D.N.Y. 1993); and the numerous successful challenges to implementation of IRCA legalization programs (*see, e.g., Reno v. Catholic Social Services*, 125 L.Ed. 2d 38, 49, 51–52, 1993; *McNary v. Haitian Refugee Center*, 498 U.S. 479, 1991).

My questions are: What is the INS afraid of? Why do the sponsors of these bills want to give the INS *carte blanche* to engage in unauthorized or illegal actions? Who can justify refusing to let the courts review and decide the legality of INS conduct?

CONCLUSION

The provisions in the Senate and House bills that abrogate procedural protections and deny meaningful judicial review are not just an attack on the rights of immigrants or the organizations that represent them. They are thinly-veiled attacks on the courts themselves, and their significance extends far beyond the immigration field. These proposals are an attempt to prohibit the courts from enforcing individual rights and civil liberties guaranteed by the Constitution and our laws.

The last time Congress considered such a blatant effort to deny the courts jurisdiction to hear fundamental claims concerning individual rights was during the civil rights era of the 1960s. At that time, numerous proposals were introduced to "strip" the federal courts of jurisdiction over school desegregation cases and over the authority to order busing as a remedy for segregation. In one respect the proposals we face today are even more extreme because in the desegregation cases the proponents contended that state courts should hear civil rights cases to enforce the Constitution. Under these proposals, no court would have jurisdiction to hear the claims of immigrants denied due process or a fair hearing.

The effort to strip the courts of jurisdiction to prevent them from enforcing constitutional rights is a fundamental threat to democracy and civil liberties. Barbara Jordan spoke of the "rule of law" as essential to our immigration policy. In our society, the courts are the guarantor of the rule of law and are essential to protecting individual rights, especially in times of public hostility.

Presidential-contender Patrick Buchanan called the judges who have prohibited implementation of California's Proposition 187 "little dictators in black robes" (Bennet, 1996). The supporters of these restrictions on judicial review are expressing the same sentiment; they just won't say so out loud. Republicans and Democrats alike should be raising a hue and cry against these "Buchananite" proposals. Until they do, they should look at themselves before calling someone else an extremist.

NOTES

[1]This paper has been revised slightly to take into account modifications to H.R. 2202 made upon its adoption by the House of Representatives on March 21, 1996, and to S. 269/1394 made upon its approval by the Senate Judiciary Committee on April 10, 1996. The analysis does not reflect changes that occurred after those dates through Senate floor action, by the House/Senate Conference Committee, or otherwise.

[2]The Supreme Court has drawn a sharp distinction between the substantive and procedural rights of noncitizens. It has further distinguished between aliens who are outside the United States, those who are at the border as "excludable" aliens, and those who have made an entry into the country and qualify as "deportable" aliens. The relevance of the plenary power doctrine is at its nadir when deportable aliens challenge the procedures governing their deportation, and it is at its apex when aliens outside the country challenge a substantive basis for denying their admission. In between is a vast area in which immigration status, ties to the United States, physical location, and the particular right at issue affect the degree of protection afforded by the Constitution. These comments address proposals in the legislation that either abridge individuals' opportunity for a full and fair hearing on their claims to remain in the United States or restrict judicial review of the government's action in the immigration arena.

[3]H.R. 2202 at 73, § 304 enacting § 240A(b)(1). The House also imposes a numerical limit on the number of suspension applications that may be granted each year (H.R. 2202 at 75, § 304 enacting § 240A(b)(3)). The Senate bill requires aliens who entered without inspection (EWI) to show "exceptional and extremely unusual hardship" and ten years physical presence in the United States in order to qualify for suspension (S. 1665 § 302).

[4]H.R. 2202 at 45, § 302; S. 269/1394 § 141. The House bill provides that § 302 applies to any arriving alien deemed inadmissible under existing INA § 212(a)(6)(C), (a)(7). *See* H.R. 2202 at 45, § 302 enacting § 235(b)(1)(A); S. 269/1394 § 141 enacting § 235(e)(1)(A)–(C). Section 235(e)(1)(A)(ii) would apply summary exclusion to aliens excludable under new § 212(a)(6)(C)(iii), which amends INA § 212(a)(6)(C) to render excludable any alien who seeks to enter without documents or presents false or fraudulent documents. *See* S. 269/1394 § 132.

[5]*See* S. 269/1394 § 141 enacting § 235(e)(1), (6), (7); H.R. 2202 at 45–46, 48, § 302 enacting § 235(b)(1)(A)(i), (C); H.R. 2202 at 102, 110, § 306 enacting § 242(a)(2), 242(f).

[6]S. 269/1394 § 141 enacting § 235(e)(5); H.R. 2202 at 46, § 302 enacting § 235(b)(1)(B)(ii). The House bill requires that "asylum officers" conduct the credible fear determination (§ 302 enacting § 235(b)(1)(B)(i)) and requires that they receive "professional training in country conditions, asylum law and interview techniques" (§ 302 enacting § 235(b)(1)(E)(i)). H.R. 2202 at 46, 49, § 302. As noted below, these requirements and definitions are unenforceable.

[7]S. 269/1394 § 141 enacting §§ 235(e)(1)(C)(3)(A), 235(e)(1)(C)(4). The Attorney General is authorized to invoke the provisions of the extraordinary migration situation for a 90-day period and for an additional 90-day period after consultation with the Judiciary Committees of the House and Senate.

[8]H.R. 2202 § 511, at 285, § 526 enacting § 208(f)(1)(A)(i). The bill allows a later filing "only if the alien demonstrates by clear and convincing evidence changed circumstances in the alien's country of nationality . . ."; H.R. 2202 § 511, at 285–286 enacting § 208(f)(1)(A)(ii).

[9]The right to representation by counsel (INA § 292) does not provide for appointed counsel for indigent respondents. The INA provides that "the person [in deportation or exclusion proceedings] shall have the privilege of being represented (at no expense to the Government) by such counsel . . . as he shall choose." The statute, therefore, protects the right to counsel for aliens who can afford to retain private counsel or who are able to find *pro bono* representation.

[10]A study of immigration litigation in the federal courts found that the courts sustained more than 40% of the affirmative challenges to agency actions based on statutory or constitutional rights and that aliens prevailed in approximately 28% of the cases seeking judicial review of final orders of deportation or exclusion (Schuck and Wang, 1992)

[11]H.R. 2202 at 110, § 306 enacting § 242(f)(3); S. 269/1394 § 142 enacting § 106(f)(3). The Senate bill also restricts decisions related to § 208(e), § 212(a)(6)(iii), and § 235(d) to habeas review.

[12]S. 269/1394 § 142 enacting § 106(f)(2)(B); H.R. 2202 at 110, § 304 enacting § 242(f)(2). *See also* H.R. 2202 at 102, § 306 enacting § 242(a)(2).

REFERENCES

Bennet, J.
1996   "Politics: The Challenger: Looking Ahead to California Vote. Buchanan Lashes Out at Immigrants," *The New York Times*, March 20, D21.

General Accounting Office, U.S. (GAO)
1992   "Immigration Control: Immigration Policies Affect INS Detention." GAO Report to Congress, GAO/GGD-92-85.

Schuck, P. H. and T. H. Wang
1992   "Continuity and Change: Patterns of Immigration Litigation in the Courts, 1979–1990," *Stanford Law Review*, 45(115).

5

1996 Update on Employer Sanctions Legislation

MARY E. PIVEC
Proskauer Roe Goetz & Mendelsohn, Washington, DC

LEGISLATIVE PROCEDURE

On March 21, 1996, the House of Representatives approved H.R. 2202, entitled the "Immigration in the National Interest Act of 1996," by a vote of 333–87. Also on March 21, the Senate Judiciary Committee concluded markup of Title I of a package of immigration reforms,[1] which language was substituted into H.R. 2202 and then passed by the Senate almost unanimously on May 2. Both the House and Senate measures contain significant new initiatives to deter illegal immigration to the United States, particularly with respect to the reform and funding of employer sanctions enforcement programs. The following is an analysis of the approved legislative changes made by the House and the Senate.

PROPOSED INCREASES IN ENFORCEMENT STAFFING

If the employer sanctions program has been less than effective since its implementation in May 1987, in no small part it has been because Congress had failed to fund adequately the staff functions necessary to make the program work. The Clinton Administration attempted to rectiFYthis situation by seeking larger appropriations for enforcement functions, and Congress responded even more generously than requested despite budget shortfalls in other federal programs. In fiscal year (FY) 1996, INS received a 24 percent increase in enforcement funding, a substantial portion of which was allocated to employer sanctions enforcement efforts. President Clinton's proposed 1997 budget allocates a record $3.1 billion to strengthening our immigration system, with $30 million targeted at reducing employment of illegal immigrants.

Both the House and Senate bills guarantee even higher levels of funding for sanctions activities. The Senate version mandates appropriations to the Department of Justice for 350 new full-time equivalent (FTE) employer sanctions investigators and support staff in each fiscal year from 1996 through 1998, a total of 900 new employer sanctions field staff positions. An amendment by Senator Edward Kennedy (D. MA) stipulates that up to 150 of these positions be allocated to investigate LCA complaints. In addition, the Senate bill authorizes an increase of 1,000 FTEs per year for fiscal years 1996 through 2000 for border patrol and support staff, merely a reiteration of the new personnel already authorized in President Clinton's Crime Bill. By comparison, the House version, §404, calls for an increase of 500 sanctions investigative positions in FY1996. The Senate bill also authorizes hiring of an additional 300 staffers to investigate visa-overstayers.

In addition, the Senate version calls for hiring an undesignated number of additional Assistant U.S. Attorneys to be used primarily for the prosecution of employment immigration crimes, including not only pattern and practice violations of the sanctions laws but also document fraud and a panoply of criminal provisions codified in Title 18 of the U.S. Code dealing with immigration crimes. There is no comparable provision in the House bill.

Both the House and Senate measures authorize state and local law enforcement agencies to enforce the nation's immigration laws. An amendment introduced by Senator Charles Grassley (R. IA) in the Judiciary Committee markup would allow the U.S. Attorney General to enter into agreements with states and localities to enforce immigration laws, with the Attorney General controlling and administering these programs. A Kennedy amendment during floor debate requires that the local law enforcement agency and its officers be certified that they have adequate training in immigration law. On the House side, Representative Tom Latham (R. IA) sponsored a successful amendment that would grant authority to local law enforcement officers to apprehend and detain for transfer to federal authorities aliens violating a deportation order. This amendment also authorizes the deputizing of local officials by the Justice Department in written voluntary agreements with the individual states.

In the en bloc technical corrections amendments debated and accepted by the House was a reiteration of the importance of workplace enforcement.

Amendment 11 by Representative Benjamin Cardin (D. MD) reemphasizes the focus on worksite enforcement of employer sanctions as "a top priority," with the Attorney General required to report back within one year regarding additional authority or resources needed to enforce § 274A of the Immigration and Nationality Act (INA) and the Clinton Executive Order requiring debarment of federal contractors found guilty of violating the employment provisions of INA § 274A.

An indication of the importance of the interdiction of illegals was passage of the floor amendment by Senators Diane Feinstein (D. CA) and Barbara Boxer (D. CA) providing for an additional $12 million to enhance the fenced "no man's land" south of San Diego.

NEW BUREAUCRATIC ENTITIES

Despite intense efforts to downsize federal government agencies, S. 269, now part of the Senate immigration bill, envisioned the creation of two new bureaucracies within the Immigration and Naturalization Service (INS). The following measures probably will not be resurrected in the conference committee.

During floor debate Sen. Bill Bradley (D. NJ) failed in his attempt to reinstate the establishment of the Office for the Enforcement of Employer Sanctions (OEES), to be funded with an initial appropriation of $100 million. The functions of the OEES would have included the investigation and civil prosecution of substantive and paperwork violations of the employer sanctions laws, as well as employer compliance education as to both verification and employment requirements and avoidance of unlawful discrimination. Since there is no comparable proposal in the House measure, this provision is probably defunct.

S. 269 had required the establishment of an automated verification system for employment and government benefit eligibility within twelve months of enactment to be maintained by yet another new bureaucracy – the Office of Employment and Government Benefits Eligibility Verification (OEGBEV) within the Justice Department. Instead, eleventh hour amendments during floor debate by Senator Alan Simpson (R. WY) have amended the authorization of seven pilot projects to become a mandate for at least three diverse project types. Likewise, there is no comparable proposal in the House measure.

ELECTRONIC AND TELEPHONIC VERIFICATION SYSTEMS

The Immigration Reform and Control Act of 1986 (IRCA) Pilot Verification Program

IRCA called for the establishment of a pilot telephone verification system to be used by employers in confirming the identity and work eligibility of non-U.S. citizen employees in connection with completion of the I-9 Employment Verification Form. The telephone verification pilot has been re-dubbed the Verification Information System (VIS) by INS, which currently has a pilot program underway in Orange County, California, which is being used by approximately 250 employers. Funding for VIS in FY1996 is expected to enable the program to expand to 800 employers in the Orange County area.

Prior to implementation of the VIS program it was necessary for INS to create a secure and accurate database for employer access purposes. According to the pilot director, John Brechtel, new INS activity impacting on the employment eligibility of foreign workers nationwide is downloaded on the INS data system housed in Orlando, Florida, on a daily basis. Employers participating in the VIS program receive training in INS facilities in Laguna Niguel on the use of specialized software developed for the VIS program.

Under the VIS program, employers input information regarding the identity of non-U.S. workers for computer verification. If the computer indicates that the database cannot provide a match to the information provided by the employee in completing the I-9 form, then the employee is subject to secondary verification by INS office staff in the Orange County office. The normal turnaround for secondary verification averages two days. Employees are eligible to continue working during the secondary verification period, and employers are specifically instructed not to terminate or suspend employment pending completion of the secondary verification process. Should the Orange County office fail to veriFYeligibility, employer participants are notified that the subject employees are to report to the Orange County office for questioning as to identity and eligibility. Thus far, almost all referred workers have been arrested for carrying fraudulent documents.

Employers participating in the VIS program are required to sign an agreement under which they commit to proper utilization of the system information, including a commitment to use the data only after an offer of employment has been made and solely in connection with the initial verification of an employee's eligibility for U.S. employment. Participants are not excused from completion and retention of Form I-9 nor are they otherwise relieved from their obligations under the IRCA.

New Senate Enforcement Bill

Due to amendments during floor debate, the new Senate enforcement bill authorizes implementation of seven pilot projects for employment eligibility verification. Moreover, it mandates the implementation at a minimum, the following three pilot projects: telephone verification of social security numbers; counterfeit-resistant driver's licenses in a state already using the social security number on its licenses; and verification of work authorization for noncitizens only, with citizen attestations of citizenship. While the citizenship attestations appear to be a weak enforcement tool, an earlier amendment makes a false representation of citizenship adequate basis for deportation and permanent exclusion. Under the terms of these amendments, employers could not be held liable for any penalty for knowingly hiring or continuing to employ unauthorized workers provided they followed prescribed procedures including the secondary verification process and promptly discharged aliens when notified by INS that their work eligibility could not be verified. However, amendments have rendered employer participation in the program voluntary. During the course of the pilot projects, the Attorney General is to evaluate for accuracy and maintenance of individual privacy rights. If she determines that a project is highly accurate in its verification reporting and still maintains privacy, the pilot project requirements will supersede those under current law for participating employers. Additionally, the Attorney General has been empowered to make participation mandatory under the new requirements for some or all employers in the pilot project area for the remainder of the duration of the project.

H.R. 2202

Both the House and Senate versions of H.R. 2202 contain the following provision, which would obviate some employer anxiety about the validity and adequacy of the documents presented to them by potential workers. The bill reduces the number of documents acceptable for I-9 verification purposes from 29 to 6. A Kennedy floor amendment to the Senate version would have specified several criteria to establish employer good faith compliance with employment eligibility requirements, whereby, in Kennedy's words, "the employer is off the hook for employer sanctions on discrimination"; however, this clarification was killed during floor debate.

By comparison, the House version contains more significant changes to the current employment verification system. The House bill mandates the creation of an employment eligibility Confirmation Process by INS in at least five of the seven states with the highest number of undocumented workers. Employer and recruiter participation in the process would be purely voluntary through a system of election regulated by the Attorney General. In sanctions enforcement proceedings, employers who complied with the Confirmation rules would be entitled to a rebuttable presumption of compliance with respect to confirmed workers. Employers could be rejected for participation by the Attorney General due to lack of resources or for noncompliance with the Confirmation rules. Employers would also be able to withdraw from the program at any time.

The Confirmation Process specified in the House bill, to be implemented no later than one year following enactment, would call for additional checks on both U.S. citizen and alien hires. Participating employers would be required to obtain the social security number of U.S. citizen declarants and both the social security number and INS identification number of alien declarants. This additional information would be submitted by the employer or recruiter via electronic or computer processes to the INS data bank within three working days of hire, subject to extension due to INS inaccessibility. Upon receipt of appropriate confirmation, the employer would be required to record a confirmation number on the face of the I-9 form for future inspection. If confirmation is not received, the employer loses the presumption of compliance. If the employer continues to employ the subject employee, the employer is required to give notice to the INS of its employment of the worker and to prove that the worker is, in fact, authorized to work for the employer.

The House bill contains very limited worker protections in the event they apply to work for a participating employer. Although the House bill requires the Attorney General to provide a timely process for challenging nonconfirmations, not to exceed ten working days, employers are permitted to terminate workers because of a failure to have work eligibility confirmed after the ten-working-day period in which a final confirmation or nonconfirmation has been sought, or sooner if the employer has other unrelated grounds for termination. If an employee is dismissed from employment due to error in the confirmation system, the employee has a cause of action against the federal government pursuant to the Federal Tort Claims Act. Employer participants are insulated from liability under any law, including the Civil Rights Act of 1964, the Fair Labor Standards Act, the Americans with Disabilities Act, and the Age Discrimination in Employment Act, for any action taken in good faith reliance on information provided in the Confirmation Process. A prior version of H.R. 2202 reported out of the House Judiciary Committee contained provisions for implementation of a "tester program" to identiFYemployers who were violating the civil rights of employees and applicants through the modified verification process. The tester provisions were deleted prior to presentation of the voluntary employer confirmation program by the bill's sponsor, Representative Lamar Smith (R. TX).

The House bill also contains a provision authorizing employer members of a multi-employer bargaining unit to rely upon the verification performed by another employer member of the bargaining unit for a period of up to five years for permanent residents and three years for work-authorized aliens. Notwithstanding this provision, such employers can still be held liable for a knowing hire violation if the alien proves to be unauthorized, unless it can demonstrate through clear and convincing evidence that it did not know and could not reasonably have known of the employee's unauthorized status at the time of hire.

Not later than 180 days after enactment, the House bill requires the Attorney General to issue regulations authorizing employers to electronically store I-9 forms. Under current regulation, such storage is not permitted.

Additionally, the House bill requires INS to provide an in-person explanation of the deficiencies in I-9 verification forms, followed by a ten- day waiting period, prior to reverifying employer paperwork for fine purposes. Only employers accused of a pattern or practice of knowing hire or continuing to employ unauthorized workers would be deprived of the benefits of the I-9 cure provisions found in the House bill. Unlike the other changes discussed herein, the I-9 cure provisions will be effective upon enactment.

ALTERATIONS IN THE INA DOCUMENT ABUSE PROVISION

Regardless of which version is passed, both the House and Senate bills greatly reduce the number of documents which prove work authorization. INA § 274(B)(a)(6) renders it an unfair immigration-related employment practice to require "more or different documents than are required" under INA § 274A(b), or to fail "to honor documents tendered that on their face reasonably appear to be genuine." Both the Senate and House bills seek to amend the circumstances under which employers may be held liable for "document abuse."

The Senate bill amends INA § 274B(a)(6) in three significant ways. First, the amendment narrows the relief available by altering the proof standard applicable to claims of document abuse by requiring proof of a specific intent to discriminate against an individual based on national origin or citizenship status. Under current administrative interpretations, there is strict liability for requiring additional documents without regard to intent. Senator Kennedy has expressed strong opposition to this aspect of the amendment, but his amendment to strike this section was voted down in a close vote in the Judiciary Committee. Employers, on the other hand, welcome the change in the proof standard because of the difficult burden they face in verifying initial and continuing employment eligibility.

Second, the amended language requires proof that an alleged victim falls within the class of individuals otherwise protected from discrimination in referral, hire, and termination. The Office of Special Counsel for Immigration-Related Unfair Employment Practices has followed a policy of prosecuting employers for document abuse notwithstanding the status of the affected job applicant.

Third, the amendment clarifies that relief will be available in connection with hire, recruitment, or discharge of a protected individual. INA § 274B(a)(6) currently applies, on its face, solely to hiring activity, as opposed to referral or reverification actions. Thus, employers have argued, mostly unsuccessfully, that they cannot be prosecuted for overdocumentation following hire, *e.g.*, for reverification of an alien with a temporary work document.

The House version retains the current language of INA § 274B(6), but § 407 of the House bill provides that the following exemptions be added. First, the House bill allows employers to request a document authorizing renewal of employment authorization when an individual has previously submitted a time-limited document for verification purposes. Under current law, such a practice has been held violative of the INA document abuse provisions. Second, the House bill authorizes an employer to challenge the work authorization of employees presenting work eligibility and identity documents which are facially valid, if the employer has a good faith reason for doing so. Under such circumstances, the employer is obligated to inform the employee of the question about the document's validity and of the employer's intention to veriFYthe validity of the work document; the employer is authorized to dismiss the employee upon receipt of confirmation that the work authorization document is invalid.

NEW DOCUMENT FRAUD DEFINITIONS AND PENALTIES

Section 212 of H.R. 2202 and §132 of the original S. 269 expand the activities prohibited under INA § 274C to include the preparation, filing, or assistance in preparation or filing of any application for benefits or any document required by the INS, with knowledge or in reckless disregard of the fact that the application or document was falsely made. This provision would negate the effect of the decision of the Chief Administrative Hearing Officer in *United States v. Ramileh*, 5 OCAHO 724 (Feb. 7, 1995) holding that the attestation of an employee to false information on the Form I-9 does not constitute the creation of a falsely made document in violation of INA § 274C. Under the proposed amendment, employers also would be subject to prosecution for document fraud for alterations of I-9 forms, including but not limited to backdating.

The Senate immigration bill also calls for enhanced civil money penalties against violators of the document fraud provisions of up to two times the prescribed level of penalties where the employer has been found, pursuant to a final determination by the Secretary of Labor or a court of competent jurisdiction, to have committed willful or repeated violations of the Fair Labor Standards Act (governing payment of minimum wage and overtime), the Migrant and Seasonal Agricultural Worker Protection Act, and the Family and Medical Leave Act.

DOCUMENT IMPROVEMENTS

The Senate version of this bill mandates changes in state-issued driver's licenses to make them counterfeit proof, with the changes to be developed and implemented by the year 2000, a date suggested by the National Governors' Association, with a six-year phase-in period. Changes in state- and locality-issued birth certificates will have a two-year lead-in period after a report to Congress, with safety paper, the seal of the issuing agency, and other fraud reducing measures to be taken. The President is charged with designating an agency to develop guidelines for minimum standards for birth certificates. Also, there is a requirement that no state agency issuing driver's licenses or identification cards can accept a birth certificate unless it is issued by a state or local government and conforms to federal standards. Additionally, a project would be piloted in five states to determine the feasibility of reporting deaths within 24 hours to state vital statistics offices. Another Simpson amendment funds state efforts to match birth and death records, with a notation "deceased" made on copies of pertinent birth certificates, thus rendering impractical fraudulent use of duplicate birth certificates.

H-1B NONIMMIGRANT WORKER EMPLOYERS

The House bill mandates additional requirements for some employers of H-1B nonimmigrant workers. It would create two classes: H-1B "depend- ent" employers and H-1B "nondependent" employers, with additional attestation and other requirements imposed on H-1B dependent employ- ers. The Senate version does not address H-1B issues.

Additionally, the House version specifies that determination of the prevail- ing wage level for employees of higher learning institutions should consider only employees of similar institutions in the area of employment.

INCREASED CIVIL AND CRIMINAL PENALTIES

Despite much touted efforts to increase the cost of violating the employer sanctions laws, neither the House nor Senate enforcement bills includes increases in penalties.

Senate Judiciary Committee markup sessions resulted in the deletion of the provisions calling for increasing civil money penalties by as much as 400 percent. By way of affirmative relief to employers who could be cited for paperwork violations where I-9 forms were lost or destroyed by natural disaster, Senators Kennedy and Jon Kyl (R. AZ) agreed on amendment lan- guage that would shield such employers from liability in such cases. However, also in markup, employer liability was extended to state employment agencies, requiring them to veriFYthat prospective employees are eligible for employ- ment before sending them out to job interviews.

Although civil money penalties will not be affected by the reform legislation, criminal penalties for immigration law violations which may be charged along with an employer sanctions pattern or practice violation could well be increased. In the Judiciary Committee, Senator Kennedy sponsored a successful amendment requiring the U.S. Sentencing Commission to review and significantly increase sentencing guidelines for smuggling, harboring, or inducing aliens to enter the United States. Moreover, the Kennedy amendment instructs the Sentencing Commission to examine and amend as necessary the guidelines for crimes of peonage, involuntary servitude, and slave trade, as contrasted with kidnapping and alien smuggling.

The House Rules Committee contravened the recommendations of the Congressional Task Force on Immigration Reform by eliminating from consideration on the House floor increased employer sanctions. This action, validated by a floor vote on the rules, eliminated from consideration the amendment by Representative Anthony Beilenson (D. CA) providing for severely increased civil and criminal penalties for the gamut of employer violations, from mere paperwork violations to pattern and practice violations.

ASSET FORFEITURE PROVISIONS

Perhaps no aspect of the enforcement provisions of the Senate bill has aroused as much antipathy from the business community as the asset forfeiture provisions.

If the proposed asset forfeiture provisions were to become law, INS would be empowered to seize any employer property, real or personal, "which facilitates or is intended to facilitate, or is being used in or is intended to be used in the commission of" a violation, or the conspiracy to violate, the criminal provisions of Title 18 of the U.S. Code dealing with the unlawful procurement of U.S. citizenship or permanent resident status (§ 1425), counterfeiting of citizenship papers (§ 1426), sales of citizenship papers (§ 1427), and the false use of visas, permits, and other documents used for admission or employment in the United States (§ 1546).

Employer property could be seized even if the employer-owner is unaware of the unlawful immigration activity supporting the seizure, provided an employer or agent of the employer-owner committed the violation with the intention of furthering the business interests of the owner or conferring any other benefit upon the owner. In order to effect the seizure, the Attorney General need only provide notice and an opportunity to be heard to the owner of the property, in accordance with such regulations as the Attorney General shall prescribe.

During markup in the Senate Judiciary Committee, the committee deleted authorization for asset seizure in connection with the alleged commission of the knowing hire or continuing employment proscriptions of the INA. The asset forfeiture provisions of the House bill were also deleted at the committee level. This issue will probably not be revived.

The Senate version still provides for the criminal forfeiture of assets against any person "convicted" of violating various criminal provisions of Title 18 of the U.S. Code dealing with immigration. Hence any employer charged with civil violations of the substantive provisions of the INA would be well advised to contest violations, lest its property be subject to seizure.

NOTE

[1]This package originated as S. 269, 141 Cong. Rec. S. 1453 (daily ed. Jan. 24, 1995) and S. 1394, 141 Cong. Rec. S. 16669 (daily ed. Nov. 3, 1995). These bills were later merged, then subsequently divided. This issue is so controversial and multifaceted that the language of S. 1664, dealing only with illegal immigration, was subjected to 156 amendments. The language resulting from the floor debate was then substituted in a strike-everything procedural motion so that when the Senate passed H.R. 2202, it was passing the language contained in S. 1664, thus moving the legislation but necessitating a conference committee to negotiate the final language of the bill, which must then be revoted by both houses of Congress. As we go to press, the Senate conferees are appointed: Republican Senators Simpson, Grassley, Kyl, Specter, Hatch, and Thurmond and Democrats Kennedy, Feinstein, Simon, Kohl, and Leahy. House conferees are to be appointed by the Speaker.

6

Deficient Visas: Permanent Residents' Limited Marriage Rights in United States Immigration Law

GUNNAR BIRGISSON
Duke University

Imagine a foreign citizen coming to the United States to pursue university studies. Following graduation, he accepts a professional job in his occupation and eventually obtains permanent residency in the United States through his employment. After living in the United States for five years as a permanent resident he avails himself of the opportunity given by U.S. immigration law to become an American citizen. Now suppose that sometime during this period, the individual marries someone from his home country who has neither a U.S. immigrant nor nonimmigrant visa. If he does so while a student or a foreign working professional, or after becoming a U.S. citizen, he can bring his spouse to the United States within a few weeks or months, as the immigration laws have provisions allowing families of nonimmigrants and citizens to be reunified in the United States. Were he, however, to marry while a permanent resident – an immigrant to the United

States – he could not bring his wife to the United States within a short period of time, as the immigration laws provide a permanent resident with no such right. The permanent resident's only option is to sponsor the spouse for an immigration visa. But the wait for such a visa is several years because of quotas limiting the number of yearly immigrants to the United States. During this waiting period, the alien spouse cannot in any way benefit from the permanent resident's spouse status to legally reside in the United States, and can only come to the United States on a visa unrelated to the permanent resident's visa. Nor is this problem limited to the permanent resident's alien spouse. Should they have children who are not themselves permanent residents or have another type of visa, the children also must wait for years before being allowed to come to the United States.

At this point, an important distinction is warranted. The problem addressed in this paper can affect an individual who becomes a permanent resident before he is married as well as his subsequent spouse. But for couples who are married before either obtains permanent residency, there is ordinarily no such problem, because the two can simultaneously be granted permanent residency if they are both listed on the application. Still, there are many thousands of families that are penalized by the former situation, and it is their plight to which this paper addresses.

It is contended in this paper that denying a permanent resident the right to bring a spouse to the United States within a short period of time constitutes a flaw in U.S. immigration law that is unfairly discriminatory against permanent residents. As a consequence of the law, spouses can be separated for several years, or marriages can be unduly delayed until the permanent resident spouse acquires U.S. citizenship. The delays cause hardship and inflict an arbitrariness on the marriage and family planning of permanent residents and potential immigrants.

In reviewing the marriage rights of permanent residents, this paper will examine the marriage rights provided by immigration law to U.S. citizens, permanent residents, and nonimmigrants; analyze this issue in light of the importance of marriage as expressed in U.S. constitutional law and international law; and examine the relationship, if any, to the perceived marriage fraud immigration problem in the United States. Finally, three alternative solutions will be proposed. The first alternative consists of clearing the backlog of pending applications. The second is to give permanent residents the same right as citizens to bring a spouse to the United States within a short period of time. The third is to allow the alien spouse to come to and reside in the United States but deny him or her certain immigration benefits such as employment authorization until the time when he or she obtains permanent resident status according to the current provisions of the immigration laws.

CITIZENS AND PERMANENT RESIDENTS

Permanent residency is defined in the Immigration and Nationality Act (8 U.S.C. § 1101(a)(20)) as "the status of having been lawfully accorded the privilege of residing permanently in the United States as an immigrant in accordance with the immigration laws, such status not having changed." Permanent residents have the right to live and work in the United States for an indefinite period of time, but lack many of the voting rights citizens hold. Additionally, unlike citizens, permanent residents cannot live abroad for long periods of time and return to the United States without risking loss of their status since maintaining permanent resident status requires an intent to reside in the United States.[1]

With the Immigration Act of 1990, Congress increased the number of immigrant visas available to relatives of citizens and permanent residents. As in earlier versions of the Act, there is no limit on the number of spouses of U.S. citizens who may immigrate each year. Accordingly, there is no backlog of unprocessed applications of spouses waiting for immigration visas. Any delays alien spouses of citizens experience are just those resulting from preparation and processing of the necessary applications. Family-sponsored immigrants who are not immediate relatives of U.S. citizens fall into one of four preference categories (8 U.S.C. 1153(a)). Spouses of permanent residents are classified in the second preference category, subcategory 2A.[2] Immigrants in these preference categories are subject to quota restrictions that have the effect of delaying the availability of an immigrant visa for several years.

The Immigration Act of 1990 established a yearly overall cap on the number of family-sponsored immigrants. Immediate relatives of U.S. citizens are counted towards this cap even though they are exempt from the numerical limits (8 U.S.C. §§ 1151, 1153). Consequently, the more immediate relatives of U.S. citizens immigrate in a given year, the fewer other individuals eligible for family-sponsored immigration will be granted immigration visas that year. There is a floor on that decrease, however, so that preference category relatives will be allocated a minimum number of visas yearly.

From October 1994 onward the cap governing the number of yearly family-sponsored immigrants is set at 480,000. The minimum number of visas available to all preference category immigrants is 226,000 per year. The second family-sponsored preference is allotted up to 114,200 immigrant visas annually, plus any unused visas from the first family-sponsored category.[3] A minimum of 77 percent of these visas must be given to spouses and unmarried children of permanent residents. The exact number of these visas varies from year to year, but it fails by a large margin to meet the demand. Because of the many applicants for immigration visas in the family-sponsored categories, applicants in the 2A category have to wait for several years before obtaining their immigration visas. In October 1996, the INS was preparing to grant visas to parties on whose behalf applications were filed in January 1993 – a wait approaching four years.[4]

Until a spouse's application becomes current, no alternative visa is specifically made available to him or her. In fact, having applied for permanent residency may actually harm efforts of the alien spouse to obtain a different visa. For example, the principal visa given to visitors to the United States, the B visa, specifically requires that the visitor not intend to permanently settle in the United States – the very thing a permanent resident's spouse intends to do. And while a fiancé of a citizen can avail himself or herself of the K visa to travel to the United States to marry a citizen, no such visa is available to the fiancé of a permanent resident.

It should be pointed out that a permanent resident can eventually qualify for U.S. citizenship. Once he does indeed become a U.S. citizen, his spouse is freed from the burden of the quotas and can qualify for first preference processing. But to qualify for citizenship the permanent resident must first reside in the United States for five years after obtaining his immigrant visa. So this does not offer much relief to the individual who has recently obtained permanent residency status and the spouse desiring to join him or her in the United States.

PERMANENT RESIDENTS AND NONIMMIGRANTS

In contrast to the restrictive treatment of permanent residents, immigration law does provide visas for spouses (and other immediate family members) of various types of nonimmigrants dwelling in the United States, without subjecting nonimmigrants' spouses to the lengthy delays experienced by immigrants' spouses. For example, spouses of students with an F-1 visa can obtain an F-2 visa, thus enabling both spouses to reside in the United States. Aliens coming to the United States to participate in exchange-visitor programs are eligible for J-1 visas, and their spouses can in turn obtain J-2 visas. Spouses with J-2 visas can even get employment authorization, so long as it is not necessary for support of the J-1 visitor. It should be noted, however, that approval of J and F visas is not guaranteed for either the student or the spouse. Applicants must convince the INS that they intend to dwell only temporarily in the United States and have no intention of abandoning their foreign residence. If the immigration officer in charge of reviewing the visa application suspects an alien is intending to settle permanently in the United States, the visa may be denied.

Nonimmigrant aliens who come to the United States to engage in specialty occupations for which they are qualified by virtue of their education and abilities may receive H-1B visas. Spouses and children can obtain H-4 visas to reside in the United States with the professional worker. A maximum of 65,000 H-1B visas may currently be granted each year. This is not discriminatory against the spouse, however, because if an H-1B visa is granted, the corresponding spousal visa would normally be issued along with it – meaning that either both or neither of the spouses would be granted visas. Family members of recipients of other kinds of H visas, which includes H-3 visas for trainees, are also eligible for H-4 visas.

Significantly, whether the INS issues a visa in any of the aforementioned nonimmigrant categories does not depend on the timing of a nonimmigrant couple's marriage. This constitutes a key distinction between the rights of a permanent resident and a nonimmigrant. As discussed earlier, the problem addressed in this paper arises for an individual who obtains permanent residency before getting married. If the couple is already married, both spouses ordinarily receive immigrant visas at the same time. For nonimmigrants, the timing of the marriage has no such crucial importance. As with permanent residents, if a couple is already married when the primary visa holder obtained his visa, the spouse can simultaneously obtain a visa. But if the couple marries after either party already has a nonimmigrant visa, the other is nevertheless eligible for a spousal nonimmigrant visa, *e.g.* a J-2, and is not subject to delays of many years. Likewise, it is irrelevant whether the primary visa holder is already in the United States and the spouse is still in the foreign country. In fact, a nonimmigrant can obtain a B-2 visa to come to the United States to marry a nonimmigrant, after which a visa derivative from the spouse's status can be obtained, *e.g.* an F-2 visa if the spouse has an F-1 visa. In essence, both nonimmigrants and citizens can thus sponsor an engaged partner to come to the United States, but a permanent resident cannot.

The fundamental distinction between these nonimmigrant visas and immigration visas is the absence of quotas having the effect of keeping the spouses apart. The purpose of quotas in immigration law is primarily to limit the number of immigrants. Nonimmigrants such as students and tourists (but not some workers) are largely exempt from such numerical restrictions. The absence of restrictive quotas means that the immigration laws afford nonimmigrants a much better opportunity than permanent residents to bring their new spouses to the United States.

Overall, it may seem justifiable that in some respects permanent residents have lesser rights than U.S. citizens, but in this respect permanent residents have even lesser rights than nonimmigrants. This is particularly odd in light of the fact that aside from these marriage rights, in other areas of the law permanent residents are better situated than nonimmigrants. This includes the right to live, work, vote and receive social benefits in the United States, but apparently not the right to marry and live in this country with a spouse who happens not to be a permanent resident or citizen.

RELATIONSHIP TO MARRIAGE FRAUD CONCERNS

Some may believe the restrictions imposed on permanent residents bear some relationship to the issue of "green card marriages," *i.e.*, cases where a citizen or permanent resident marries a nonresident alien in order to bestow on him or her the privileges of permanent resident status. In fact there is no direct relationship between the quota restrictions on spouses of permanent residents and the congressional response to the problem of marriage fraud. The Immigration Marriage Fraud Amendments were passed into law in 1986 in response to perceived abuses of immigration laws by which citizens and permanent residents married aliens solely to provide them with immigration benefits. Under the statute, if a citizen or permanent resident marries an alien and sponsors the spouse for permanent residency, the alien spouse's permanent residence is conditional for the first two years of the marriage. During this period the INS will ascertain that the marriage is bona fide and does not exist solely to provide an immigration benefit to the alien spouse. In case of marriage fraud, the alien spouse is stripped of his or her conditional permanent residency and is placed in deportation hearings, and the permanent resident or citizen spouse faces penalties. Although this is a separate issue from the one addressed in this paper, marriage fraud concerns have a looming presence in the area of spousal sponsorship and fear of abuse of more favorable laws is a potential obstacle to much needed reform in the area of marriage rights.

RIGHTS-BASED REMEDIES: CONSTITUTIONAL AND INTERNATIONAL LAW

The United States Supreme Court has repeatedly affirmed that the right to marry is one of the fundamental liberties protected by the U.S. Constitution,[5] and one of the "basic civil rights of man."[6] In the immigration context the Court has stated that rejoining one's immediate family is "a right that ranks high among the interests of the individual" (*Landon v. Plascencia*, 459 U.S. 21, 34 1982). In light of the strength and clarity of such pronouncements, the difficulty permanent residents have in bringing their spouses to the United States, particularly in comparison to the relative ease afforded to both citizens and nonimmigrants in this regard, might appear to be discriminatory against permanent residents. Specifically, since the right to marry is considered one of the fundamental rights protected by the United States Constitution, impeding permanent residents' right to marry is arguably a violation of the Fifth Amendment.

The author is not aware of any cases directly challenging the constitutionality of this aspect of the immigration laws. Even if such a case were brought, it would appear unlikely to meet with success because of the extensive power courts acknowledge Congress to possess over the field of immigration law. Although immigration as such is not specifically mentioned in the Constitution, Congress' power over the field has been attributed to several portions of the Constitution, such as the Naturalization Clause, as well as from implied constitutional powers incidental to United States sovereignty and foreign relations. But regardless of the exact source of its power over immigration law, Congress' "plenary power to make rules for the admission of aliens"[7] is a well-established part of Supreme Court jurisprudence.

The Supreme Court has gone so far as to state that "[o]ver no conceivable subject is the legislative power of Congress more complete than it is over" the admission of aliens.[8] Furthermore, the Court has explicitly sanctioned unequal treatment of aliens and citizens: "[i]n the exercise of its broad power over naturalization and immigration, Congress regularly makes rules that would be unacceptable if applied to citizens. . . . The fact that an Act of Congress treats aliens differently from citizens does not in itself imply that such disparate treatment is 'invidious'" (*Matthews v. Diaz*, 426 U.S. 67, 80–81 1976). In light of this extreme deference by the courts to Congress, a judicial challenge to the constitutionality of this aspect of the immigration law would likely be futile. There are additional obstacles to a rights-based remedy: the fact that permanent residency is not an individual's immutable characteristic such as race or gender since permanent residents can become citizens after the requisite period of time; the quota system has been an established part of immigration law for three-quarters of a century; and also, permanent residents are not directly denied the right to marry, which likely would be unconstitutional, but instead are subjected to hinderances in bringing their spouses to the United States.

As regards international human rights law, its principles support the basic notion that the freedom to marry shall be protected by nations, but it provides but general support for an argument that the United States immigration laws violate the human rights of permanent residents. International law expresses the importance of the family in a number of conventions and other instruments. Article 23 of the International Convention on Civil and Political Rights, to which the United States is a party, states that:

1. The family is the natural and fundamental unit of society and is entitled to protection by society and the State.

2. The right of men and women of marriageable age to marry and to found a family shall be recognized.

This language makes no distinction between spouses of different nationalities, marriages of different lengths, or families of different sizes. Nevertheless, it would constitute overreaching to read into the Convention's general language any obligations regarding the marriage rights of permanent residents in the United States or elsewhere. U.S. courts have held that even though treaties such as this one are the "supreme law of the land" under the Constitution, treaty articles phrased in broad generalities do not create judicially enforceable rights in the United States (*Frolova v. U.S.S.R.*, 761 F.2d 370, 7th Cir. 1985).

The Helsinki Accords do address the issue of marriage between citizens of different states, but under their provisions states need only deal with family reunification applications "in a positive and humanitarian spirit" and "as expeditiously as possible."[9] Although this may be more detailed than the International Convention on Civil and Political Rights provisions, specific requirements with which states must comply are not set out.

LEGISLATIVE REMEDIES

The relative disadvantage immigration law imposes on permanent residents planning to marry aliens does not appear to be a deliberate choice made by the United States Congress. The marriage rights of immigrants, nonimmigrants, and citizens have not been considered together as a single issue by Congress. Instead, separate laws for each category of people have been passed at different times, with the unfortunate result that permanent residents have been left with lesser rights than citizens and nonimmigrants. This may give hope that Congress would favorably consider a remedy to this inequitable legislative scheme.

Several alternative legislative solutions are possible. One is to clear the backlog of pending applications by making all permanent resident spousal applications current. The obvious advantage of this is simplicity. But such a remedy would only address the current consequences of a problem rather than the problem itself. Eventually the backlog would again build up and a growing number of spouses would be waiting for visas.

The other alternatives would be to put permanent residents on equal footing either with citizens or with nonimmigrants. The former option would liberate permanent residents' spouses from the delays caused by the quota system, and thus give permanent residents the same rights as citizens to bring a spouse to the United States. The basis of this proposal is that the spouse of a permanent resident already has the right under the U.S. immigration law to immigrate, but is the victim of delays caused by restrictive quotas on the number of immigrant visas issued yearly. Terminating the quota provision would simply provide without delay what the spouse is eventually entitled to anyway under the immigration laws.

The reasonableness of granting permanent residents the same rights as citizens in this respect is aptly demonstrated by the fact that this is the law in Canada, which like the United States is a country that is largely constituted of immigrants and descendants of immigrants. Permanent residents of Canada enjoy exactly the same right as Canadian citizens to sponsor a spouse for permanent residency. Furthermore, permanent residents also share with citizens the ability to sponsor fiancés for permanent residency. There are no quotas limiting the number of yearly family-sponsored immigrants, so neither the spouse of a citizen nor of a permanent resident has to wait for years abroad for an immigration visa.

An alternative, less radical, solution would enable spouses to reunite in the United States while yet preserving the integrity of the immigration quota system. This would require creating a new nonimmigrant visa – or transitional visa – for spouses of permanent residents. Such a visa would let a spouse come to and reside in the United States but could deny him or her the right to work or receive other benefits afforded to permanent residents. In this respect the spouse would be similarly situated to spouses of most nonimmigrants. The alien spouse would then be able to reside in the United States until the immigration visa became available and he or she could become a permanent resident and obtain a wider range of rights. Although this second option would be less satisfactory to pro-immigration advocates, it would better serve to appease those who believe that the United States currently allows too much immigration.

Neither of these options need be incompatible with or undermine the marriage fraud laws. Under either scheme the INS could remain as vigorous as it currently is in ensuring that marriages between aliens and permanent residents are in fact bona fide.

It should also be pointed out to potential adversaries of either of these proposals that from an economic point of view, it seems possible that during the time an alien spouse waits for an immigrant visa, a larger portion of the permanent resident's earnings are likely to be sent abroad if the spouse resides there. Remedying this situation might thus help keep money in the U.S. economy.

CONCLUSION

Although it does not appear that Congress intended to discriminate against permanent residents, it is nevertheless true that immigration law greatly restricts the ability of permanent residents, when compared with that of citizens and nonimmigrants, to bring an alien spouse to the United States. The resulting lengthy wait for an immigration visa for a spouse is an inappropriate obstacle to spousal unity and represents an unwarranted intrusion into the private affairs of permanent residents, whose marriage rights should be respected and supported by the law to the same extent as the marriage rights of citizens and nonimmigrants. Congress should consider this matter and enact legislation to remedy it by granting permanent residents the right to sponsor a spouse to immediately come to the United States.

NOTES

[1]Contrary to what the term itself indicates, individuals can be deprived of permanent residence, for example if the INS determines that an individual has abandoned his permanent resident status in the United States (*Matter of Huang*, 19 I&N Dec. 749, BIA 1988).

[2]Permanent residents' unmarried children under the age of 21 are also in the 2A category. Permanent resident's children who are 21 or older can apply in the 2B category. The first category covers unmarried sons and daughters of U.S. citizens. The third category applies to married sons and daughters of U.S. citizens. The fourth family category covers brothers and sisters of adult U.S. citizens.

[3]Only 23,400 first-preference visas are given yearly. This makes it unlikely that any surplus visas will be available for second-preference applicants.

[4]State Department, *Visa Bulletin,* Number 67, Vol. VII (Oct. 1996).

[5]*See e.g.*, *Zablocki v. Redhail,* 434 U.S. 374, 386 (1978), *Moore v. City of East Cleveland,* 431 U.S. 494, 499, 503–504 (1977), *Stanley v. Illinois,* 405 U.S. 645, 651 (1972).

[6]*Loving v. Virginia,* 388 U.S. 1, 12 (1967), citing *Skinner v. Oklahoma,* 316 U.S. 535, 541 (1942).

[7]*Kleindienst v. Mandel,* 408 U.S. 753, 765 (1972); citing *Boutilier v. INS,* 387 U.S. 118, 123 (1967).

[8]*Kleindienst* id, citing *Oceanic Navigation Co. v. Stranahan,* 214 U.S. 320, 339 (1909).

[9]Conference on Security and Cooperation in Europe: Final Act, Aug. 1, 1975, 73 *State Dep't Bulletin* 323 (1975), reprinted in 14 *ILM* 1292 (1975).

PART II

WELFARE REFORM: WHAT BENEFITS FOR IMMIGRANTS?

7

Welfare Reform: A New Immigrant Policy for the United States[1]

MICHAEL FIX
WENDY ZIMMERMANN
The Urban Institute

The Personal Responsibility and Work Opportunity Reconciliation Act of 1996 (Public Law 104-193), significantly scales back welfare benefits for the poor and disabled and gives states greater responsibility for designing assistance programs for needy families. The new law singles out immigrants for especially deep cuts while giving states new powers to determine immigrants' eligibility for public services.

New restrictions on legal immigrants' eligibility for benefits represent a radical shift in the nation's immigrant policies, *i.e.*, those policies that influence immigrant integration. By treating immigrants differently than other groups, the welfare law transforms U.S. immigrant policy from a laissez-faire or hands-off set of policies that treat legal immigrants on largely the same terms as citizens, to an explicit policy of exclusion.

Congressionally enacted limits on the public services available to immigrants were accompanied by equally significant limits imposed on immigrants' due process rights by the Illegal Immigration Reform and Immigrant Responsibility Act of 1996 (Public Law 104-208) and the Anti-Terrorism and Effective Death Penalty Act of 1996 (Public Law 104-132). These latter two laws significantly limited the rights of those seeking asylum in the United States, illegal immigrants who are apprehended in the United States, and legal immigrants who commit crimes.

When viewed collectively, welfare reform, illegal immigration reform, and the antiterrorism bill differ in important ways from congressional efforts to reform immigration over the past three decades. First, the reforms attempt to mitigate the purportedly negative impacts of immigration by restricting the benefits and rights available to immigrants, not by reducing the number or changing the characteristics of new immigrants. Indeed, attempts to limit legal immigration during the 104th Congress were stymied by opposition from an unusual coalition of immigration advocacy groups, libertarian think tanks, and high-tech employers fearful of losing highly skilled international workers (*see* Fix and Zimmermann, 1995).

Second, unlike the other landmark immigration laws enacted over the past 30 years which balanced inclusionary and exclusionary forces, the 1996 reforms are overwhelmingly exclusionary in character.[2] It could be argued that the reforms set out in the welfare, illegal immigration, and antiterrorism laws represent the most exclusionary turn in immigration policy since establishment of the national origins quota system in the nativist 1920s.

Third, each embraces a policy of what has been termed immigrant exceptionalism – one that seeks to deepen the differences between the rights and entitlements of citizens and noncitizens. In so doing, the laws tend to elevate the power and authority of the government over that of the individual. As a result, they represent a sharp retreat from important trends in immigration law that began to emerge in the 1970s – trends that vested legal and illegal immigrants with expanding rights and privileges and embraced more universalistic visions of membership (*see* Schuck, 1984).

As we imply above, the immigrant provisions in welfare reform – the primary focus of this study – carry broad policy implications for individuals and institutions that go well beyond changes in immigrants' eligibility for public benefits. They represent a redefinition of citizenship, a departure from past refugee policy, a reformulation of the role of immigrant families and sponsors, and an expansion of the immigration-related enforcement duties of public and private service providers. The law also signals a dramatic shift in the roles of federal, state and local government in the integration of immigrants and in the distribution of their costs and benefits across federal, state and local governments.

The broad new restrictions on immigrants could have a profound effect on future integration patterns. However, many crucial policy choices remain that will determine how much of the safety net is left for immigrants and the degree to which welfare reform promotes or retards integration.

We begin by examining the political evolution and policy context of the welfare reform's immigrant restrictions. We then review some of the law's expected impacts. The following section examines some of the policy implications and implementation issues that stem from the reforms. As we proceed, we suggest some of the ways in which the welfare reform, illegal immigration, and antiterrorism laws interact.

BACKGROUND

Political Evolution

Federal proposals to broadly restrict legal immigrants' eligibility for public benefits have a long and thoroughly bipartisan history. President Clinton's original proposal for welfare reform introduced in 1994 included restrictions on immigrants that were nearly as restrictive as those included in the version of the bill that became law. The initial restrictions were later broadened by the Personal Responsibility Act, a centerpiece of the Republicans' 1994 Contract for America. A modified version of the restrictions was later included in immigration reform proposals in both the House and Senate. Finally, a Republican-sponsored welfare reform law passed the Congress and was signed by the President. While the version finally signed by the President was one of the most restrictive proposed, a nearly identical set of restrictions sponsored by Senator Alan Simpson poised to become law under the rubric of immigration reform failed.

The primary rationale for all proposals to curb immigrants' access to benefits was the need for federal budget savings. Nearly half the $54 billion in estimated savings from welfare reform is expected to come from the immigrant exclusions. Although the President has publicly stated that he signed the bill despite the immigrant restrictions and that he intends to try to "fix" the provisions in the next Congress, the fiscal and political costs of doing so are likely to prove too great for sweeping policy reversals.

Policy Context

What developments made such restrictive, potentially far-reaching reforms possible just a few years after Congress voted to increase legal immigration by 40 percent?

Growing Numbers and Concentration. The first half of the 1990s has seen larger numbers of immigrants entering the United States than ever before, with over 1 million immigrants entering and staying each year. This figure includes about 700,000 legal immigrants, 100,000 refugees, and 200,000 to 300,000 illegal immigrants. The force of these flows has been magnified by its concentration in a handful of states, with over three-quarters of recent immigrants living in just six states (Fix *et al.*, 1994).

Debate Focused on Immigrants' Costs and Use of Welfare. Over the past several years the debate over immigration has become increasingly visible. But the tenor of the current debate differs from earlier periods, focusing less on the number and qualifications of new immigrants and more on their costs. Immigrants' participation in welfare and other public assistance programs has been at the core of that debate – which may help explain the use of welfare rather than admissions policy to limit immigration's perceived negative impacts. The political debate over migrants' use of public benefits in the 104th Congress returned repeatedly to a number of questions: Are immigrants more likely to use benefits than natives? Do immigrants come to the United States for benefits? Do they contribute more in taxes than they use in services? Are the families of immigrants assuming responsibility for the relatives they sponsor?

The answers to these questions depend on the analytic approach adopted. Although immigrants have slightly higher overall levels of welfare use than natives, their welfare use is heavily concentrated among two subpopulations. One is refugees, who enter the United States under different and more trying circumstances than other immigrants. The other is elderly immigrants, many of whom use Supplemental Security Income (SSI) because they have not worked enough quarters to qualify for social security, and because SSI represented a bridge to Medicaid and health insurance. By contrast, nonrefugee, working-age immigrants use welfare at rates that are comparable to those of working-age natives, although their use has increased somewhat in recent years.

The unit of analysis also matters: when immigrant-headed households are compared to native-headed households, immigrants show higher rates of use than natives. This is because many immigrant households contain native-born citizens who use welfare and because immigrant households are larger than native households (*see* Fix, Passel and Zimmermann, 1996a, 1996b). Results can also differ because "welfare" can be defined in many ways. Conventionally, welfare refers to cash assistance programs. But it can also be defined to include a wide variety of public assistance programs ranging from Medicaid, to the reduced-price school lunch program, to housing assistance. But even when these broader measures are included, higher individual use of benefits among immigrants (versus natives) for individual programs is only evident for SSI.

The concentration of immigrant welfare use among refugees and the elderly suggests that the immigrant restrictions have not been driven by the same behavioral goals that have animated welfare reform more generally – that is, moving single mothers into the workplace and discouraging out-of-wedlock births. Rather, the immigrant restrictions in the welfare bill are more likely the product of fiscal imperatives coinciding with an increased tolerance for anti-immigrant measures.

The immigrant restrictions should also be viewed in the context of a shrinking welfare state that is allocating losses rather than gains to almost all vulnerable populations. We see, then, that welfare reform narrows SSI disability criteria and imposes a three-month limit on able-bodied adults' use of food stamps in any three-year period. Looking beyond the welfare context, we see similar trends. While the immigration and antiterrorism laws restrict immigrants' due process rights, the Congress and the courts have been limiting the reach of legal services and class action litigation for the general population. Still, while immigrants confront the same limits on services as other groups, they must also contend with the additional restrictions on rights and benefits for which they have been singled out.

WELFARE REFORM AND IMMIGRANT ELIGIBILITY FOR PUBLIC BENEFITS

The welfare reform legislation makes five key sets of changes to immigrants' eligibility for public assistance programs. First, it bars legal immigrants for the first time from receiving most federal means-tested public benefits. The legislation places more severe restrictions on future immigrants (*i.e.*, those entering on or after August 22, 1996) than on immigrants living in the United States when the law was passed (referred to as current immigrants). Both current and future legal immigrants are barred from receiving SSI and food stamps. Future legal immigrants are barred from receiving most federal means-tested benefits for their first five years in the country.

Second, the law increases sponsors' responsibility for the immigrants they bring into the United States. When legal immigrants are admitted to the country they must demonstrate that they will not become a "public charge," or a burden on the U.S. coffers. One way to do so is to have a relative or friend sign an affidavit promising to support the immigrant. Although the affidavit is used in considering an immigrant's application for admission, the courts have ruled that those that were previously in force were not legally binding. Thus, sponsors who failed to support immigrants could not be sued. Welfare reform requires that a new affidavit of support be designed that is legally enforceable. (There is, however, some question as to whether this is legally feasible.)

The new law also expands sponsor-to-alien deeming, under which the sponsor's income is deemed to be available to the immigrant when determining eligibility for public benefits. Prior to the passage of the 1996 welfare law, a portion of the sponsor's income was deemed to the immigrant for three major programs: AFDC (Aid to Families with Dependent Children), SSI, and food stamps. The deeming period lasted for three years after entry for AFDC and food stamps and five years for SSI. Under the new law, deeming is expanded to most federal means-tested programs and will last until the immigrant naturalizes. The new deeming requirements will not go into effect until after the five-year bar on federal means-tested programs has run for new immigrants.

The recent illegal immigration reform bill imposed new requirements on sponsors, requiring that they earn at least 125 percent of the poverty level. While no firm income requirements were applied under former law, the poverty level was used to assess a sponsor's ability to support an immigrant. It could be the case that the new income threshold will prohibit many low-income persons from sponsoring family members, potentially altering future legal immigration flows.[3]

Third, the legislation bars aliens categorized as "not qualified" aliens from most federal, state and local public benefits. These include undocumented immigrants and others with temporary authority to remain in the United States. The legislation provides a broad definition of the types of programs from which these unqualified aliens are barred.[4]

Fourth, the new welfare law dramatically alters state authority to set eligibility rules for immigrants. It gives states new flexibility to determine eligibility for legal immigrants for three major programs: AFDC (or Temporary Assistance for Needy Families – TANF – which replaces AFDC under the new welfare reform law), Medicaid, and the Title XX Social Services block grant. It also grants the states the power to restrict legal immigrants' access to their own-funded public benefit programs.

Fifth, the legislation requires that service providers verify that those applying for federal public benefits are qualified aliens. Although states already verified the eligibility of noncitizens for most of the major benefit programs, the new law expands these verification requirements to a much broader set of organizations and programs.

Reforms Not Enacted

Although these recent policy changes are quite far-reaching, it is also worth noting that a number of equally far-reaching proposals advanced in earlier welfare and immigration bills did not become law. (They are, however, likely to be taken up again in the next Congress.) A proposed 40 percent reduction in legal immigration levels was pulled out of a comprehensive immigration bill, voted on separately and, to many observers' surprise, defeated. A proposal to allow states to bar undocumented immigrant children from public schools was stricken from the illegal immigration bill in order to ensure Presidential approval. Proposals that would have extended sponsor-to-alien deeming beyond citizenship were abandoned, along with proposals that would have required that sponsors have incomes equal to at least 200 percent of the poverty line – a requirement that would have made it impossible for one-half of United States citizens to sponsor a family member.

Many Choices and Questions Remaining

It is a generally unappreciated fact that much of the final shape and impact of the reforms depend on a series of crucial, defining actions still to be taken by both federal and state governments. Perhaps the most important is how the Executive Branch will choose to define the scope of the means-tested federal benefits programs from which future legal immigrants will be barred. A narrow definition would include only a handful of programs; a broad one would fold in the 60 or more programs once specified in the Personal Responsibility Act. Similarly, the breadth of the safety net provided to illegal and other "not qualified" immigrants depends on how the opaque phrase "federal, state and local public benefits" will be defined.

Beyond these definitional choices, the legislation explicitly leaves it to states to decide whether qualified immigrants will be eligible for TANF, Medicaid, and Title XX Social Services. As of this writing, only 5 of the 30 states that have submitted plans for implementing TANF intend to bar legal immigrants from the program.

Other far-reaching implementation decisions that remain include determining what criteria the federal government will use to establish that someone has worked 40 quarters. States must decide how quickly they will begin implementing the new immigration restrictions. (Only California, which tried to cut off undocumented women from receiving state-funded prenatal care, has so far moved to bar undocumented immigrants from state services.) Federal and state governments will have to determine how rigorously they will monitor whether programs are correctly verifying status.

The law's impacts, both in terms of federal budget savings and the number of people affected, depend on the extent to which immigrants naturalize; this in turn, depends on the success of the Immigration and Naturalization Service (INS) in processing the growing numbers of naturalization applications. The INS implementation of a new waiver for the disabled from the required English and civics tests, as well as a waiver for those who cannot afford the $95 application fee will affect many benefits recipients, since large numbers are poor, disabled, and non-English speaking. Whether immigrants will be naturalized quickly enough to avoid losing benefits may also be affected by a new INS initiative to institute stricter FBI checks of each applicant's criminal background.

Finally, the considerable impacts of the bill may be tempered if the Clinton Administration keeps its pledge to fix, or at least soften, the immigrant restrictions. Although it appears unlikely that new legislation will be enacted that reverses the broad changes made, the Administration could make marginal improvements to the bill by, for example, exempting some of the most vulnerable populations (disabled SSI recipients, *e.g.*) and by defining key terms narrowly.

EXPECTED IMPACTS OF REFORMS

The many decisions still to be made regarding definitions, eligibility, and implementation make it difficult to assess the impacts of the new welfare law. Some data, however, are available that provide a glimpse of possible effects on individuals, poverty, and on states.

Perhaps the most telling figure is the Congressional Budget Office (CBO) calculation that 44 percent of the $54 billion in estimated savings from the welfare bill can be attributed to the bars on immigrant eligibility. Although immigrants account for only about five percent of all welfare users, they account for nearly half of the savings from welfare reform.

The bars on SSI and food stamps to both current and future legal immigrants will result in significant numbers of people losing benefits. The CBO estimated that approximately 500,000, or three-quarters of current noncitizen SSI recipients would lose their benefits under the new restrictions. They also estimated that about 1,000,000 current noncitizen food stamp recipients, or about 56 percent of all noncitizen recipients, would lose benefits (CBO, 1996).[5]

These restrictions are likely to affect some of the most vulnerable immigrant populations. Although much of the rhetoric behind the restrictions for SSI focused on keeping newly arrived elderly immigrant parents off the welfare rolls, 40 percent of immigrants who receive SSI are disabled (Ponce, 1996). In addition, the bar on food stamps is likely to affect large numbers of immigrant children: 64 percent of food stamp households headed by a noncitizen contain children (Smolkin, Stavrianos and Burton, 1996).

The eligibility restrictions on SSI are also likely to have a direct effect on immigrant eligibility for Medicaid. Many SSI recipients receive Medicaid through their eligibility for SSI. When they lose SSI they lose Medicaid, unless they can establish eligibility some other way. The CBO estimates that about 300,000 immigrants will lose Medicaid eligibility by 1998.[6] About 165,000 legal immigrants may lose access to Medicaid as a result of the SSI bar and another 135,000 will lose Medicaid because of the restrictions on unqualified aliens and the five-year bar on future immigrants.[7] These figures, however, represent a comparatively small share of the more than 2 million noncitizens covered by Medicaid in 1995.[8]

The restrictions on immigrant eligibility for benefits are also likely to move significant numbers of families into poverty – families that contain both citizens and noncitizens. A study conducted by the Urban Institute estimated that the immigrant restrictions in the welfare bill will account for nearly half of the persons – 1.2 out of 2.6 million – to be moved into poverty as a result of the law. The bars on immigrants also account for 450,000 of the 1.1 million children expected to be pushed into poverty because of the new law (Zadlewski et al., 1996). These figures include both citizens and noncitizens because of the large share of noncitizen-headed households that contain citizens (50 percent).

Because immigrants are so heavily concentrated in just a handful of states, the impacts of the eligibility restrictions on immigrants will also be highly concentrated. Forty-one percent of all noncitizen SSI recipients live in California, another 33 percent live in New York, Florida, and Texas (Ponce, 1996). Further, several of the states containing large numbers of immigrants have comparatively high benefit levels, including California and New York. As a result, those states are slated to lose even larger amounts of federal money and, if they provide state-funded assistance to immigrants, their costs of providing assistance to immigrants will also be higher relative to other states.

POLICY IMPLICATIONS

In exploring some of the more and less remarked upon implications of the recent changes to immigrant eligibility for public benefits, we examine their implications for individuals – for social membership and citizenship, access to the social safety net, and for integration. We then sketch some of their implications for institutions – for federalism and for the agencies that provide benefits to immigrants.

Membership and Citizenship

By drawing the kind of bright line between legal immigrants and citizens that was formerly drawn between illegal and legal immigrants, our social welfare policies now single out legal immigrants and their families for harsher treatment than the other poverty populations who lose benefits under welfare reform. For immigrants, welfare reform represents more than an alternative service delivery model; it represents a fundamental redefinition of their membership in the society. By imposing new restrictions on noncitizen access to a host of federal, state and local benefits ranging from income support to higher education assistance, welfare reform demotes the civic status of legal immigrants. It does so by conditioning membership (in the form of access to public benefits) on citizenship, military duty, or sustained work (40 quarters or 10 years) in covered employment.

Legal permanent residents are not the only class of immigrants to have their civic status effectively demoted by welfare reform. By segmenting the immigrant population into two broad categories – qualified and unqualified immigrants – the law seeks to make the rules governing aliens' rights to benefits clearer and simpler than they have been. But by taking this approach, the law expressly relegates several classes of immigrants in the United States lawfully (such as applicants for asylum or adjustment of status, or aliens granted temporary protected status), to the same unqualified status as the undocumented (Wheeler, 1996). It thereby blurs distinctions between immigrants here with the consent of government and others here without it.[9]

One of the principal ways that welfare reform redefines membership is by transforming the meaning of citizenship. Welfare reform may represent the most important – if largely undebated – reconsideration of the importance of citizenship since the passage of the Fourteenth Amendment. By making citizenship the gateway to benefits ranging from Medicaid to mental health to child care services, welfare reform makes citizenship important in a nation where its value has been extremely limited. In the past, citizenship has been required only to exercise political rights (to vote and hold office, *e.g.*), to hold some government jobs, and to make it easier to bring immigrants' relatives to the United States. But access to the welfare state has not generally turned on citizenship. Now, in the wake of welfare reform and the reductions in due process protections set out in illegal immigration reform, citizenship is not only the gateway to public benefits. It also represents a shield against the immigrant's expanded vulnerability to deportation. Viewed together, these changes beg the question whether it is rational policy to induce citizenship out of fear or expediency rather than allegiance to the nation.

The new distinctions between differing classes of immigrants and natives created by welfare reform raise a number of practical and equity concerns. By differentiating between newcomers and natives, the new law could deepen existing divisions within the society. It may also deepen divisions within families, making differing streams of benefits (food stamps, income support, Medicaid, *e.g.*) available to citizen and noncitizen family members. In particular, older children born outside the United States who are noncitizens may find themselves disadvantaged relative to their younger citizen siblings. These divisions within families may be aggravated by the immigration reform's restrictions on adjustment of status (such as those that make suspension of deportation more difficult or that dismiss any outstanding legal claims for legalization under the 1986 amnesty program) that will make it harder for undocumented family members to legalize.

Further, it is not yet clear whether states will have the legal authority to discriminate among differing classes of qualified immigrants in determining eligibility for services. Although it may not want to provide state assistance to all qualified aliens, a state (*e.g.*, Maryland) may wish to protect certain immigrant populations, such as children. The states will not only face constitutional constraints in their ability to draw distinctions between subclasses of legal immigrants, the authorizing legislation for programs such as Medicaid may make such fine classifications impossible.[10]

What Remains of the Social Safety Net?

At the most basic level, the immigrant restrictions built into welfare reform remove the social safety net from some of the most vulnerable members of the immigrant community. These include:

- Noncitizen children receiving food stamps;

- Elderly noncitizens receiving SSI;

- Disabled noncitizens receiving SSI;

- Refugees, who have been in the United States for five years or more, who continue to suffer from physical or psychological impairments as a result of their war experiences.[11]

The policy instrument chosen to restrict immigrants' access to many benefits – i.e., bars – also has implications for the extent to which the safety net is available to immigrants. The bar remains in place regardless of need, applying with equal force to the disabled, single adults, and to elderly immigrants with intact family members able to help support them. These bars represent a sharp departure from the deeming restrictions on immigrant use of public benefits that were in place prior to welfare reform. While deeming shifted responsibility for immigrant support to the sponsor for a period of years, if the sponsor became bankrupt or died, the immigrant could receive services. Since program bars preclude such need-based exceptions, immigrants will have to find other sources of support.

One strategy taken by welfare reform framers to try to mitigate the law's impact was to create a set of population exceptions. These exceptions could be viewed as reflecting the greater equities that some classes of immigrants are perceived to have to benefits. Thus benefits eligibility has not been curtailed for veterans, because of the sacrifices they have made; immigrants who have worked for 40 quarters, because of their contributions to the labor market and public coffers; and refugees, asylees, and aliens whose deportation has been withheld, because of their special needs and the express consent the nation has shown to their presence.

The new illegal immigration reform bill also exempted two other groups. Battered women and children who are unqualified aliens are made eligible for the same programs as qualified aliens, and legal immigrant battered women are exempted from deeming. Legal immigrants who are abandoned by their sponsor and so would otherwise go without food or shelter can receive a one year reprieve from deeming.

In addition to these population exceptions, the framers of the welfare law built in a number of program exceptions for qualified immigrants, reflecting a mix of safety net and, as we indicate below, human capital concerns. These include:

- Emergency medical care under Medicaid;

- Short-term, noncash emergency relief;

- Services provided under the National School Lunch Act;

- Services provided under the Child Nutrition Act;

- Immunizations, testing, and treatment for communicable diseases;

- Foster care and adoption assistance;
- Student assistance under the Higher Education Act or Public Health Service Act;
- Means-tested programs under the Elementary and Secondary Education Act;
- Head Start;
- Job Training Partnership Act.

The Congress also carved out a limited number of program exemptions that apply to "not qualified" aliens. The excepted programs are a subset of the programs available to qualified immigrants: emergency medical care under Medicaid; short-term, noncash emergency relief; and immunization, testing, and treatment for communicable diseases.

Both qualified and unqualified immigrants remain eligible for a variety of community programs that: provide in-kind assistance; are delivered at the community level; do not base eligibility on income; and provide assistance necessary for the protection of life and safety. The reach and effectiveness of this exception – like the other definitional issues noted above – depends on how broadly it is defined through regulation.

These exceptions suggest that the safety net that has been expressly erected for qualified (and for that matter, unqualified) immigrants is driven by public health and child nutritional concerns, and by concerns about the possible hunger and homelessness that might result from welfare reform.

Viewing the welfare reform law more broadly, it becomes clear that many of the safeguards intended to moderate the law's impacts on citizens will not benefit noncitizens. For example, although there is a lifetime limit of five years on receipt of benefits under TANF, refugees are allowed to receive benefits for only their first five years in the United States. Thus, a refugee who receives benefits for two years and goes off welfare cannot go back on three years later as a citizen would be able to do. This inequity may provide a perverse incentive for refugees to receive benefits for longer periods during the time they are eligible.

While federal law permits states to exempt 20 percent of their caseload from the five-year time limits because of hardship, no hardship exemption can be extended to noncitizens. Further, a provision exempting child-only units (in which payments are provided only to the children in the unit and not the parents) from the five-year limit on TANF payments is of little value to legal immigrant children, who will be ineligible for benefits.

What Is the Impact on Immigrant Integration?

In addition to the straightforward safety net concerns, we would add the less-noted concern that welfare reform could delay immigrant social and economic integration. Take, for example, restrictions imposed on immigrant use of Medicaid. According to a recent study, although low-income Latino immigrants are less likely to have low-birth-weight babies than low-income native women, the prevalence of illness among San Diego's low-income Latino infants born in Mexico was comparable to that of non-Latino infants raised in central Harlem (New York City) and other disadvantaged communities. Moreover, the infants experienced high rates of illness despite the widespread availability of public health insurance coverage (Medi-Cal) and timely well-baby check-ups (Guendelman, 1995). Presumably, these health outcomes would be worse in the absence of such care and insurance, potentially inhibiting the healthy development of these children and reducing their school participation and success.

Just as welfare reform addresses safety net concerns, the law also addresses human capital and other immigrant integration issues. Not surprisingly, the programs that are safeguarded are only available to the legal immigrant or qualified alien population. These programs include: preprimary education (Head Start); means-tested programs in elementary and secondary education; federal loans and grants for higher education; and access to Job Training and Partnership Act (JTPA) programs.

But while these are clearly liberalizing provisions intended to protect programs that represent the proverbial hand-up rather than hand-out type of benefits, they produce a number of anomalous policy results. If it makes sense to pursue immigrant integration as an objective, why allow noncitizen children to participate in Head Start but give states the option of barring them from child care programs funded under the Title XX Social Services block grant? Why protect employment and training services delivered under JTPA, while restricting job training financed under Title XX? Why permit states to deem sponsors' income for higher education loans and grants?

Further, looking beyond welfare reform it could be the case that new provisions in the illegal immigration law make it more difficult for legal immigrants to challenge discrimination they may encounter when seeking to enter the labor force. These new provisions loosen antidiscrimination protections put in place by earlier legislation.

How Well Does Welfare Reform Address Federalism Concerns Raised by Immigration?

The new welfare reform law is striking not only for the new lines that it draws between classes of immigrants, but for the power that it vests in states to draw those lines. In this regard welfare reform represents a reversal of Supreme Court doctrine that barred states from discriminating on the basis of legal status or alienage in their public benefit programs (*Graham v.*

Richardson, 403 U.S. 365, 1971). The law allows states to decide what mix of services they will extend to legal noncitizens and what tools they will use (bars, deeming) to do so. In short, the states will now play a central role in determining societal membership – a right that was formerly reserved to the federal government.

The concept of federalism that animates the immigration provisions of welfare reform, however, can be viewed as a somewhat schizophrenic one, reflecting a tension between the competing imperatives of devolution and curtailing illegal immigration. In general, states have been given greater flexibility when it comes to determining legal immigrants' eligibility for public benefits, but less flexibility when it comes to policies affecting illegal immigrants. Constitutionality concerns, however, surround both sets of changes.

Welfare reform constrains state discretion in at least three ways. First, the law bars unqualified aliens from state and local services. States can only extend benefits to unqualified immigrants if they pass a law expressly authorizing themselves to do so. However, no sanctions were written into the welfare reform law that can be brought against states that do not comply with this constitutionally dubious provision (*see* Chemerinsky, 1996). Second, states are barred from retaining "sanctuary laws" that prohibit state or local personnel from communicating with the INS. This prohibition has already provoked a Tenth Amendment challenge by New York City's Mayor Rudolph Giuliani. Third, state agencies administering federal housing, SSI, and TANF programs must furnish the INS, four times each year, with the name, address and other identifying information on aliens whom the state "knows is unlawfully in the United States."[12]

Debates over federalism have not only focused on questions of authority but also money. As we have seen, welfare reform reshuffles federal and state roles, leading to mixed results when it comes to new state discretion over immigrants' benefits. In the fiscal domain, the results may be quite different – leaving states without even a mixed victory. What began as an effort to secure impact aid that would offset immigration's costs has yielded new restrictions on immigrants' access to services that, ironically, could exacerbate rather than improve the intergovernmental fiscal inequities that flow from immigration.[13]

Overall, according to the CBO estimates, the federal government will be sending about $23 billion less to state and local governments as a result of the immigrant restrictions (CBO, 1996). The effects of these reduced flows will be heavily concentrated within a few states. By its own analysis, California alone stands to lose $6.8 billion over the next six years (California Legislative Analyst's Office, 1996). Further, the two federal programs from which current and future immigrants are barred – SSI and food stamps – are financed with federal funds, limiting possible savings to states.

Moreover, the political impetus for providing states with impact aid could have been shunted aside by welfare reform. In fact, the recently enacted illegal immigration reform bill contained a provision for 100 percent reimbursement to public and some nonprofit hospitals that provide emergency care to unlawfully present immigrants. However, no funds were appropriated for any such reimbursement for the current fiscal year.

Devolution to the states will inevitably lead to further devolution to counties and other local units of government, possibly driving new fiscal arrangements. In California, for example, the General Relief Program is 100 percent county-funded, leaving only counties to pay for cash assistance to needy immigrants that was previously funded primarily by the federal and state governments. Although the legislation gives states the authority to bar immigrants from state and locally funded programs, California's counties are required by state law to be the provider of last resort.

Finally, it is clear that devolution will exaggerate differences across states in the amount of safety-net services available – to immigrants as well as other populations. The safety-net services available to immigrants in New York are likely to be quite different from those provided in Texas. In Texas, unlike New York, immigrants losing federal benefits have no General Assistance program to turn to. Moreover, unlike New York and most other states, Texas has very few optional Medicaid categories under which the state can provide coverage once an immigrant's SSI eligibility is terminated.

What Impact Will Welfare Reform Have on Implementation and Verification?

In addition to federalism concerns, the new welfare reform law's immigrant restrictions raise a number of other institutional issues. In the first place, they substantially expand the number of benefit-granting agencies that must verify the legal status of claimants in order to determine if they are "qualified." Prior to passage of welfare reform this verification requirement was limited to a few major federal programs such as AFDC and food stamps. While the framers of the illegal immigration reform bill made clear that nonprofits would not be subject to these verification requirements, it remains to be seen whether they will be forced to verify in order to be reimbursed for federal or state-funded services rendered.

This expanded verification is illustrative of the ways in which efforts to control illegal immigration and mitigate immigration's impacts are altering the day to day working of domestic institutions. In that sense both welfare reform and illegal immigration control can be seen as conscripting a widening circle of state and local officials into service as what has been termed "junior immigration inspectors." Welfare reform enlists the service of a host of benefits providers who had been exempt from these obligations. The illegal immigration reform bill permits the federal government to deputize state police and other law enforcement officials to serve as immigration inspectors. At another level, welfare reform will mean that intake workers will administer not one but a host of new eligibility regimes, compelling them to identify:

- noncitizens (versus citizens); qualified (versus unqualified) aliens;
- lawfully present aliens for the purpose of qualifying for Social Security;
- immigrants who arrived before August 22, 1996;
- immigrants arriving after August 22, 1996;
- refugees and asylees in the United States less than five years;
- immigrants who have worked 40 quarters in covered employment;
- sponsored immigrants;
- immigrants whose sponsors have abandoned them or whose support levels are so low as to deny them adequate food and shelter;
- veterans, their spouses and children.

From an implementation standpoint, these subtle, often hard-to-police distinctions demonstrate how complex it will be for public and private institutions to screen for benefits eligibility. Further, the new verification imperatives may also beg the question whether poor natives can readily produce evidence of citizenship.

The complexity introduced by the new law imposes heavy information demands on government. These demands led the framers of both the welfare and illegal immigration reform bills to authorize the creation of linked electronic verification systems to determine legal status and citizenship. As a consequence, both move the nation toward a system where all individuals will have to provide information on their citizenship and legal status to a much broader set of service providers and law enforcers. Some would also argue that these changes also move us closer to a national identity card.

Finally, there will be a continuing tension between the goal of restricting unqualified immigrants' access to benefits and promoting the public health. Requirements that agencies report, or at least be allowed to report, to the INS information about aliens known to be unlawfully in the United States – as well as the verification requirements themselves – are likely to chill the willingness of unqualified aliens' to be tested and receive treatment for communicable diseases or to receive emergency medical services.

CONCLUSIONS

Taking a step back and examining the many far-reaching policy shifts embodied in the welfare law as well as the illegal and antiterrorism laws, it becomes clear that the 104th Congress has moved us closer than ever before to a new era in immigrant and immigration policy. The three laws dramatically restrict the benefits, individual rights, and due process protections available to both illegal and legal immigrants. In the process, they draw a new, hard line between citizens and noncitizens, treating noncitizens more uncharitably than they have been treated since the nativist period of the early twentieth century.

Through the exemptions to the broad bars on immigrant eligibility for benefits, the welfare reform law has effectively created new criteria for membership in U.S. society. The only legal immigrants to have access to the same safety net as the rest of the population are those who have shown a strong attachment to the U.S. labor force by working (and presumably paying taxes) for ten years, those who have served honorably in the U.S. military, and those who were admitted to the United States for humanitarian reasons. The latter group's membership is actually significantly diminished under the new law, which limits their eligibility for services to their first five years in the country.

The programmatic exemptions to the bars have left a minimal – and not always coherently designed – safety net for immigrants. The services for which they remain eligible relate solely to public health, child nutrition and emergency services. An investment in legal immigrants' future integration is maintained, to some extent, through continued eligibility for selected human capital programs such as job training. The extent of the social safety net that remains in place for noncitizens depends, however, on a series of important decisions that have yet to be made in federal, state and local legislation, regulation, and implementation.

In addition to rewriting the criteria for membership and shrinking the safety net, the new laws have reshaped the role of the immigrant family. They have done so in two ways. First, they impose more stringent income requirements on those who wish to bring relatives to the United States. Second, the bars on eligibility and the new deeming requirements place responsibility for the support of needy and disabled immigrants squarely on the shoulders of their families, who are expected to bear a burden far greater than that borne by citizens' families.

The three new laws hold great significance not only for immigrants and their families but also for the roles that federal, state and local governments play in immigration policy. The devolution of responsibility to state and local governments for setting immigrant policy and implementing immigration policy can be viewed as a major challenge to the principle of federal preemption that has controlled in this area. The approach taken, however, is two-pronged, with states gaining authority over decisions regarding legal immigrants' eligibility for services and losing authority when it comes to illegal immigrants.

All levels of government will now have greater access to information about both citizens and noncitizens and will be required to use that information when providing a much wider set of public services. The welfare law authorizes some state and local workers, and requires others, to report to the federal government information about those not lawfully in the United States.

Taken as a whole, these new laws attempt to reduce any negative fiscal and economic effects of legal immigration through domestic or welfare policy rather than through immigration policy – *i.e.*, by reducing the number, or changing the composition of legal immigrant flows. These changes are also a departure from immigration reforms of the past three decades in that they are solely exclusionary and do not reflect the balance that previous immigration reforms maintained between inclusionary and exclusionary pressures.

Of course, it is significant that the numbers of immigrants coming to the United States has not been reduced and that immigration continues to be primarily for the purpose of family reunification. The United States still has a relatively liberal immigration policy by historical and international standards when it comes to how many immigrants it admits. But in terms of the welcome the nation provides to immigrants, its arms are no longer open quite so wide.

NOTES

[1] The opinions are those of the authors and not those of the directors or trustees of the Urban Institute. This paper has been prepared with support from the Andrew W. Mellon and William and Flora Hewlett Foundations.

[2] For example, the Immigration Reform and Control Act of 1986 (IRCA) imposed sanctions on employers who hired illegal immigrants; at the same time it established a one-time amnesty program for illegal immigration.

[3] The immigration legislation requires that the person petitioning to bring a relative into the United States sign the affidavit of support, but if the petitioner cannot meet the income requirement it allows another person who can do so to sign an affidavit as well.

[4] The welfare reform legislation defines public benefits as any retirement, welfare, health, disability, public or assisted housing, postsecondary education, food assistance, unemployment benefit, or similar benefit for which payment or assistance is provided to an individual, household or family eligibility unit by an agency of the federal, state or local government or by appropriated funds of the federal, state or local government (§§ 401, 411).

[5] The authors of this report note that these estimates depend on a number of assumptions that may not hold true. For example, although the CBO builds into their estimates assumptions about people who would naturalize and therefore retain eligibility, it is difficult to know how many people will choose to and be able to successfully naturalize. The data on which these estimates are based are also imperfect. For example, the SSI data include an unknown number of persons who became citizens after enrolling in SSI but for whom the Social Security Administration did not update their citizenship status.

[6] This figure would be significantly higher if states took the option they are provided under welfare reform to bar their legal immigrant populations from the program.

[7] Conversation with authors of November 1996 Congressional Budget Office Report. Certain groups of immigrants who previously were eligible for Medicaid are considered not qualified aliens under the new law and are no longer eligible. They include immigrants who are considered permanently residing under color of law (PRUCOL), such as aliens granted an indefinite voluntary departure, a stay of deportation, or suspension of deportation.

[8]Medicaid coverage is based on data from the March 1996 Current Population Survey.

[9]Sharp distinctions drawn between aliens deemed to be qualified and unqualified when it comes to federal means-tested benefits are blurred when it comes to determining eligibility for Social Security. For those benefits, new distinctions are created between aliens who are "lawfully present" and those who are not. Lawfully present aliens include asylum applicants granted work authorization and aliens granted temporary protected status, among others. *See*, Wheeler, 1996:1251.

[10]The welfare bill does not repeal Medicaid rules requiring states to provide the same "amount, duration and scope" of medical services to all who qualify for assistance based on each state's rules (Wheeler and Bernstein, 1996:7).

[11]Because asylees and refugees do not enter as sponsored immigrants, they will not be subject to federal or state deeming requirements after their five years of program eligibility has lapsed. Presumably they would be subject to any state-imposed bars on noncitizen benefit eligibility.

[12]It remains to be seen how broadly this knowledge requirement will be interpreted. Under current agency and congressional interpretation such knowledge does not arise until the alien is under a final order of deportation. Only the Food Stamp Program now requires reporting of household members. *See*, generally, Wheeler and Bernstein, 1996.

[13]According to some scholars immigration generates a net surplus for the federal government, a net deficit for local governments, and mixed results for state governments depending on the state's differing tax and service structure. *See* Rothman and Espenshade, 1992.

REFERENCES

California Legislative Analyst's Office
1996   "Federal Welfare Reform (H.R. 3734): Fiscal Effect on California." Policy Brief. August 20. Sacramento, California.

Chemerinsky, E.
1996   "Memorandum on the Constitutionality of Section 411(d) of H.R. 3734." Los Angeles: University of Southern California.

Congressional Budget Office (CBO)
1996   "Federal Budgetary Implications of H.R. 3734, The Personal Responsibility and Work Opportunity Reconciliation Act of 1996." Washington, DC.

Fix, M., J. Passel, with M. Enchautegui and W. Zimmermann
1994   "Immigration and Immigrants: Setting the Record Straight." Washington, DC: The Urban Institute.

Fix, M., J. S. Passel and W. Zimmermann
1996a   "The Use of SSI and Other Welfare Programs by Immigrants. Testimony before the U.S. Senate Subcommittee on Immigration." Washington, DC: The Urban Institute.

_____
1996b   "Facts About Immigrants' Use of Welfare," March, updated April 1. Washington, DC: The Urban Institute.

Fix, M. and W. Zimmermann
1995   "Immigrant Families and Public Policy: A Deepening Divide." Washington, DC: The Urban Institute.

Guendelman, S. et. al.
1995   "Infants of Mexican Immigrants, Health Status of an Emerging Population," *Medical Care*, 33(1):41–52.

Ponce, E.
1996   "Lawfully Resident Aliens Who Receive SSI Payments: December 1995." Office of Program Benefit Payments, Social Security Administration. Washington, DC.

Rothman, E. and T. J. Espenshade
1992   "Fiscal Impacts of Immigration to the United States," *Population Index*, 58(3).

Schuck, P.
1984   "The Transformation of Immigration Law," *Columbia Law Review*, 84(1). January.

Smolkin, S., M. Stavrianos and J. Burton
1996   "Characteristics of Food Stamp Households: Summer 1994." Office of Analysis and Evaluation, Food and Consumer Service, U.S. Department of Agriculture. Washington, DC.

Wheeler, C.
1996   "The New Alien Restrictions on Public Benefits: The Full Impact Remains Uncertain," *Interpreter Releases*, 73:1245.

Wheeler, C. and I. Bernstein
1996   "New Laws Fundamentally Revise Immigrant Access to Government Programs: A Review of the Changes." Washington, DC: National Immigration Law Center.

Zedlewski, S., S. Clark, E. Meier and K. Watson
1996   "Potential Effects of Congressional Welfare Reform Legislation on Family Incomes." Washington, DC: The Urban Institute.

8

Undocumented Immigrants: Health, Education, and Welfare

STEPHEN H. LEGOMSKY
Washington University

As we all know, these are difficult times for immigrants and difficult times for welfare recipients. For the person who happens to be both an immigrant and a welfare recipient, these are excruciating times.

Under current law, those aliens who have been lawfully admitted for permanent residence (legal immigrants) are generally eligible for the major federal and state public assistance programs (*see*, U.S. Commission on Immigration Reform, 1994:116). So, too, are certain miscellaneous categories of immigrants known as PRUCOL's. They include asylees, parolees, and certain others.

Legal immigrants, however, do have some special barriers to overcome. To gain admission in the first place, they had to prove they were "not likely to become public charge[s]" (8 U.S.C. 212(a)(4)). Often this means their sponsors have to sign affidavits of support pledging to assist them if the need arises. For the moment, those affidavits are generally nonbinding, although if the immigrant applies for any of certain forms of welfare within a specified number of years after admission, the sponsor's assets and income will be "deemed" available to the immigrant for purposes of determining the immigrant's eligibility. Apart from that, an immigrant who becomes a public charge within five years after admission risks deportation (8 U.S.C. 241(a)(5)).

Legislation pending at this writing would make even legal immigrants ineligible for the major federally funded welfare programs, with just a few narrow exceptions (H.R. 4-1995, § 403(a)). I personally find these prospects dreadful (Legomsky, 1995:1453), but my topic here is a different one: public services for undocumented immigrants.

By way of background, undocumented immigrants are generally ineligible for almost all forms of federal and state welfare. There are a handful of exceptions, and they tend to be either for immediate emergencies or for public health and safety, such as inoculation against contagious diseases (Legomsky, 1995:1460; U.S. Commission on Immigration Reform, 1994:115–117; Reich, 1992).

When people talk about "welfare," they usually have in mind a whole range of federal and state government programs for the poor: income support programs like Aid to Families with Dependent Children (AFDC) and Supplemental Security Income (SSI); healthcare programs like medicaid; food and nutrition programs like food stamps, WIC, school breakfast, and school lunch; and programs that help people with housing, energy, higher education loans, legal services, and other needs.

But means-tested programs are really just one kind of governmental assistance. Today federal, state, and local governments provide an array of tax-funded benefits beyond those that are targeted specifically at the poor. We all receive police and fire protection and the free use of most roads, bridges, parks, libraries, and public schools. There are homes and services for battered women, abused children, disabled persons and others with special needs. For which public services should undocumented immigrants be eligible?

Immigrants are unpopular enough. Undocumented immigrants are even less popular. So undocumented immigrants on welfare face a triple whammy (Legomsky, 1995:1454). Not many public relations professionals would advise organizations to call themselves "Citizens for Illegal Aliens on Welfare."

So it is not surprising that there is a large and growing movement to restrict the eligibility of undocumented immigrants for public benefits. The pending federal welfare reform bill would make undocumented immigrants ineligible for all federal means-tested public benefits other than emergency assistance and certain housing programs, and it would require states to do likewise (H.R. 4-1995, §§ 401, 402, 411, 412). In California, Proposition 187, if ultimately upheld by the courts, would disqualify undocumented immigrants from almost all state health and social services, and it would disqualify undocumented children from public elementary and secondary education.

There are some respectable arguments for the general proposition that undocumented immigrants should not be eligible for the full range of government services available to citizens and to lawful permanent residents. They are, after all, not supposed to be here, and thus their claims for public benefits start off on a lower moral footing. Moreover, all levels of government operate under serious fiscal constraints, so the cost factor is a legitimate consideration. In addition, one cannot dismiss entirely the possibility that public benefits could help to attract some amount of undocumented migration.

The point I would emphasize, however, is that these arguments are not the end of the debate. They are just the beginning. There are certain government services that almost no one would really want to deny to undocumented immigrants. Police and fire protection are obvious examples. Few people today would actually argue that these services should be denied because undocumented immigrants are not supposed to be here, or because money is scarce, or because police protection is a magnet for undocumented migration. Most people recognize, at least subconsciously, that countervailing considerations exist. First, there are moral constraints; certain things would simply be too cruel to do, even to undocumented immigrants. Second, there are practical constraints that reflect our own self-interest; withholding fire protection or inoculation against contagious diseases would harm the entire community, not just the undocumented immigrants. Thus one cannot justify disqualifying undocumented immigrants from a particular public program simply by intoning "they're not supposed to be here." The only meaningful way to proceed is to consider each benefit program, one at a time, and to weigh the pros and cons of excluding undocumented immigrants from that particular program. I believe that even the most fervent immigration restrictionists, if pressed, would acknowledge this.

Certain government services fit both the moral category and the public interest category. Elementary and secondary education is the classic example because it is crucial to a child's life opportunity. When you take away a child's education, you do damage that can never be undone. I would object to doing this even to those children who have committed grave moral errors. What is so astonishing about Proposition 187 is that the children whom it punishes are morally innocent. Whatever one's view of the parents' actions, the children have done only what any other children would do – accompany their parents when the family moves. And even if one could somehow construct a moral justification for destroying the life of an innocent child in order to punish the parents, self-interest alone would counsel against doing so. Who in his or her right mind would want to create a permanent underclass of uneducated, soon-to-be unemployable adults?

So my view is that, in the end, measures like Proposition 187 solve nothing, inflict lifelong suffering on innocent children, and harm everyone around them in the process.

Apart from public education, those undocumented immigrants who are indigent are now squeezed by multiple forces, and the pressure will worsen if pending reforms are enacted. As mentioned earlier, undocumented immigrants are already ineligible for almost all welfare programs. Those who are here because they are waiting for their asylum claims to be processed might eventually receive permission to work but, as a result of reforms instituted in 1994 (59 Fed. Reg. 62284-62303), not for 180 days. Legal aid agencies may not use Legal Services Corporation (LSC) funds to serve undocumented immigrants; in the future, agencies that receive LSC funds might be barred from serving undocumented immigrants even with non-LSC funds (Kerwin, 1996). Other charities, hampered by general funding cutbacks, will have fewer and fewer resources for immigrants, documented or otherwise.

Again, some members of the public will respond that this is precisely the idea. Undocumented immigrants, they will say, are not supposed to be here in the first place and therefore do not deserve public funding. Moreover, they will add, we want to make life uncomfortable for undocumented immigrants so that those who are thinking about coming here will stay away and those who are already here will leave.

What was said before applies here as well. Some undocumented immigrants are children, innocent of moral wrongdoing. Many others are asylum claimants who, through no fault of their own, must often wait long periods for their claims to be heard. Still others are waiting for their priority dates to become current so that they can legally rejoin their husbands or wives and their young children in the United States.

But even with respect to those undocumented immigrants who are not adults, asylum claimants, or immigrants awaiting family reunification, surely there are moral limits to the consequences a civilized society can assign to violation of law. All I am suggesting is that we examine those limits carefully before we do something of which we will later be ashamed.

REFERENCES

Kerwin, D. M.
1996   "Don't Give Me Your Tired, Your Poor or Your Huddled Masses: The Impact of Pending Legislation," *Interpreter Releases*, 73:181, 183–184. February 12.

Legomsky, S. H.
1995   "Immigration, Federalism, and the Welfare State," *UCLA Law Review*, 42.

Reich, P. L.
1992   "Jurisprudential Tradition and Undocumented Alien Entitlements," *Georgetown Immigration Law Journal*, 6:1.

U.S. Commission on Immigration Reform
1994   "U.S. Immigration Policy: Restoring Credibility," *Interpreter Releases*, 71.

9

Impact of Welfare Reform Proposals on Health Programs and Civil Rights of Migrant Farmworkers

CYNTHIA G. SCHNEIDER
Migrant Legal Action Program, Inc., Washington, DC

WHO ARE MIGRANT FARMWORKERS?

Before one can discuss the impact of welfare reform proposals on healthcare programs for migrant farmworkers, one needs to have a sense of the size of this population, whether they have dependents in the United States, their levels of income, immigration status, and where they live and work in the United States. The best data on farmworkers is from a series of studies conducted by the U.S. Department of Labor (1991a, 1991b, 1993a, 1993b, 1994). These studies, which are based on interviews with farmworkers, are commonly referred to as the National Agricultural Worker Survey or NAWS.

There is no universally accepted definition of migrant farmworker. Generally, migrant farmworkers are people who cross geographic boundaries and stay away from home in order to perform farm work for wages (Martin and

Martin, 1992:1). The NAWS study defined migrant as a person who traveled at least 75 miles from their home to seek work in agriculture within the last year (Department of Labor, 1994:1).

The number of farmworkers, let alone migrant farmworkers, is also a disputed issue. There is no accepted national count of farmworkers (Department of Labor, 1994). However, some numbers do exist. NAWS researchers use the figure 2.5 million farmworkers (year-round and seasonal, including migrant) in the United States, which is the number reported in 1993 by the Commission on Agricultural Workers (1993).

The NAWS estimates that 64 percent of all farmworkers (or 1.6 million workers) are seasonal farmworkers (including migrants). Of these, NAWS further estimates that 42 percent of all farmworkers, or 670,000 persons, are migrants (Samardick, 1995a). Migrant farmworkers work in every state except Alaska (*see* Larson and Plascencia, 1993).

The majority of migrant farmworkers are what NAWS calls "back and forth" migrants (Department of Labor, 1994:16). That is, they travel from their home base to one job site in the United States. The majority of these back and forth migrant farmworkers (83% or 480,000 persons) have their permanent home abroad. NAWS estimates that 13 percent of migrant farmworkers, or 210,000 persons, are "follow the crop" migrants, that is, those who fit the stereotypic notion of a migrant farmworker. Sixty-four percent of this group are U.S. based.

The lack of full-time and year-round work, combined with low wages, relegates two-thirds (63%) of migrant farmworkers to living below the poverty line (Department of Labor, 1994:31). This compares to a 52 percent poverty rate among all seasonal farmworker households (Samardick, 1995b:10).. Both figures are well above the actual poverty rate of 12 percent. Migrants work an average of only 29 weeks per year, 25 of them in farm work, yielding a median income of $5,000 a year (Department of Labor, 1994:31). The median family income for all seasonal farmworkers is between $7,500 and $10,000 (Department of Labor, 1991a:54).

NAWS estimates that there are 2.1 million dependents of farmworkers in the United States, 1.3 million of whom are children. The vast majority of these children (78% or 1 million) do not migrate. Forty percent of the children who do migrate have both parents doing farm work. Seventy percent of the children who migrate live in poverty (Samardick, 1995a).

NAWS reports that most migrant farmworkers (71% in 1991) have legal authorization to work in the United States (Department of Labor, 1994:19). The numbers of undocumented migrant farmworkers have steadily increased over the years. In 1989, 17 percent of migrant farmworkers reported being undocumented; in 1990 and 1991, these figures were 23 percent and 26 percent, respectively.

NAWS has not broken out the immigration status of the 71 percent of the migrants who in 1991 were legally authorized to work in the United States. However, 1990 NAWS data for all farmworkers shows 40 percent of all farmworkers to be U.S. citizens, 15 percent to be permanent resident aliens, 23 percent to be temporary resident aliens, 12 percent to be unauthorized, and 10 percent to be in other immigration categories (Department of Labor, 1991a:13).

CURRENT MIGRANT FARMWORKER PARTICIPATION IN THE MEDICAID PROGRAM

One would assume that since the majority of farmworkers are poor and have documented immigration status, they would receive health care through the Medicaid Program, which is the primary federal program providing health care to low-income persons. This is not the case. While no data exists on farmworker receipt of Medicaid benefits, the NAWS data shows that migrant farmworkers and their dependents vastly underutilize federal benefit programs. Only 20 percent of migrant farmworker households reported to the NAWS researchers that they received food stamps, WIC, AFDC, general assistance, or public or subsidized housing in a two-year period preceding the interview (Samardick, 1995b:13). Since migrant farmworker households underutilize these benefit programs, it is fair to assume that migrant farmworker households no doubt participate in the Medicaid Program in small numbers. The underutilization of public assistance programs by migrant farmworker households is also true of all farmworker households. Only 21 percent of all farmworker households reported receiving any public assistance benefit (Samardick, 1995b:11).

The low level of participation of adult migrant farmworkers in the Medicaid program is to be expected. Medicaid is not available to most adult migrant farmworkers. To be eligible for Medicaid one must be receiving or eligible to receive AFDC or SSI, the two federal cash public assistance programs (42 U.S.C. 1396a(a)(10)). When they are working, migrant farmworkers are not eligible for these programs. Only in a few instances are migrant farmworkers eligible for Medicaid when they are not working.

However, migrant farmworker children and pregnant migrant farmworker women are eligible for Medicaid. Under federal law, children born after September 30, 1983, living in families with incomes below the poverty line, are eligible for Medicaid (42 U.S.C. 1396a(a)(10)(A)(III)).

Despite their eligibility, migrant children and pregnant farmworker women may not participate in the Medicaid program for several reasons. One reason could be the lengthy application process. A family may have left an area by the time their application is acted upon. Second, farmworker families may not carry with them documentation complete enough to have their Medicaid application processed. Third, since Medicaid benefits are not transferrable from state to state, a follow-the-crop migrant farmworker must reapply for the program in each new state the family enters. The farmworker family may feel it is not worth their time and effort to apply for the program.

CURRENT MEDICAID REFORM PROPOSALS

House Speaker Newt Gingrich announced in March that proposals for changes in welfare and Medicaid, which were supported by the National Governors' Association (NGA), will shortly be introduced in the House. Besides the NGA proposal, ongoing discussions among conservative Democrats and moderate Republicans in the House and Senate could lead to yet alternative welfare proposals. What those proposals will look like, no one knows at this time.

Governors' Proposal

Eligibility. The NGA proposal would end the entitlement status of Medicaid and turn the Medicaid Program over to the states in the form of a block grant with very few federal requirements as to whom the state must serve and as to the scope of healthcare benefits. Under the NGA proposal, only pregnant women and children under age six with incomes below 133 percent of the federal poverty line and children aged six through twelve with incomes below 100 percent of the poverty line would be guaranteed coverage. This aspect of the NGA plan would greatly impact upon farmworker children. Federal law currently requires coverage of children up to age thirteen on September 30 (42 U.S.C. 1396a(a)(10)(A)(III)). Current law is phasing-in the coverage of all poor children with complete coverage to age eighteen being achieved in 2002. The NGA proposal would repeal the expansion of Medicaid benefits to poor children. Further, while the NGA proposal allows a state to broaden its coverage, there are no financial incentives to do so. In fact, under the NGA's funding mechanism, states would be discouraged from expanding coverage to poor children. Many states now provide Medicaid coverage to poor children up to age eighteen.The NGA proposal took no position on immigrant eligibility for Medicaid benefits.

Benefits. While the NGA proposal guarantees coverage for certain categories of people, it repeals virtually all federal standards relating to the health services which states must cover under their Medicaid Programs. Under the proposal, a state would have to offer some hospital care, physician services, home health care, laboratory services, and other specified benefits. But all current rules (42 U.S.C. 1396a(a)(10)(B)) on the amount, duration, and scope of healthcare services that must be covered would be dropped. For example, a state could limit hospital care to five days of care annually.

The NGA proposal could restrict the rules governing the Early and Periodic Screening, Diagnostic and Treatment (EPSDT) component of the Medicaid Program. This is a very important and useful program for children participating in Medicaid. Under current law, children found to be suffering from a medical problem detected during a routine screening must be provided with the treatment necessary to address the problem notwithstanding the fact that the state's regular Medicaid Program may not otherwise cover the treatment (42 U.S.C. 1396a(a)(43)(C)). The NGA proposal could greatly scale back the treatment guarantee.

Further, current law requires that all benefits must be the same for a group of persons within a state. The NGA proposal is silent on this requirement, but it can be read to allow discrimination against certain groups within a state or within areas of the state.

Current law protects low-income families by limiting the amount of any copayment or other cost-sharing requirements which can be charged to Medicaid recipients. This could disappear under the NGA proposal.

Program Access. Current law contains a broad definition of residency which must be used by all states. A migrant farmworker is a "resident" of a state where she is seeking work or is working as well as being a resident of a state where she lives. This allows the farmworker to qualify for benefits either in her home state or the state in which she is working. It is unclear how the NGA proposal would deal with the residency issue. It is quite possible that without a federal definition, each state could narrowly define "residency" that could result in a migrant farmworker being eligible for Medicaid only in their home-base state.

One of the major efforts in extending Medicaid coverage to migrant farmworkers within the last several years has been the encouragement of interstate migrant compacts (Wright and Fasciano, 1994). These compacts allow farmworker families to receive Medicaid benefits as they travel around the country without the need to reestablish eligibility in each new state. Under the NGA proposal allowing diverse state plans and few minimum national standards for eligibility, it is highly doubtful that states would enter into interstate migrant compacts, which again would result in farmworkers being covered only in their home state.

Migrant and Community Health Clinics. Migrant and community health clinics serve all low-income persons in their service area. Both clinic systems are vastly underfunded. Migrant health clinics receive funds sufficient to serve only 15 percent of the need (GAO, 1992). These clinics currently seek Medicaid reimbursement when they treat a Medicaid patient. Under the NGA block grant proposal, these federally funded clinics would see Medicaid reimbursement reduced, thus further limiting the numbers of persons the clinics are able to serve.

Immigration Reform Bills

Besides the National Governors' Association proposal, the immigration reform bills which are pending in the House and Senate impose new restrictions on a noncitizen's participation in the Medicaid Program. If enacted into law, the immigration reform bills' provisions, restricting immigrant access to Medicaid, would continue to apply should the Medicaid Program be redesigned through welfare reform legislation. Several of the immigration reform provisions would directly impact upon immigrant farmworkers' and their families' access to the Medicaid Program.

Both bills redefine the definition of eligible immigrants.[1] One current category of eligible immigrants – those "permanently residing in the United States under color of law" (42 U.S.C. 1396b(v)(1)) – would be eliminated. The exact number of immigrant farmworker women and children who qualify for Medicaid under this alien category is unknown. Yet, since this category is a fairly broad catch-all category, it has the potential for dramatically impacting upon immigrant farmworker families.

Current law allows women, ineligible for Medicaid due to their immigration status, to receive some pregnancy-related benefits through the Medicaid Program. The Senate bill would allow ineligible alien women to receive prenatal and postpartum services under Medicaid only if they can establish proof of continuous residence in the United States for periods of not less than three years. Since it is quite common for Mexican farmworkers to return to Mexico in the off-season, this provision probably eliminates any chance of otherwise ineligible Mexican farmworker women from receiving pregnancy-related services under Medicaid.

Several other provisions of both bills could harm migrant farmworker families. The House bill would provide open-ended authorization for state and local officials to report undocumented people to the INS. An undocumented migrant parent of U.S. citizen children may choose not to apply for Medicaid for their children under this bill, fearing that they will be reported to INS. Another House provision would also chill an immigrant's ability to apply for Medicaid benefits. That provision would permit deportation on public charge grounds based on receipt of Medicaid; the Senate bill contains a similar provision. However, neither bill would allow deportation based upon receipt of forms of emergency Medicaid assistance allowed for ineligible aliens.

The vetoed budget reconciliation bill and the earlier welfare reform bill (H.R. 4) contained provisions limiting immigrants' access to nonemergency Medicaid. Under these vetoed bills new immigrants who enter the United States after the date of enactment would have been barred from Medicaid for their first five years in the country. In addition, states would have been given the option to bar any or all other legal immigrants with a few exceptions, which would not apply to migrant farmworker households. The constitutionality of this provision is highly questionable. Further, these bills would have denied new legal immigrants, who enter the United States after the date of enactment, access to the Maternal and Child Health Care Block grant programs, family planning, and community and migrant health clinics, among other means-tested programs.

These vetoed bills also would have denied SSI benefits to most legal immigrants. This would have greatly impacted upon retired migrant farmworkers. Receipt of SSI guarantees receipt of Medicaid benefits. Many retired farmworkers do not qualify for social security retirement benefits because their employers failed to report their earnings to the Social Security Administration. The loss of SSI to retired immigrant farmworkers would mean not only a loss of their sole source of income but also the loss of healthcare benefits.

The President's welfare reform proposals do not change immigrant eligibility for Medicaid.

State Reform Efforts

A final aspect of Medicaid "reform" is occurring in the states. Many states are requiring Medicaid participants to enroll in managed care programs (*see* Perkins and Melden, 1994). Managed care is seen by the states as a way to reduce Medicaid spending. States must receive approval from the U.S. Department of Health and Human Services to move Medicaid participants into managed care programs.

Managed care programs present several problems for migrant household Medicaid participants. First, access in rural areas to a managed care provider may be difficult for farmworker families. Second, in many low-income communities federally funded community and migrant health centers are the only source of primary care for these families. If these centers are not part of the managed care system, the centers will lose an important source of revenue and the Medicaid patients will lose a provider who is not only accessible but also culturally and linguistically sensitive to their needs.

In sum, given what is currently being considered in Congress, the impact of welfare reform efforts on migrant farmworker health programs would be a giant leap backwards from what is currently available. And that is not to say that what is currently available affords universal coverage to migrant farmworker households. It certainly does not.

If legislation is enacted which turns the Medicaid program over to the states, work must be done in each state to see that the migrant farmworker population is not intentionally or unintentionally denied coverage and access to services. If the special needs and unique work circumstances of farmworkers are not considered in designing a state's Medicaid Program, it is very likely that they will not be covered.

NOTE

[1]On March 21, 1996, the House passed its version of the Immigration Reform Bill, H.R. 2202. On April 15, 1996, the Senate Judiciary Committee's version of this bill, S. 1664, was brought to the Senate floor.

REFERENCES

Commission on Agricultural Workers
1993   *Report of the Commission on Agricultural Workers.* Washington, DC: Government Printing Office.

Department of Labor, U.S.
1994   "Migrant Farmworkers: Pursuing Security in an Unstable Labor Market." Research Report No. 5. Washington, DC: U.S. Department of Labor, Office of the Assistant Secretary for Policy.

_____
1993a   "A Demographic and Employment Profile of Perishable Crop Farm Workers." Research Report No. 3. Washington DC: U.S. Department of Labor, Office of the Assistant Secretary for Policy.

_____
1993b   "U.S. Farmworkers in the Post-IRCA Period." Research Report No. 4. Washington, DC: U.S. Department of Labor, Office of the Assistant Secretary for Policy.

_____
1991a   "A Demographic and Employment Profile of Perishable Crop Farm Workers." Research Report No. 1. Washington, DC: U.S. Department of Labor, Office of the Assistant Secretary for Policy.

_____
1991b   "A Demographic and Employment Profile of Perishable Crop Farm Workers." Research Report No. 2. Washington, DC: U.S. Department of Labor, Office of the Assistant Secretary for Policy.

Government Accounting Office (GAO)
1992   "Hired Farmworkers: Health and Well-Being at Risk." Washington, DC: Government Accounting Office.

Larson, A. C. and L. Plascencia
1993   "Migrant Enumeration Project." Unpublished.

Martin, D. A. and P. Martin
1992   "Coordination of Migrant and Seasonal Farmworker Service Programs." Administrative Conference of the United States.

Perkins, J. and M. Melden
1994   "The Advocacy Challenge of a Lifetime: Shaping Medicaid Waivers to Serve the Poor," *Clearinghouse Review,* 28:864.

Samardick, R.
1995a   "The National Agricultural Workers Survey (NAWS): Recent Findings Relevant to Policy Development and Program Planning and Evaluation." Washington, DC: U.S. Department of Labor. January 19.

_____
1995b   "Lessons Learned from the National Agricultural Worker Survey (NAWS)." Washington, DC: U.S. Department of Labor. March 8.

Wright, G. and N. Fasciano
1994   "Feasibility Study for a Demonstration to Improve Medicaid Coverage of Migrant Farmworkers and Their Families: Design Report." Draft. Mathematica Policy Research, Inc., Washington, DC. September 25.

10

Human Rights and Ethics in Immigration Policy

JOHN ISBISTER
University of California, Santa Cruz

Americans are sharply divided about immigration policy. On one question, however, most are agreed: the proper criterion for judging the issue, they believe, is the national interest.

I want to suggest a different set of criteria. How would our opinions about immigration change if we looked at it from the perspective of human rights or ethics? (*See* Weiner, 1995; Gibney, 1988; Carens, 1987, 1988, 1991, 1992; IMR, 1996; Isbister, 1996; Brimelow, 1995.)

On what basis can one think of immigration as an issue of human rights? It is not immediately obvious. When thinking about human rights, one normally turns to the United Nations Conventions on the subject. They establish rights that are universal, but they do not establish the right of people to cross international borders to secure those rights. This is the case even with refugees; to qualify under the U.N. definition of a refugee, a person must be outside his or her national boundaries to begin with. While the United Nations accords certain rights to refugees, including the right to nonrefoulement once having crossed an international border, it accords no right to cross a border in the first place (*see* UNHCR, 1993; Loescher and Scanlan, 1986; Zolberg, Suhrke and Aguayo, 1989). The U.N. gives us little help, therefore, in thinking about immigration as a human right.

So we need to turn elsewhere. The ideas that all people are equal, that human rights are inherent, and that governments are bound to protect those rights come not from the U.N. but from the Enlightenment of the eighteenth century.[1] Among the many declarations concerning rights from that era, it may be most appropriate for Americans to ponder the Declaration of Independence:

> We hold these Truths to be self-evident, that all Men are created equal, that they are endowed by their Creator with certain unalienable Rights, that among these are Life, Liberty and the Pursuit of Happiness.

This sentence may seem banal to an American schoolchild, but if we are to follow it any distance, it has extraordinary implications. It does not say "all Englishmen" or "all residents of the thirteen colonies" are created equal. Its subject is "all Men" and, whatever Thomas Jefferson may have thought, today we understand this to mean "all people." According to our country's founding document, it is self-evident – it does not require proof – that everyone in the world has equal moral standing. Americans do not have superior rights. All people are equal.

Suppose that we take the founding sentence of our republic seriously. What would it mean for immigration policy? We may divide the question in four: 1) the case for open borders, 2) the question of priority categories, 3) the treatment of undocumented immigrants, and 4) the right to citizenship.

First, can we defend any immigration restrictions at all? Border controls seem to violate the principle of equal worth. Freedom of movement is surely central to the liberty that the Declaration of Independence holds to be an unalienable right of all people. We would not tolerate restrictions on the movement of Americans within the United States; how can we reconcile ourselves to restrictions of movement across national borders? Does the equal worth of all people not require us to admit to this country everyone who would like to live here? The case is strong. The principle of equal treatment requires us, I think, not to discriminate against people because of the accident of birth.

But does equal worth necessarily require equal treatment? Not always. Programs of preferential treatment based on race, for example, may be justified if they break down a system of racial injustice (Wasserstrom, 1986). A moment's consideration will reveal, however, how different the preferential treatment of affirmative action is from the preferential treatment of immigration controls. The purpose of affirmative action is to benefit people who have been disadvantaged. U.S. immigration controls do the opposite. They protect the privileges of the already privileged, Americans who live in a prosperous country, at the expense of relatively disadvantaged potential immigrants.

The ethical case against border controls is, therefore, not just that they treat equals unequally, but that they do so in an egregious way, by sheltering the privileged at the expense of relatively disadvantaged potential immigrants. Americans maintain immigration laws because they fear that unrestricted entry would drive down their own standard of living. No doubt it is in the interest of the privileged to protect their privileges, but it cannot be ethical if that protection has the effect of further disadvantaging the unprivileged.

This is the strongest case against immigration controls, but it is not necessarily completely valid. Many arguments have been mounted on the other side of this question, some of which I have attempted to refute elsewhere (Isbister, 1996). I cannot, however, completely refute what I regard as the strongest argument against open borders.

What if it can be shown that open borders would exacerbate inequalities among morally equal human beings? Not all Americans are privileged. Some are disadvantaged: the poor, the unskilled, and many members of minority ethnic groups. It must be conceded that the research that has been conducted so far on the impact of immigration on disadvantaged Americans is not definitive (*see* Isbister, 1996; Borjas, 1994). Nevertheless, it is likely that an increased and unending supply of low-wage labor from poor countries would keep the earnings of unskilled American workers low and profits high (*see* Briggs, 1992). If so, some people argue, immigration should be curtailed.

I cannot refute this argument. The American poor are genuinely needy and unfairly impoverished. It cannot be right to take conscious action to worsen their plight. We are obliged, I think, to protect the welfare not just of the most disadvantaged people in the world but of all who suffer disadvantage.

The argument in favor of border controls which is based on the disadvantage of some U.S. residents is therefore valid. So, however, is the previous argument for open borders. We are left with a conflict of rights.

Resolution of it is not easy. I think that morality demands from us an increased commitment to reduce domestic poverty. It demands an increase in the flow of immigrants to the country, so that more people in the world have an opportunity to share in the benefits of American life. At the same time, however, some restrictions on immigration may be required, or at least the authority to impose restrictions if the flow of immigration becomes too large to be absorbed without serious harm to the American poor.

In the end, the case for completely open borders can probably not be sustained. But rich and middle-class Americans – the majority in this country – should bear some sacrifice on behalf of their equally worthy but disadvantaged brethren in the world, rather than using immigration policy in pursuit of their own advantage.

Since some border restrictions are probably required, we are brought to the second issue of rights: which foreigners are to be allowed in? (*See* also Briggs and Moore, 1994.)

Under current law, the largest number of entries is reserved for relatives of American residents. Lesser provision is made for people with labor market skills, for refugees, and for a few other groups. Are these the best priorities Americans can choose? I think not.

Reunification of families is an important goal, but the overwhelming priority given to it in U.S. law is unjustified. While the demands of kinship are worthy, they are narrow. Since so many of the scarce slots are allocated to family members, a severe shortage of openings exists for other types of immigrants.

Some have argued that the interests of Americans would be served by admitting a higher proportion of people based on their labor market skills (*e.g.*, Becker, 1990; Briggs, 1992). This is debatable. Skilled immigrants do not necessarily improve the well-being of Americans in general. They help some Americans, by generating new production, jobs and income, but they harm others by lowering the wages in their professions and blocking the advancement of some Americans to those professions.

Furthermore, an emphasis on labor market skills has no relationship to the ethical and human rights goals of immigration. The United States will not do more good in the world by giving priority to people with more education and skills. If anything, the contrary is true since such people often have good opportunities in their home countries. In fact, the admission of highly skilled people may actually constitute exploitation of poorer countries by the United States, as the extensive literature on the brain drain suggests.

What about refugees? Expansion of the refugee category might harm the economic interests of Americans, since refugees are more likely than other immigrants to require state assistance. On the other hand, the moral obligation of the United States lies in the admission of refugees, particularly when refugee status is a consequence of American actions. I would like to argue, however, that we have a moral obligation to admit refugees even when their status has no relationship to our foreign policy.

Recall that the strongest moral objection to any restriction on immigration is that it harms people who are on average disadvantaged. For no group of foreigners is this truer than for refugees. They are people in great danger. American immigration policy could have no higher purpose than helping to find a permanent home for victims of oppression.

The third issue has to do with the rights of undocumented immigrants. What rights should they have? Neither of the two extreme answers to the question can stand.

The first extreme answer is that since the undocumented have no right to be in the United States, they have forfeited all their rights here. This is obviously wrong, for if it were true, Americans would be justified in treating them in any arbitrary way they wanted – killing them or enslaving them, for example. The other extreme view is that since the undocumented are human beings, with the same moral worth as everyone else, they have exactly the same rights as legal American residents. This cannot be true, however, as long as border controls exist, since the meaning of border controls is that some people do not have the right to live in the United States.

Consideration of the rights of the undocumented reveals, therefore, another argument against the very existence of immigration restrictions. Border controls necessarily create two classes of people in the United States with unequal rights: the legal and the illegal. It is no answer to say that this dilemma would disappear if the border were policed more effectively, since border controls can never be fully effective. In fact, some evidence exists that increased controls on the border actually result in a larger undocumented population in the United States because once people have successfully entered the country, they are less likely to return to their country of origin and then face the perils of another attempted entry in the future (Kossoudji, 1992).

If, in spite of this understanding, we are going to maintain restrictions on immigration, we must face the fact that those restrictions impose unequal rights on morally equal people – not just out there in the world but right here in River City. The undocumented are subject to deportation if discovered. They must therefore try to avoid contact with authorities who might threaten their residency. This means that they are inhibited from reporting violations to which they are subject – for example, sexual harassment, domestic violence, or unfair labor practices.

The dilemma cannot be resolved completely, but I propose a reform that goes in the opposite direction from California's Proposition 187. Why not assure undocumented immigrants that if they identify themselves to the authorities for the purpose of reporting illegal treatment – for example, domestic abuse or violations of the minimum wage law – they will not thereby be subject to deportation? This might substantially improve the respect for human rights in the United States, and it would hardly reduce deportations at all since these sorts of abuses are seldom reported now.

More generally, we need an enforceable international "bill of rights" for migrant workers. They come to work; they come because some people in the host countries want them to. They are not going to disappear, their moral standing is equal to that of all other people, and they deserve a legally binding statement about their rights (*see* IMR, 1991).

The fourth issue has to do with citizenship – and here I do not mean to be critical of current U.S. law but to pose a warning. The Fourteenth Amendment to the Constitution provides that, "all persons born or naturalized in the United States, and subject to the jurisdiction thereof, are citizens of the United

States. . . ." Pete Wilson, Pat Buchanan, and others have proposed changing this amendment so that the American-born children of undocumented immigrants would not be citizens. I believe this would be disastrous (*see* Chapman, 1996; *cf.* Schuck and Smith, 1985).

The Fourteenth Amendment is the vehicle by which the slaves were granted citizenship, following the Civil War. Symbolically, any tinkering with this provision would have grave consequences for race relations in the United States.

The objections go beyond symbolism, however. We have a number of examples in the world of citizenship laws similar to those preferred by Wilson and Buchanan, and they are not happy ones. In Germany, for example, merely the fact of being born in the country does not convey the right of citizenship. The consequence is that some people who can trace their ancestry back three or four generations within the country have no right to German citizenship. They are second-class noncitizens, without voting rights and many other rights in the only country they know as home. They are punished in perpetuity for a crime committed not by themselves but by their parents or grandparents (*see* Kurthen, 1995). This cannot be reconciled with the principle of equal worth, and we should resist it in the United States.

I have no illusion that the United States will abandon its national interest and adopt an immigration policy based on universal human rights. I think, however, that we could move in the direction of human rights without abandoning our national interest. Moreover, when the two perspectives come into conflict, and when we choose national interest over universal rights, we should at least have the decency to concede that our use of immigration policy to enhance our own interests is immoral.

NOTE

[1] A philosophical basis for equality and human rights, and their relationship to immigration, can be found in many other places. Political theorist Joseph Carens (1987) bases the case for open borders on three philosophical traditions, those of Robert Nozick, John Rawls, and the utilitarians. Carens argues that Nozick's individualist philosophy is inconsistent with immigration controls because those controls are an action of the state to prevent autonomous individuals – who may reside initially on different sides of a border – from making voluntary contracts with one another. From Rawl's perspective, immigration controls are invalid because they enforce an inequality that is not to the advantage of the least well off, namely the people who wish to immigrate but are prevented from doing so. The utilitarian case for open borders, Carens argues, is that it allows people to locate where their productivity, gains, welfare, and happiness are greatest, thus maximizing global utility.

REFERENCES

Becker, G. S.
1990   "Opening the Golden Door Wider – To Newcomers with Knowhow," *Business Week.*
             June 11, 12.

Borjas, G. J.
1994   "The Economics of Immigration," *Journal of Economic Literature,* 1667–1717.

Bosniak, L. S.
1991   "Human Rights, State Sovereignty and the Protection of Undocument Migrants under the International Migrant Workers Convention," *International Migration Review*, 25(4):737–770.

Briggs, V. M., Jr.
1992   *Mass Migration and the National Interest*. Armonk, NY: M. E. Sharpe.

Briggs, V. M., Jr. and S. Moore
1994   *Still An Open Door?* Washington, DC: American University Press.

Brimelow, P.
1995   *Alien Nation, Common Sense About America's Immigration Disaster*. New York: Random House. Chapter 13.

Carens, J. H.
1992   "Migration and Morality: A Liberal Egalitarian Perspective." In *Free Movement, Ethical Issues in the Transnational Migration of People and Money*. Ed. B. Barry and R. E. Goodin. London: Harvester Wheatsheaf. Pp. 25–47.

———
1991   "States and Refugees: A Normative Analysis." In *Refugee Policy, Canada and the United States*. Ed. H. Adelman. Toronto: York Lanes Press. Pp. 18–29.

———
1988   "Immigration and the Welfare State." In *Democracy and the Welfare State*. Ed. A. Gutmann. Princeton, NJ: Princeton University Press. Pp. 207–230.

———
1987   "Aliens and Citizens: The Case for Open Borders," *The Review of Politics*, 49:251–273.

Chapman, S.
1996   "Birth Control," *The New Republic*. April 8, 11–14.

Gibney, M., ed.
1988   *Open Borders? Closed Societies? The Ethical and Political Issues*. Westport, CT: Greenwood Press.

International Migration Review (IMR)
1996   "Special Issue: Ethics, Migration, and Global Stewardship," *International Migration Review*, 30(1).

———
1991   "Special Issue: U.N. Convention on the Protection and Rights of All Migrant Workers and Members of Their Families," *International Migration Review*, 25(4).

Isbister, J.
1996   *The Immigration Debate: Remaking America*. West Hartford, CT: Kumarian Press.

Kossoudji, S. A.
1992   "Playing Cat and Mouse at the U.S.-Mexican Border," *Demography*, 159–180.

Kurthen, H.
1995   "Germany at the Crossroads: National Identity and the Challenges of Immigration," *International Migration Review, 29(4)*:914–938.

Loescher, G. and J. A. Scanlan
1986   *Calculated Kindness: Refugees and America's Half-open Door, 1945 to the Present*. New York: The Free Press.

Schuck, P. H. and R. M. Smith
1985   *Citizenship Without Consent: Illegal Aliens in the American Polity*. New Haven, CT: Yale University Press.

United Nations High Commissioner for Refugees (UNHCR)
1993   *The State of the World's Refugees 1993: The Challenge of Protection.* New York: Penguin
          Books.

Wasserstrom, R.
1986   "One Way to Understand and Defend Programs of Preferential Treatment." In *The
          Moral Foundations of Civil Rights.* Ed. R. K. Fullinwider and C. Mills. Totowa, NJ:
          Rowman and Littlefield. Pp. 46–55.

Weiner, M.
1995   *The Global Migration Crisis, Challenge to States and to Human Rights.* New York: Harper
          Collins.

Zolberg, A. R., A. Suhrke and S. Aguayo
1989   *Escape From Violence: Conflict and the Refugee Crisis in the Developing World.* New York:
          Oxford University Press.

PART III

REDEFINING THE ROLES OF LOCAL AND STATE GOVERNMENT IN IMMIGRATION

11

Framing the Issues: Immigrant Policy the Role of State and Local Government

ANN MORSE
Immigrant Policy Project[1]
National Conference of State Legislatures, Washington, DC

The Immigrant Policy Project has been examining the role of states and localities in the resettlement of immigrants and refugees since 1992. This paper outlines some of our project's goals and activities, provides an overview of immigration trends driving state and local involvement in immigration, describes the major issues for states and localities (*e.g.*, fiscal, constitutional and service delivery issues), and provides examples of successful programs at the state and local level.

THE IMMIGRANT POLICY PROJECT

The Immigrant Policy Project is a collaborative research effort undertaken by the State and Local Coalition on Immigration. The Coalition is comprised of the National Governors' Association, the National Conference of State Legislatures, the National Association of Counties, the United States Conference of Mayors, the American Public Welfare Association and, most recently, the National League of Cities.

Begun in 1992, the Project's goal is to address the role of state and local governments in the resettlement of immigrants and refugees. The Project performs research and education, acts as a central source of information for the Coalition, and provides information to Coalition constituents. The Project seeks to document immigration trends, innovative policies and programs, and priorities for state and local government.

Perspectives

The Project benefits from several advisory groups: a National Advisory Board of elected and appointed officials, a Governing Board of the executive directors of the participating organizations, and an expert panel. Each of these groups of advisors has been critical to our development and to our success in providing research for state and local policymakers. Our National Advisory Board, for example, is composed of two elected or appointed officials from each of the organizations. The Coalition constituents have a broad range of perspectives on immigration, reflective of the national debate. We seek to provide our constituents, of all perspectives, with the information they need to help them in their rational assessment of immigration issues in their state, city, or county. While there is a range of individual beliefs by policymakers on the benefits or costs of immigration, there is a coalescence over issues of federalism and accountability. Federal jurisdiction is clear for immigration policy, and, in the view of our constituents, the federal responsibility for immigrants is equally clear. State and local policymakers believe strongly in federal responsibility and fiscal accountability for its policy decisions on immigration.

Immigration vs. Immigrant Policy

Our focus is on "immigrant" rather than "immigration" policy. Although the federal government has exclusive jurisdiction over immigration policy, that is, the terms and conditions for entry into the United States, federal decisions have direct and indirect effects on state and local governments in the form of their budgets, the composition of their citizenry, the utilization and quality of their services, and the general social, political and economic character of their communities. In brief, states and localities have a role in understanding and responding to the needs of immigrants after their arrival in the United States.

IMMIGRATION TRENDS

Why are states and localities involved in immigration? At the risk of this not being "news" anymore, the United States is at a peak level of immigration:

9.5 million immigrants arrived in the 1980s, compared to 8.9 million during the last peak in U.S. immigration at the turn of the century. These 9.5 million newcomers migrated from more than 100 countries, mostly from Asia and Latin America, in contrast to the traditional sending countries of Europe. According to the 1990 census, the foreign-born population of the United States is approximately 21 million in a total population of 258 million, or about 8.5 percent compared to about 15 percent in 1890 (Fix and Passel, 1994).

Everyone also knows that six states receive most of the immigrants: California, New York, Florida, Texas, New Jersey, and Illinois. This is historically true, that immigrants tend to settle in large urban areas in these states – Los Angeles, New York City, Miami, Chicago. What is new, however, is the unexpected settlement of immigrants in smaller cities and communities: Lowell, Massachusetts, for example, where 1 in 7 residents is a recent immigrant; Monterey Park, California, whose population changed from two-thirds white in 1970 to 88 percent Asian and Hispanic by 1990; or Atlanta, Georgia, whose Asian and Hispanic population grew from 20,000 in 1980 to 200,000 by 1992. Other "unexpected" settlements are Guatemalans in Sussex County, Delaware; Vietnamese and Mexicans in Garden City, Kansas; Vietnamese in Louisiana; Soviet Pentecostals in Oregon; and Hmong and Ethiopians in Minnesota. Over a relatively short period of time, school systems and hospitals in these communities were trying to serve people who spoke dozens of unfamiliar languages and had very different cultures.

Second trend – although the numbers of immigrants are increasing, the federal government has reduced or constrained the few programs that assist newcomers in integrating into the economic, social and civic life of the United States. Federal funding for refugees, the newly legalized (the "amnesty aliens" granted legal status in the 1986 Immigration Reform and Control Act), and immigrant education programs have been substantially cut or delayed (Fix and Passel, 1994).

Third, state and local responsibility for newcomers has increased in the last fifteen years due to new legislative or judicial mandates to provide services: the Refugee Act of 1980 required states to provide cash and medical assistance to refugees; the 1986 Immigration Reform and Control Act allowed access to public assistance, education and health services; and a mandate under the federal Medicaid program requires emergency medical services for undocumented immigrants. States and localities implement programs required by federal law, provide services mandated by the courts, and initiate programs and policies to serve the specialized needs of their new citizens (Morse, 1994).

Fourth, a proliferation of confusing immigrant categories and benefit eligibility complicates state and local government ability to determine eligibility for assistance. New categories, such as temporary protected status, allow foreigners to enter the country but prohibit access to federally funded public assistance. This patchwork of eligibility standards ignores the reality of a family in need of assistance, where the family members may have entered under several different immigrant categories, but only one or two may be eligible for public assistance.

To recap – more immigrants; less federal support; new mandates on states and localities; and complex eligibility schemes for public assistance.

MAJOR ISSUES FOR STATES AND LOCALITIES

Funding

Call it a cliché or a mantra, states and localities rally around the cause of "no unfunded mandates." For immigration, this means that the federal government should live up to the costs of its decisions in terms of their effects on state and local programs. Immigration decisions are clearly within federal jurisdiction, but for states and localities, the denial of federal benefits to immigrants is primarily a question of unfunded federal mandates for services and a continuation of cost-shifts for immigrant programs.

We saw this cost shifting over the 1980s in the refugee program (where a 36-month federal promise dropped to zero reimbursement for AFDC-eligible refugees and eight months for others, e.g., single refugees). We saw it in the SLIAG program, with restricted reimbursement and funding continually delayed. We saw it in immigrant education programs: Michael Fix at the Urban Institute notes that funding for immigration education fell by half in the 1980s; that Title VII bilingual education for limited English proficient children fell by half; and that refugee education assistance has been unfunded since 1988 (Fix and Zimmermann, 1993).

Congress seems poised to further abrogate the federal responsibility for the effects of its decisions in immigration policy, in both welfare reform proposals and in immigration reform legislation.

Welfare Reform

In welfare reform proposals, Congress would initiate a permanent bar to the federal SSI and Food Stamp Programs for legal immigrants and bar new arrivals from all federal means-tested programs for five years (including programs such as child nutrition, energy assistance, substance abuse; current law limits immigrant access for three to five years for three programs: AFDC, Food Stamps, and SSI). Should this legislation pass, look out for the ripple effect, such as loss of Medicaid eligibility, effects on children's programs, and a cost-shift to state and local general assistance/emergency relief programs. The legislation would also add burdensome administrative and reporting requirements to states and localities in determining citizenship, immigrant and sponsor income, immigrant status, work history, time-in-country, and time-on-aid.[2]

Immigration Reform

In the immigration reform bills now on fast-track, the Senate would require a minimum of five years deeming for all federal needs-based programs. Deeming means that the entire income of the immigrant's sponsor (and that of the sponsor's spouse) is considered available to the immigrant in determining the immigrant's eligibility for public benefits – it effectively denies public assistance.

The likely implication for states and localities is that immigrants would turn to general assistance programs as they lose access to federal programs. The Immigrant Policy Project conducted a study of general assistance programs in 24 localities. We found that state and local general assistance programs are serving significant numbers of needy immigrants and refugees. All 24 have programs that would serve immigrants dropped from SSI, and 14 would serve immigrant families made ineligible for AFDC. The survey established that cuts in federal welfare eligibility for legal immigrants are easily translated into cost-shifts for state and local welfare programs (NCSL, 1995).

The attempt by Congress to allow states and localities to bar or deem raises both federal and state constitutional questions. In 1971, the Supreme Court decided in *Graham v. Richardson* that states may not discriminate against immigrants in determining eligibility for benefits, under the equal protection clause in the U.S. constitution. State constitutions also contain obligations to serve the needy and to protect privacy.

Intergovernmental Roles

An open question remains as to the appropriate intergovernmental roles – federal, state, and local – in funding immigrant policy. Studies show the inequity in revenue-sharing of immigrant taxes: two-thirds of revenues provided by immigrants flow to the federal level, while only one-third flows to states and localities. Yet states and localities provide two-thirds of services to immigrants, primarily in education and health care.[3] Local jurisdictions are finding it increasingly difficult to pay for immigrant services. Georges Vernez of RAND finds that the fiscal burden of immigrants increases as the size of the jurisdiction decreases, ranging from neutral or even positive at the national level, to neutral to negative at the state level, to negative at the county/city level (Vernez and McCarthy, 1995).

EXAMPLES OF PROGRAMS AT THE STATE AND LOCAL LEVEL

In the first two years of the project, The Immigrant Policy Project convened regional meetings of state and local policymakers, private sector organizations, and associations representing immigrants and refugees, to understand the priority issues and where we should focus research. We examined service delivery issues, health care concerns, employment and training programs. One of the most often noted concerns was how to address the language barrier for newcomers to begin the process of getting resettled, to help access programs, to obtain jobs, to get help in emergency situations. We heard that there are not enough translators or interpreters, particularly at hospitals or schools; that children are being asked to take on roles as interpreters, upsetting parental authority in the family; that five of the largest school systems are serving students from over 100 language backgrounds. Meeting participants often noted the lack of sufficient classes for English as a Second Language or the lack of work-specific English classes, and that English classes are universally oversubscribed. Many states and localities have established language banks, hired interpreters/translators, or contracted with telephone interpreter services. Perhaps there is an appropriate federal role in funding and developing new curricula, interpreter training, and appropriate language programs to break down the language barrier.

Language differences are the major source of tension between newcomers and established residents. Robert Bach, author of *Changing Relations: Newcomers and Established Residents in U.S. Communities*, found that language serves as a source of intergroup conflict, tension, and distance because people are unable to communicate with each other. However, he notes, "participation works." When groups of different ethnicities or cultures work together toward common goals, such as Neighborhood Watch or Safe Street programs, good community relations result. These localized activities benefit all community residents, improve communication among different ethnic groups, and help overcome perceptions of mistrust (Bach, 1993).

One myth about language acquisition is the belief that earlier immigrants adjusted without any special assistance. In fact, a number of private and public organizations organized and provided language classes for immigrants. New Jersey passed legislation in 1907 to support English and civics classes for the foreign born. In New York, a Bureau of Industries and Immigration was established in 1910 to promote the effective employment of immigrants and their development as useful citizens. In 1914, the federal bureau of naturalization sponsored citizenship classes in the public schools. Social clubs, labor unions, and businesses also supported language and civics class for newcomers in the early twentieth century (Fuchs, 1990).

EXAMPLES OF STATE AND LOCAL PROGRAMS: TWO MODELS FROM THE REFUGEE PROGRAM ON WELFARE-TO-WORK

Merced County, California, is home to a sizable refugee population, about 15,000 in a total county population of 173,000. In 1994, 35 percent of the total county population received public assistance of some sort; the unemployment rate was 15.5 percent and, while job growth was good, the population growth was better, at 20 percent. The refugee population was largely Hmong, a nomadic population from southeast Asia that has only had a written language since the 1950s. Prior to arriving in the United States, the Hmong practiced traditional agrarian techniques of slash and burn and moved frequently in search of new land, skills, and methods not exactly transferable to California.

No materials existed for Merced's service providers, and communication was extremely difficult. However, Merced was able to create new services to respond to the refugees' needs, including orientation, acculturation, crisis intervention, English as a Second Language, and vocational training. Merced began "mainstreaming" refugees into the JOBS/GAIN program, which provided basic education, on-the-job training and work experience.

In public policy, we are always asking "what works." Merced County says, "this works": employment-specific English language courses; multiple wage earner strategies that assist the second parent and eldest child to enter the workforce; creating networks with businesses, refugees, and educators; and work experience, noting that 90 percent of refugees' first jobs is part-time (Baker, 1995).

When Wisconsin decided to initiate a series of work-based welfare reforms, staff in the state refugee program worked hard to make sure refugees would continue to receive appropriate services under the new system. The state adapted its successful Key States Initiative Program (funded under the federal Office of Refugee Resettlement) and persuaded the state and local JOBS agencies that funding refugee agencies was the best way to serve refugee welfare recipients (and to meet the work participation requirements of the new system). The JOBS agencies came to recognize that refugees are part of the welfare caseload and realized that unless the population was served, they would have difficulty meeting the work participation requirements. Finally, there was commitment from the state legislature to appropriate funds in order to meet the new welfare to work requirements. The refugee clients were not easy to serve: 88 percent were Hmong; the families were larger than average; 75 percent had less than one year of work experience and an average of 5.5 years of education (compared to the AFDC client average of 11.3 years). Yet, welfare dependency was reduced from 73 percent to 37 percent, and welfare savings were estimated at $15.8 million over the seven years. The program's success was attributed to a focus on family self-sufficiency; a bilingual, bicultural service system operated by the Mutual Assistance Associations; and integration with Wisconsin's JOBS and welfare reform programs (NCSL, 1995).

THE GLOBAL ECONOMY

Former California State Senator Art Torres sees opportunity in the newcomers' ties to their country of origin as assets for international trade and economic development. These ties can help a local community compete in an increasingly interconnected global economy. The language skills and familiarity with a trading partner's culture can be tapped from immigrants to support new business ventures. The ease and low cost of transportation and communications facilitate ties between new and old cultures, and these ties can contribute to economic growth both in the United States and in the immigrants' country of origin. In 1984, when an immigrant family from Mexico started a wood products company in San Diego, they were able to export a substantial amount of goods into Mexico because of their bicultural heritage and knowledge of Mexican business opportunities. Similar cultural advantages have benefited California companies in Silicon Valley and other high-tech firms that are owned or operated by immigrants.

Governor William Weld of Massachusetts has stated that Massachusetts depends heavily on the intellectual capital that flows into Massachusetts' borders: to teach students the key skills for the workplace of tomorrow, to fill technology gaps that help their companies compete in a global economy, and to help their research hospitals make the scientific breakthrough that will end a deadly disease (Weld, 1996).

Current Initiatives

Despite the often hostile national debate on immigration, few initiatives have been undertaken at the state and local level that would be detrimental to immigrants. States and localities are seeking responses that are within their jurisdiction to solve problems related to immigration. These responses vary. California's Proposition 187 to deny services to illegal immigrants is one end of the spectrum, and the Project will need to assess the potential for its replication in other states. The Project has been active in advising lawmakers of the content of the California proposition and potential effects of its implementation in areas such as public health and public education. Few states join California at this end of the spectrum in restricting services to immigrants. The majority of states with high immigrant populations have developed responses that would adapt programs or services in order to assist the integration of newcomers. For example, states and localities have undertaken citizenship initiatives that support language and civics training for would-be citizens. They have also created state offices or special legislative committees, modified service delivery, and established public education campaigns. Examples include the Maryland Office for New Americans; a committee in Oregon that was established to understand migration issues and develop policy recommendations; legislation in Illinois that requires interpreters at public hospitals; citizenship campaigns in Chicago, New York, and Maryland to assist newcomers to traverse the barriers to naturalization; and an Immigrant and Refugee Policy Council established by the Virginia legislature to focus on immigration issues.

During 1995, policymakers focused mainly on two areas: issues related to citizenship and issues related to illegal immigration. As applications for citizenship soared, several states and cities established programs to assist in the process, such as one-stop naturalization workshops, videos, and outreach to immigrants who have not yet naturalized.

Citizenship Initiatives

The Illinois Department of Public Aid developed a Refugee and Immigrant Citizenship Initiative to facilitate access to and success in the naturalization process for those residents who desire the full rights and responsibilities of citizenship. New York State and the City of Chicago also undertook programs to help immigrants become citizens. In Maryland, 367,000 of the state's population (7.3%) is foreign born. Last year, the legislature agreed to support citizenship promotion, appropriating funds for community organizations to provide application assistance and public education on the responsibilities and benefits of citizenship.

Illegal Immigration

States continued to seek federal reimbursement for the incarceration costs of undocumented criminal felons and started new partnerships with the INS to deport prisoners promptly. There are very strong concerns at the local level, where communities experiencing large numbers of new arrivals, often undocumented, with little response from the federal government to investigate, deport, or pay. Recently, states and the INS have started new cooperative agreements to expedite deportation of immigrants who entered illegally and were convicted of felonies. To ease prison crowding and cut costs, Florida became the first state in the nation to deport illegal alien criminals imprisoned for nonviolent crimes. This program was created in cooperation with the INS in mid-1994. Last year, states also scored a fiscal victory, winning federal reimbursement for the costs of incarcerating undocumented immigrants (the State Criminal Alien Assistance Program). States estimated their total incarceration costs for this population at $796 million; the first year appropriations was $130 million, or 16 percent of the total cost.

Given federal action and control of immigration policy, states and localities are by default creating immigrant policy – developing programs and services that assist immigrants in resettling in their new communities. The question facing us is how to jointly address issues of common concern and how to improve and restore the federal, state and local partnership in successfully resettling immigrants and refugees.

NOTES

[1]The Immigrant Policy Project of the State and Local Coalition on Immigration is funded by the Andrew W. Mellon Foundation.

[2]NCSL conducted a study in April 1996 of the implementation costs for the new deeming requirements in S.1664. The study found that the cost of deeming for only 10 programs (of a possible 50 federal means-tested programs) would result in a $744 million unfunded mandate.

[3]The Illinois Immigrant Policy Project released a new study in May 1996 that found the federal government collects 70.8 percent of the major taxes paid by immigrants, yet pays for only 35.2 percent of the major welfare and education services received by immigrants.

REFERENCES

Bach, R. L.
1993   *Changing Relations: Newcomers and Established Residents in U.S. Communities.* New York: Ford Foundation.

Baker, A.
1995   "Meeting the Challenge," *Immigrant Policy News . . . The State-Local Report,* 2(1). May 12.

Dunlap, J.
1995   "Federal Welfare Reform and Cost Shifts: A Survey of Legal Immigrant Eligibility for General Assistance." Memo. Washington, DC: Immigrant Policy Project, State and Local Coalition on Immigration.

Fix, M. and J. Passel
1994   *Immigration and Immigrants: Setting the Record Straight.* Washington, DC: The Urban Institute.

Fix, M. and W. Zimmermann
1993   *After Arrival: An Overview of Federal Immigrant Policy in the United States.* Washington, DC: The Urban Institute.

Fuchs, L.
1990   *The American Kaleidoscope: Race, Ethnicity and the Civic Culture.* Hanover, NH: The University Press of New England.

Morse, A., ed.
1994   *America's Newcomers: An Immigrant Policy Handbook.* State and Local Coalition on Immigration, Immigrant Policy Project. Denver, CO: National Conference of State Legislatures.

National Conference of State Legislatures (NCSL)
1995   "Wisconsin: Welfare Reform and Refugees" *Immigrant Policy News . . . The State-Local Report,* 2(2). December.

Vernez, G. and K. McCarthy
1995   *The Fiscal Costs of Immigration: Analytical and Policy Issues.* Santa Monica, CA: RAND.

Weld, W. F.
1996   "Immigration Brings Intellectual Capital to Massachusetts' Shore," *Immigrant Policy News . . . Inside the Beltway,* 3(1). February 29.

12

Health Issues of Immigrants and Refugees: Local Experience and Response in a Changing Political and Economic Climate

SUSAN ALLAN
Arlington County Health Director

The experience of Arlington County, Virginia, with a rapid and dramatic influx of immigrants from all over the world is useful for examining local experience and policy issues concerning immigrant health services. Immigrants to the United States are generally unexpectedly healthy as a group. Health services that are most useful include health education and screening shortly after arrival in this country; preventive health care for children; communicable disease control; and family planning and maternity services. Although there is a role for specific, targeted programs, communities can best serve immigrant populations when the general human services programs are strong and well funded, with capacity for adaptations for language and culture. Federal and state government support for local programs should include adequate funding for the general programs, technical expertise, translations and training, and minimization of policy and procedural barriers to services. Because most immigrant services are provided through those programs serving the general population, the most important federal and state role is providing resources for a strong general human services network.

ARLINGTON COUNTY, VIRGINIA: FROM SOUTHERN SUBURB TO INTERNATIONAL URBAN COMMUNITY

Like many other communities in this country, Arlington County is a strikingly different community now than it was in 1960. Perhaps the most significant change has been the dramatic influx of foreign-born immigrants, which began around 1960 but became a powerful demographic shift in the last two decades. Before 1960, Arlington was a suburban southern community, with a minority community consisting only of the longstanding African-American population which had held fairly steady as the white population swelled with people drawn to the federal job market. In the 1960 census, less than one percent of the Arlington population was noted as being a race other than white or black. The 1990 census shows a very different community (see Figure I): 21 percent of the Arlington population are foreign born, about two-thirds having arrived in the United States since 1970. These new immigrants represent an amazing array of countries of origin, languages, and cultural traditions.

This dramatic change has affected most aspects of community life, including the services the local government provides and the manner in which those services are provided. Certainly one of the biggest changes in the community is in the languages spoken (see Table 1). According to the 1990 census, 24 percent of Arlington County residents speak a language other than English at home, with a tremendous variety of languages represented. While there is some clustering of recent immigrants or non-English speakers in certain neighborhoods, the 1990 census found immigrants residing throughout all sections of the county (Data Analysis and Research Team, 1994a, 1994b, 1994c; Northern Virginia Planning District Commission, 1993).

The age distribution of recent immigrants differs from that of the U.S.-born Arlington residents in that immigrants are generally young family units or adults in their childbearing years. Although Arlington immigrant families usually have at most two or three children, because Arlington overall has an unusually small percentage of children in the population, a disproportionate number of the children in the community are recent immigrants or children of immigrants. As a result, perhaps the most visible impact of the immigrants has been on the local public schools. The schools are also the source of some of the

Figure I.   Minority Population of Arlington County, Virginia: 1900–1990.

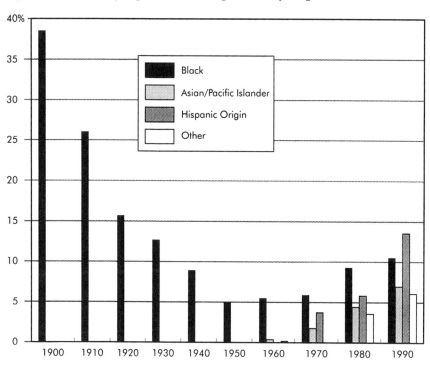

most detailed and accurate information about the recent immigrant families. In the Arlington Public Schools, 20 percent of the children in the system overall are currently enrolled in some form of special classes for English language support. In almost half of the elementary schools, 30 percent or more of the students are enrolled in special English language support classes (Arlington Public Schools, 1995). It may be that more than 40 percent of all the students live in households where English is not the predominant language.

HEALTH ISSUES OF IMMIGRANTS AND REFUGEES

There is generally more speculation than actual information about the health issues and health status of immigrants and refugees. The discussion here represents our local experience, confirmed by the limited number of specific studies we have been able to find and consistent with extensive general data about health status, morbidity, and mortality for a variety of population groups and communities. Although the available information is sometimes frustratingly incomplete, it is also surprisingly consistent.

TABLE 1

LANGUAGES AND COUNTRIES OF LIMITED ENGLISH PROFICIENT STUDENTS: SEPTEMBER 30, 1995

Language	Country[a]	Language	Country[a]
Aderinya	Ethiopia	Mongolian	Mongolia
Akan	Ghana	Nepali	Nepal
Albanian	Albania	Pampango	Philippines
Amharic	Eritrea, Ethiopia	Pashto	Afghanistan, Pakistan
Arabic	Algeria, Egypt, Iraq, Mauritania, Morocco, Saudi Arabia, Sudan, Syria, Tunisia, United Arab Emirates	Polish	Poland
		Portuguese	Angola, Brazil, Cape Verde, Portugal
		Punjabi	India
Bengali	Bangladesh	Quechua	Bolivia
Bulgarian	Bulgaria	Romanian	Romania
Burmese	Myanmar	Russian	Belarus, Kyrghistan, Latvia, Russia, Ukraine
Catalan	Spain	Serbo-Croatian	Bosnia-Herzegovina, Yugoslavia
Cebuano	Philippines	Shona	Zimbabwe
Chewa	Malawi	Sinhala (Sinhalese)	Sri Lanka
Chinese	China, Hong Kong, Philippines, Taiwan, Vietnam	Slovene	Croatia
		Somali	Somalia
Creole English	Jamaica	Spanish	Argentina, Bolivia, Chile, Colombia, Costa Rica, Cuba, Domican Republic, Ecuador, El Salvador, Guatemala, Honduras, Mexico, Nicaragua, Panama, Paraguay, Peru, Puerto Rico, Spain, Uruguay, Venezuela
Creole French	Haiti		
Fang	Equatorial Guinea		
Fanti	Ghana		
Farsi/Persian	Afghanistan, Iran, Pakistan		
French	Belgium, France, Zaire		
Ga-Adangme-Krobo	Ghana	Swahili	Kenya
Georgian	Republic of Georgia	Tagalog	Philippines
German	Switzerland	Telugu	India
Hindi	India	Temne	Sierra Leone
Ilocano	Philippines	Thai	Thailand
Indonesian	Indonesia	Tigrinya	Eritrea, Ethiopia
Italian	Italy	Tshiluba	Zaire
Japanese	Japan	Turkish	Turkey
Kannada	India	Ukranian	Ukraine
Khmer	Cambodia	Urdu	India, Pakistan
Kisii	Kenya	Uzbek	Uzbekistan
Korean	Korea	Vietnamese	Vietnam
Lao	Laos		
Macedonian	Macedonia		
Maithili	Nepal		

Source: Survey of Limited English Proficient Students, Arlington Public Scholols: School Year 1995–1996.

[a]This listing does not include all countries where the languages are spoken.

In any discussion of immigrants and refugees, it is important to acknowledge the remarkable diversity of the immigrant populations and to recognize that no generalizations will apply to all. Also, because the majority of the immigrants in Arlington and across the country are not refugees, the subsequent discussion deals primarily with nonrefugee immigrants. The special issues of refugees will also be noted.

The common belief is that immigrants have high healthcare needs and bring many diseases and health problems into this country. Indeed, we know that the countries from which most of the recent immigrants come have lower life expectancies and higher rates of many diseases than the United States. Yet, although there are a few specific health problems more common among immigrants, the available information and our local experience consistently show that immigrant populations overall are remarkably healthy and, in fact, are healthier in most respects than the general U.S.-born population (Business Week, 1994; Ebrahim, 1992; Department of Health and Human Services, 1994). Their life expectancy is longer, with lower rates of the most common causes of death, including heart disease, stroke, and cancer (Meyer, 1992). Immigrant women, despite frequent poverty and lack of prior health care, have healthy pregnancies, low-risk deliveries, and healthy newborns (Guendelman *et al*, 1990; Meyer, 1992). And despite conspicuous media coverage of a few sensational cases, those studies looking at healthcare utilization show that immigrants use medical services about half as frequently as U.S.-born residents (Business Week, 1994).

An especially interesting finding is that this health advantage holds primarily for the first generation of immigrant families and the advantage is more marked for recent immigrants than for long-term immigrants (Kliewer, 1992; Department of Health and Human Services, 1994). In subsequent generations, life expectancy, diseases rates, and pregnancy outcomes are increasingly comparable to the U.S. rates for their particular socioeconomic level (Guendelman, 1990). While the research is limited and has not been done for all immigrant populations, this finding supports the common hypothesis about why first generation immigrants are so healthy. Most immigrants come to the United States seeking employment and to make a better life for themselves and their children. Therefore, those who make this choice and who are able to find a way to come to the United States are those with the physical and mental resources to travel, to work, and to plan for their futures (Ebrahim, 1992:184). They leave behind the less healthy living and working environments of their original countries, but bring with them many of the aspects of their lifestyles that are healthier than the U.S. habits: their diets are better, they are less likely to smoke cigarettes or use drugs (Amaro *et al*, 1990; Mavleides *et al*., 1990), their daily activities include higher levels of exercise. For many, these healthy habits may in fact initially be reinforced by their relative poverty in this country: they continue a diet based on carbohydrates and vegetables because they are unable to afford large amounts of meat or fast foods, and the employment they find often involves higher levels of physical activity than the jobs they or their children later move into.[1]

For the most part, the health issues for immigrant populations are those health concerns typical for families with children and for adults of childbearing age. The women need family planning services and prenatal care. The children need preventive and developmental "well child" care. The men may have health issues related to their employment, such as musculoskeletal strains or skin rashes from exposure to chemicals or cleaning fluids.

The special health concerns of immigrants derive from the diseases endemic in their countries of origin (Ebrahim, 1992; Kliewer, 1992). Many arrive in the United States having been exposed to tuberculosis. Although they are not actively ill and present no immediate risk to others, people infected with tuberculosis may develop active disease at some point in the future. This risk can be greatly reduced if preventive medication is taken, so it is helpful both to the immigrant and to the community to provide tuberculosis screening and treatment services soon after their arrival in the United States. To put the risk in context, however, Arlington County has nearly 40,000 foreign-born residents, but only a total of 30 to 35 cases of tuberculosis a year, so the overall rate of active tuberculosis is very small.

Many immigrants arrive with a variety of parasitic diseases. These diseases are generally easily diagnosed and treated; they present no hazard to the general community here because the effective food and water sanitation measures in the United States eliminate the major routes for transmission of these diseases. Certain Asian and African populations, primarily refugees who have been living in crowded and unsanitary conditions, have high endemic levels of hepatitis B, which may present a health risk to family members but usually only a small risk to the general community. As with tuberculosis, this risk can be minimized by providing appropriate screening and medical services to the immigrant and the extended family at the time of their arrival in this country. Although children often were appropriately immunized in their own countries (since most countries of the world have better childhood immunization rates than the United States!), many have missed vaccinations or have lost their records in the process of moving to this country, so children often need additional immunizations.

Because of the conditions under which they have been living, refugees often do not come into the country as healthy as general immigrant populations. The number of refugees is far smaller and the impact on the community is far less than for general migration. In recent years, Arlington has been receiving about 250 to 400 new refugees per year, most from the countries of Southeast Asia or from the disrupted countries of Africa. Many of the health problems with which immigrants arrive are not chronic and, once assessed and treated, the refugee's health status may be quite normal.

For example, dental problems are very common among refugees, but are amenable to immediate dental treatment. Parasitic diseases can be promptly treated and eliminated. Tuberculosis prevention can be given, and uninfected family members can be protected from the risk of hepatitis B through vaccination. Other conditions may need longer-term treatment or attention, such as the mental health problems of persons who have been tortured or who have seen family members murdered or the growth and developmental delays of children who have been malnourished during critical years of their childhood.

LOCAL SERVICES

The important question for a local government such as Arlington County is which services are necessary or most effective for addressing the needs of the immigrants and refugees and for protecting the interests of the larger community. The special issues arise for the most part in the first few years. After that, the healthcare issues for immigrants are generally the same as those for other U.S. residents of the same socioeconomic circumstances.[2] Perhaps the most effective and important services are those provided in the first couple of years after arrival. Our local experience has been that most immigrants become well integrated into the general community within a few years and then have the economic and social ability to obtain medical care within the standard private sector healthcare system.

Transition healthcare services currently are provided to all refugees (through INS referrals) and to those other immigrants who happen to find their way into one of our local health department or community programs. These transition services include an initial health assessment, with screening and treatment for infectious diseases and parasites. The staff also provides an orientation to the U.S. healthcare system, explaining what services are available through the local health department, how insurance or medicaid works, when to use the emergency room, and how to find a private doctor. The staff provides assistance with obtaining initial healthcare services, such as making an appointment with a physician. Equally important to the long-term health and independence of the immigrant, the staff teaches them about basic healthcare practices that are different in this country than in the country of origin. Topics include nutrition, well-child checkups and immunizations, ob-gyn services, as well as domestic activities such as hygiene, how children are disciplined, and how women are treated in this country. Staff workers attempt to ensure appropriate linguistic and cultural adaptation for all services, although that is more easily provided for the larger immigrant communities than for those in which only a few individuals or families, are served.

Immigrants, like all of us, also have ongoing healthcare needs. The greatest issue is access to health care; this is an issue for immigrants in much the same way that it is a problem for all people in this country who do not have health insurance. Except for the limited medical assistance currently available to refugees at this time (eight months eligibility for Medicaid), immigrants have access to healthcare services through the same categories and channels as others living in our communities. To the extent that the poor or those with certain kinds of jobs are increasingly without access to health care, so too the immigrants, especially more recent immigrants, will be disproportionately affected (Burciaga, 1993).

FEDERAL AND STATE ROLES IN LOCAL SERVICES

What assistance from federal and state governments do we need at the local level to be able to meet the health needs of immigrants and refugees? To best provide for immigrants and refugees, local communities need a mix of special targeted programs and strong general healthcare and social services programs. Although federal and state funding for special immigrant and refugee programs is important and receives the most attention from advocates, there are other federal and state activities that may be even more important to support the provision of effective health services for immigrants and refugees at the local level. The most important federal and state contribution to local services is funding to ensure an overall human services system that is strong and effective. The federal and state governments could be a source of technical support, such as developing culturally appropriate healthcare materials, translated materials, and providing specialized training to local staff. Not enough of this is currently available. Then federal and state governments should make sure their policies don't get in the way of local efforts to reach the immigrant and refugee populations.

Support for Special Programs Targeting Refugees or Immigrants

Federal and state funding for special programs for healthcare services for immigrants and refugees was never large, and it has diminished considerably. In Arlington, at the height of the first wave of refugees, we received more than 1 million dollars in federal assistance for initial refugee services. This year, it is less than $200,000. While designated funding may help encourage initial establishment of special programs, the allocations falls far short of covering the full costs of services, and they are most realistically seen as a supplement to the general programs. Immigrants can be helped to adjust most effectively to the health practices and healthcare system of the United States through special transition or orientation programs that provide health education and health assessment. Those communities with migrant worker populations need assistance with structuring health care and establishing a medical records system for migrant workers.

Support for General Human Services Programs

Although special programs targeted for immigrants and refugees can be a valuable component of local services, most immigrant and refugee services are provided through the broader human services programs that serve the general population. Federal and state support for a strong foundation of general human services programs should include: maintaining or expanding Medicaid, state and local hospitalizations and general relief programs; ensuring effective local public health programs for communicable disease control, immunizations, and community disease surveillance; and funding for strong programs for family planning, prenatal clinics, and well-child clinics. With a strong general base, these programs can then be more flexible in making various language and cultural adaptions for the range of populations served. However, a program that is only marginally funded and is barely able to meet the basic community needs is unlikely to be able to adapt to provide effective service to immigrants or to other nonstandard individuals in the community.

Similarly, in a study of immigrant experiences in U.S. schools, the authors found that the quality of immigrant education depends on the fundamental strength and competence of the school system overall. They concluded that a school system's ability to be effective with immigrants was best enhanced not by special targeted programs but rather by enhancing the overall capacity and effectiveness of the school system (McDonnell and Hill, 1993).

Technical Support

Federal and state governments can be effective sources of technical support for local programs in a number of ways. For those local programs that are funded by the federal or state governments, documents can be provided already translated into the necessary languages. Information and training about appropriate cultural adaptations can be provided for newly arriving populations. For example, there are special cultural issues related to providing family planning and prenatal care to women from certain Middle Eastern countries, and nutrition education should be adjusted for families from Southeast Asia. When a local program develops translated or culturally adapted materials, federal and state programs can help disseminate these to other local communities serving a similar group of immigrants. Training of translators can also be organized through federal and state programs.

Assess Effect of Policies on Services to Immigrants

Ideally, the federal and state governments would attempt to assure that their various policies support and do not create barriers to the local community's ability to serve immigrants. Some of the obvious policy barriers include eligibility guidelines which exclude immigrants and prohibition of using languages other than English. The affect of other policies may be less obvious but still problematic. For example, a "utilization standard" for program evaluation may not include the extra time needed for translation, or for a detailed explanation to a newly-arrived African mother of how to read a thermometer so she can assess whether her child is having a dangerous reaction to an immunization or is seriously ill. Another well-intended policy creating an unintended barrier is the "motor voter" law which requires that all patients in local health department clinics be offered the opportunity to register to vote, and clinic staff must document that the offer was made and the patient's response. In some of our clinics where 75 percent of our patients are recent immigrants who don't speak English, this process is unduly time-consuming for the staff and confusing or even frightening for the immigrants, some of whom may interpret this as a message that we want to serve only voting citizens. Word of mouth among immigrants about this creates a danger of people becoming less willing to come into our family planning or tuberculosis clinics; this result would not serve the best interests of the community.

FINAL COMMENTS

Immigrant populations bring a complex mix of costs and benefits to a community, with the details and balance of the costs and benefits undoubtedly differing from one community to another. Often it is assumed that the costs are high, especially in areas such as healthcare needs and public health risks presented by the immigrants. Our experience, consistent with the available literature, suggests that those costs are not so large as generally assumed and that the long-term costs can be further reduced by fairly simple interventions at the time the immigrants first arrive in the country or the community.

Admittedly, the experience in Arlington is not entirely typical. The immigrant influx has been larger and more varied than in most other communities. At the same time, Arlington has demonstrated both the fiscal ability and the community willingness to adapt to many of the needs of the immigrants and to undertake explicit efforts to make them a part of the local community.

Nonetheless, the problems we have experienced and the programs we have developed in response to those problems may be applicable to many other communities as they work with their immigrant populations. We have seen many benefits to the community from our efforts to adapt to the new county residents. The most cited benefit is that the community is more interesting, with ever-expanding opportunities to experience another culture's foods, music, or ideas. We can travel the whole world without leaving our own neighborhood.

But our human services systems have also been changed in ways that will benefit every community member they serve, not just the immigrants who may first have stimulated the changes. To try to effectively serve the great variety of immigrants we encounter, we have had to learn to evaluate and respond to each immigrant individually, rather than as preestablished and standardized services. This was initially difficult and seemed more time consuming, and we have not always been successful in making those adjustments. But where we have been successful, members of our staff have found their work to be more interesting and creative, they have developed a broader range of skills, and they have created programs that are more flexible and adaptable. We are more explicit about identifying the goals we hope to achieve for each individual, and then, as much as possible, we try to structure the mix of services for those particular goals. We are finding that not only are the immigrants who were the impetus for many of these changes benefitting from this greater flexibility and individualization of services, but that all the people we serve benefit.

NOTES

[1]This finding of relatively high levels of health in immigrant populations in the United States probably is due, to a considerable degree, to the voluntary nature of their migrant status. Circumstances may be very different in those parts of the world experiencing forced mass migrations.

[2]Although Arlington does not have a migrant worker population, it should be noted that migrant workers are probably an exception to this statement that special programs are needed only for the first few years. Because of their exceptional circumstances, on-going special programs may be the only way to effectively address the healthcare needs of migrant workers.

REFERENCES

Amaro, H. *et al.*
1990   "Acculturation and Marijuana and Cocaine Use: Findings from HHANES 1982–84," *American Journal of Public Health*, 80:54–60.

Arlington Public Schools
1995   "Survey of Limited English Proficient Students: School Year 1995–1996," Arlington, VA: Arlington Public Schools.

Bach, R. L.
1993   *Changing Relations: Newcomers and Established Residents in U.S. Communities: A Report to the Ford Foundation by the National Board of the Changing Relations Project.* New York: Ford Foundation.

Burciaga, V. R. *et al.*
1993   "Insuring Latinos against the Costs of Illness," *Journal of the American Medical Association,* 269(7):889–894.

Business Week
1994   "Give Me Your Tired, Your Poor, Your Healthy," *Business Week*, March 21, 30.

Data Analysis and Research Team, Arlington County Planning Division
1994a   "Statistical Brief: Black Population 1990," Arlington County, VA: Arlington County
         Planning Division.

1994b   "Statistical Brief: Hispanic Population 1990," Arlington County, VA: Arlington
         County Planning Division.

1994c   "Statistical Brief: Asian-Pacific Islander Population, 1990," Arlington County, VA:
         Arlington County Planning Division.

Department of Health and Human Services, U.S.
1994   "Health of the Foreign-Born Population: United States, 1989–90," Advance Data 241.

Dunlap, J. C. and F. Hutchinson, eds.
1993   "America's Newcomers: Health Care Issues for New American." Issue Paper No. 2.
         Immigrant Policy Project, State and Local Coalition on Immigration, National
         Conference of State Legislatures.

Ebrahim, S.
1992   "Social and Medical Problems of Elderly Migrants," Special Issue: Migration and Health
         in the 1990s, International Migration, Quarterly Review, 30:179–191.

Edmonston, B. and J. S. Pasel, eds.
1994   Immigration and Ethnicity: The Integration of America's Newest Arrivals. Washington,
         DC: The Urban Institute Press.

Guendelman, S. et al.
1990   "Generational Differences in Perinatal Health among the Mexican American
         Population: Finding's from HHANES 1982-84," American Journal of Public Health,
         80:61–65.

Gurwitt, R.
1992   "Back to the Melting Pot," Governing, June, 31–35.

Kliewer, E.
1992   "Epidemiology of Disease among Migrants," Special Issue: Migration and Health in the
         1990s, International Migration, Quarterly Review, 30:141–155.

Mavleides, K. et al.
1960   "Acculturation and Alcohol Consumption in the Mexican American Population of the
         Southwestern United States: Findings from HHANES 1982–84," American Journal of
         Public Health, 80:42–46.

McDonnell, L. and P. T. Hill
1993   Newcomers in American Schools: Meeting the Educational Needs of Immigrant Youths.
         Santa Monica, CA: RAND.

Meyer, M.
1992   "Los Angeles 2010: A Latino Subcontinent," Newsweek, November 9, 32–33.

Morse, A., ed.
1994   America's Newcomers: An Immigrant Policy Handbook. Washington, DC: Immigrant
         Policy Project, State and Local Coalition on Immigration, National Conference of
         State Legislatures.

Northern Virginia Planning District Commission
1993   "Northern Virginia's Foreign Born: Their Numbers and Characteristics." Annadale,
         VA: Northern Virginia Planning District Commission.

Siem, H. and P. Bollini, ed.
1992   Special Issue: Migration and Health in the 1990s, International Migration, Quarterly
         Review. Vol. 30.

PART IV

REFUGEE RESETTLEMENT AND ASYLUM REFORM

13

Refugee Resettlement: A View from the Administration

PHYLLIS E. OAKLEY
Bureau for Population, Refugees and Migration, U.S. Department of State

The United States has for years played a leadership role within the international community in the field of refugee resettlement. We have no intention of abandoning this position. We have by far the largest program of permanent resettlement in the world. The United States has typically provided 50 percent of the places pledged to the United Nations High Commissioner for Refugees (UNHCR) for its priority caseloads. We continue to press other resettlement countries – both traditional and new players – to resettle those for whom no other durable solution exists.

That said, given the varied causes and massive scale of recent refugee/migrant movements as well as the changed global circumstances since the end of the cold war, it is appropriate that our approach to third country resettlement (as well as that of other concerned countries) has come under review. We continue to fine tune its use as a durable solution.

There is general agreement that, when deciding where to concentrate available refugee resources, priority must be given to sustaining human life, ensuring refugee protection, and finding solutions to refugee problems at their source or close to home. Of course, the ideal is repatriation. I think we would all agree that for large numbers of refugees, whether from Rwanda, Bosnia, or from Afghanistan or Vietnam, in the end repatriation has to be the primary focus.

We also continue to believe that, in many cases, resettlement is an important component of refugee protection. It has been said that we were used to dealing with refugees from tyranny and yet we don't really know today how to deal with refugees from anarchy. Approximately 40 low-intensity conflicts are occurring within countries in the world today – as civil war or the whole state breaking down – forcing people to leave. These cases are different from a wartime situation as well as from the former plight caused by friction between the two superpowers.

We are moving from an era of large in-country programs to one of smaller, more geographically dispersed and more ethnically diverse populations. This forces us back into the question of regional numbers and whether there are quotas for regions in the world that have a right to come into the United States.

An example of this new reality is found in Southeast Asia, where, from 1975 to 1995, the number of Indochinese refugees admitted to the United States exceeded admissions of any other region in all but two years (1977 and 1992, when Soviets accounted for the largest number of admissions).

Having averaged over 50 percent of annual admissions over the twenty year period, FY 1996 Indochinese admissions will total less than 25 percent, and this number should drop to no more than 15 percent in 1997.

In contrast, the number of African admissions, which has averaged 2.5 percent of U.S. admissions during the 1975–1995 period, will likely reach 8 percent this year and could increase further in 1997. Fourteen African nationalities were included in our FY 1995 admissions program. They were processed in ten locations across the continent.

While the U.S. admissions program will continue to include refugee groups of particular concern to the United States, as provided for under our law, the new realities also mean we will coordinate our efforts more closely with UNHCR and other resettlement countries. In Africa as well as the Near East and now Bosnia, much of the U.S. refugee resettlement effort is in response to requests of UNHCR.

We are pleased with the progress UNHCR is making in the development of a structure within which resettlement countries and NGOs come together periodically to consider how resettlement resources can best be utilized. By working together, we would hope to create a political climate internationally that recognizes the need to resettle certain refugees and other migration flows. We look forward to the consultations among governments and NGOs that UNHCR is planning for June 1996.

Closer to home, the broad support for refugee programs in the Congress and among the American people is shown by the fact that the bureau's budget was straight-lined for FY '96. It appears that we will not have the statutory limitation on annual refugee admissions. While some of these mature programs are naturally coming to an end and the refugee numbers are going down, what we really want to maintain is flexibility. We can all imagine situations where we might want to really raise those refugee numbers and make them available without having to face going to Congress and getting waivers and getting exceptions. That has been understood and certainly approved. Besides preserving flexibility, it is also necessary to maintain departmental and administrative prerogatives in the refugee area. This is a constant struggle between Congress trying to regulate and organize and tell us what to do and the desire of any Administration, Republican or Democratic, to say that we really want to maintain our own flexibility and be able to manage our own programs.

For FY 1997, the President's budget request will support an estimated 75,000 admissions. We believe that this number is appropriate to meet anticipated requirements. The decline from the 1996 level of 90,000 is due to the closing down of the program in Southeast Asia. We are beginning to work out programs to bring the CPA to a close. We have had some encouraging signs from the government of Vietnam. They are going to be willing to work with us to develop a program under ODP, in which we can have access to people who return to Vietnam who may be of special interest to the United States. The final numbers and regional distribution will be discussed in the regular process of consultation with the Congress and other interested parties.

We are closely watching proposed immigration and welfare reform legislation; the final wording of the various bills passed could have a serious impact on refugees. As the admission of refugees to this country is a federal responsibility and is tied to our overall foreign policy goals, we must continue to ensure a minimum package of integration assistance for new arrivals. We believe it is critical to ensure that refugees are placed in locations where successful initial resettlement is most likely. At the same time, refugees should not appear to be given benefits unreasonably in excess of what is available to U.S. citizens.

We believe that the program is strongest when federal agencies, state governments, and voluntary agencies collaborate in support of refugee resettlement. Working with the office of refugee resettlement at the Department of Health and Human Resources, we will encourage states to maintain refugee-specific programs. However, it is important to remember that in a small number of states where state governments have chosen to withdraw from the program, resettlement has continued with voluntary agencies taking the lead to manage local programs. This has enabled us to maintain a nationwide program.

Anticipating shifts in the U.S. welfare system, we have already begun to take steps to ameliorate the impact on refugee admissions. The Bureau of Population, Refugees and Migration is implementing policies intended to encourage earlier refugee self-sufficiency. Initial refugee placement decisions will be critical to a successful resettlement program.

To better inform and prepare all refugees for the new realities of resettlement in the United States, we recently convened a task force to assist us in realigning cultural orientation overseas. The task force participants, representing federal and state officials, national and local voluntary agencies, and refugees themselves, recommend a number of ways to better prepare refugees for the realities of resettlement.

Let me just close by saying that I think that there has been a great deal of interest in criteria for refugee admissions: How to establish new criteria in this post-cold war era? Who are the people who should be of concern to the United States when we do not see the people fleeing tyranny but really flight from anarchy and in many cases the collapse of states? At the end, it is a question of number versus criteria.

Various groups within the United States – even auditors in the State Department or on the Hill – are calling for reexamination of the criteria for refugee admissions. After lengthy discussions, we concluded that many refugees simply cannot achieve that kind of permanent protection through repatriation or even local resettlement, and therefore resettlement in third countries has to be maintained as an important element of the overall refugee policy. As we get into 1997 and prepare for 1998, we are all once again going to have to reason together and think about new criteria for refugee admissions.

14

New Priorities in Refugee Resettlement

RALSTON DEFFENBAUGH
Lutheran Immigration and Refugee Service

I well remember a time in early 1992 when Phyllis Oakley's predecessor's predecessor, Princeton Lyman, came up to New York to meet with the officers of the refugee resettlement voluntary agencies. He had another meeting in New York, but he had a couple of hours free and wanted to come over and meet with us. He had lunch with us and over sandwiches rolled up his sleeves and said, "I want to tell you about some trends that are coming in the refugee program. You and your agencies need to know about this so you can plan ahead." He set out in great detail the anticipated decline in admissions from Southeast Asia, the anticipated decline in admissions from the former Soviet Union, and said we could look ahead now over the next three, four, five years and see the programs changing quite dramatically.

We were still then in FY1992, when the admissions ceiling was 120,000. In FY1993 it went up to 130,000 and since then it has been going down – 120,000, 110,000, 90,000 – and now, for budget purposes, 75,000 for FY1997. So we have seen, as Lyman set out in his road map, a plan that has been followed pretty clearly by the Bureau for Population, Refugees and Migration.

That road map made a lot of sense at that time. The pool of eligible people from Southeast Asia was being taken up. The pool of what then seemed to be the eligible people from the former Soviet Union was being taken up. But I would question whether this forecast made for planning purposes which was based upon the refugee situation that was known in early 1992 should have become a self-fulfilling prophecy for administration of the refugee program up to today. Yes, there have been some unforeseen changes that have been accommodated. For example, in early 1992 how many of us knew of Herzegovina, or places like Banja Luka or Vukovar? And how many of us would have thought that the Sarajevo of the Olympics would have become the Sarajevo of today? The U.S. program did adjust to take in people fleeing from the fighting in former Yugoslavia. But all-in-all the program has, I think, pretty much followed that road map set out four years ago.

Now, however, I think we need to really reconsider whether that road map is still so valid. Yes it is for the Southeast Asian purposes, but for the purposes of the former Soviet Union, is the Russia today – or the Russia after the elections in June – going to be the same Russia that we were so excited about after the fall of the Soviet Union? And what about the "new refugee groups" (they are not "new" for those refugees perhaps), groups that the U.S. program has traditionally not taken in? How flexible are we in our program to offer resettlement to assist in the worldwide humanitarian effort, to offer protection for refugees that we are not so used to taking in?

There also have been changes on the United Nations High Commissioner for Refugees (UNHCR) side. Four years ago, there was a strong UNHCR trend against resettlement. We have had, in the first part of this decade, the massive outflow of Kurds from Northern Iraq, the massive flows of people from the former Yugoslavia, the Rwandan and Burundian emergencies, and other massive humanitarian crises with which UNHCR has had to deal. In the midst of these desperate needs the UNHCR response, quite understandably, has been that we don't have any time for resettlement, we just have to save these people. Indeed, the resettlement activities of UNHCR declined quite dramatically and were downgraded administratively. Very little funding or political support was devoted to resettlement. Besides the emergencies, this attitude came in part from a souring of many UNHCR people from the experience of resettlement of Southeast Asians. It appeared for many UNHCR people that they were resettling persons who were not in the same desperate need of resettlement as people in other parts of the world, in some respects helping to administer a sort of managed migration program which UNHCR people did not feel was really part of their core mission for refugee protection.

I hope now that we are turning the corner on some of this. For example, with UNHCR, the conclusion which was adopted at the Executive Committee meeting last October was much more positive than the previous conclusions about resettlement. Previous conclusions and UNHCR documents had spoken of resettlement as the least desirable of the durable solutions, a sort of last resort for refugees. But the conclusion of October said that the Executive Committee "reiterates the continued importance of resettlement as an instrument of protection and its use as a durable solution to refugee problems in specific circumstances."

In addition, UNHCR has engaged in an evaluation study of its resettlement program which has been taken quite seriously. The UNHCR global assessment of resettlement needs has been more constructive in identifying some of the urgent needs for refugee resettlement. There is new leadership in the resettlement unit of UNHCR. There is an increased emphasis on providing referrals for resettlement, not only to the United States program but to those of other resettlement countries as well.

I see the recent congressional votes, both in the Senate and the House, as being very, very significant. These votes were not close; in both chambers the proposed 50,000 refugee cap was soundly defeated. I think this bears a strong message even amidst this overall anti-immigrant sentiment in which we find ourselves. That message is: first, refugee resettlement is not part of managed migration – we Americans don't want to see refugees as being part of a quota system, or demographics, or managed immigration; second, our nation wants to be flexible to respond to new needs of refugees; third, the wealthiest, most open nation in the world wants to take in more than 50,000 refugees at this time when worldwide refugee numbers are at such high levels; and last, I think the strongest part of the message that these votes carry is that taking in refugees, being a haven for persecuted people, is part of who we are as Americans – it is part of the American nature. We are, after all, a country with a Statue of Liberty in New York Harbor. It showed that there is a strong constituency for refugees in our country, a constituency that goes all the way across the political spectrum. It was very interesting for us at Lutheran Immigration and Refugee Service (LIRS) to find ourselves in alliance on the refugee debates not only with other voluntary agencies or other religious groups, but with groups like the Christian Coalition, the "pro-family" groups, the very strong "pro-life" groups, business interests, libertarians, as well as others. It was a remarkably broad coalition of support for this humanitarian program which reflects part of the real nature of what we are as the United States of America.

For resettlement, then, I think this leads us to a number of conclusions. One is that these votes and the changes in our refugee program present a real calling for us in the United States to admit new groups, to be creative in our overseas processing, to work with UNHCR and with other countries to see which are the small groups of people for whom resettlement is protection, for whom resettlement will provide the durable solution, the alternative to an indefinite insecure stay in a refugee camp.

Second, I think we have to recognize in our domestic resettlement program the dramatic gains that we have had in the quality of resettlement and the lessons we can learn from that. For example, in the last year's score card of refugee resettlement performance that the State Department does informally, the overall employment levels for refugees were up around 80 percent or higher. (We have to measure whether at the end of six months in the United States, "free case" refugees – those who have no family in the United States – have been employed for at least six weeks.) The trend is improving. For example, last month the statistics for our agency, LIRS, were that 93 percent of our free case refugees were employed after six months in the United States. I think that is a very commendable performance in refugee resettlement. It has happened because the State Department has set goals for the agencies to achieve, they have held us accountable to those goals, and because of that we have had results. This confounds the talk about welfare dependence among refugees or refugees being a burden on our society. We don't admit refugees because we expect them to be hard workers or because we expect them to pay back to our society; we admit them because they are in need. Yet we are in the very fortunate position of having a group of people coming into our country who do in fact contribute far more than they receive.

Another lesson we can learn is one that Mark Franken mentioned, the dramatically positive effect of the early concentration of resources in resettlement. By using tools like case management – a single point of accountability for refugees once they arrive – we can have quality resettlement without significant harmful impacts on local communities. I would urge the State Department and the Office for Refugee Resettlement to pursue the efforts to try to have an extended reception and placement period so that we can concentrate more of those resources early on.

Just before concluding I think there are two great unmet needs in our resettlement program. I have no great ideas how to meet those lacks but I think it is necessary for them to be identified. One is the need for psychological services. A high proportion of refugees are suffering from post-traumatic stress disorder, many are victims of torture, many have suffered horribly. We do not now in our resettlement program have any systematic or consistently adequate way of providing psychological services for refugees. There are a few good people in a few places who are doing that on a voluntary basis, but generally those needs are unmet.

The other unmet need is perhaps a broader one for national policy, to have a system whereby we can provide temporary protection for people fleeing from places closer to our borders for whom the United States is a place of refuge but for whom, perhaps, full refugee resettlement is not needed at this time. Our law has a big gap in that area of temporary protection, and that was illustrated quite dramatically with the situation of Haitian boat people and Cuban boat people.

In conclusion, I want to say I think we are very fortunate as Americans in our refugee resettlement program. Not only is it something that is the right thing to do because we are helping people in desperate need, but we find that the refugees themselves end up bringing gifts to our nation and to our communities far greater than any resources that are given them. It is a situation of having one's cake and eating it too. We have been very fortunate in this program, and I think we can give thanks for that.

15

Legislative Developments and Refugee Resettlement in the Post-Cold War Era

KATHLEEN NEWLAND
Carnegie Endowment for International Peace

The year 1996 was a roller-coaster for legislative developments affecting refugee resettlement. In the early spring, it seemed that there was an excellent chance that the legislative framework for refugee resettlement would be radically different when the 104th Congress adjourned in the autumn. In the final analysis, less changed than had been feared by refugee advocates, but some provisions of both the welfare and immigration bills that were finally passed will have a severe impact on some refugees resettled in the United States. In particular, the welfare bill would eliminate most refugees' eligibility for welfare benefits after five years of residency, unless they naturalize. For many elderly, disabled, or traumatized refugees, both citizenship and self-sufficiency may be out of reach. These realities have no bearing on their admission to the United States, however. The welfare reforms truly change the rules of the game for refugees admitted to the United States for permanent resettlement. But we will not begin to see the full consequences of these changes until after the year 2001.

The original version of the immigration bill presented to the House of Representatives in the 104th Congress would have placed a legislated ceiling on refugee admissions to the United States at the level of 50,000 per year. A similar cap was dropped from the Senate immigration bill during its mark-up, and this provision was dropped from the House bill on March 19. A few days later, the major part of Title V of the House bill, dealing with legal immigration reform, was deleted, including the refugee cap and the strict limitations on the uses of the Attorney General's parole authority for humanitarian admissions. Provisions remaining in the bill are aimed at restricting the ability of spontaneous asylum seekers to apply for asylum in the United States, through such measures as summary exclusion procedures that allow asylum seekers to be turned back at the border if they do not have proper documents and cannot convince the immigration officers on the spot that they have a credible fear of persecution if returned. Another such measure was a one-year limit on filing an asylum application after entry. The resettlement program itself emerged from the legislative process relatively unscathed, although with reduced funding.

This remainder of this paper will focus on why it was so important to avoid a legislated cap, and also why it is important, in looking at the final version of the legislation, not to be so elated about having averted this threat that we forget the very real distortions that continue to mar our refugee resettlement program. These distortions created the vulnerability to the rigid and radical downsizing which the resettlement program has just narrowly escaped.[1] If we do not address the flaws in the program, I believe this vulnerability will continue and other attacks on the program will arise before long.

Even without the legislated ceiling on the resettlement program, there has been a consistent trend of sharp reductions in the numbers of refugees admitted for permanent resettlement in the United States. The ceiling for admission was set at 120,000 for FY 1994, at 112,000 for FY 1995. The Administration asked for 90,000 in FY 1996, and 78,000 in FY 1997. At the same time that admissions for resettlement have been going down, the funding of the State Department's Migration and Refugee Assistance account has remained at approximately the same level–quite remarkable at a time when so many programs are experiencing deep cuts. So the current situation is one of level funding and reduced admissions. As a result, the proportion of the account devoted to refugee admissions has fallen to about 13.8 percent for FY 1997, from an average of about 40 percent in 1989–1991. The money saved from lower admissions has mostly been dedicated to overseas refugee assistance, which now accounts for an estimated 72 percent of the 1997 appropriation (U.S. Committee for Refugees, 1996:11).

The logic of declining refugee admissions is based on declining needs in the large in-country programs for the former Soviet Union and Vietnam, which have dominated admissions since 1989. If conditions in these countries continue to improve steadily – a big "if" in the case of the former Soviet Union, given the persistence of anti-Semitism as well as the alarming political uncertainties there – ever higher proportions of entrants from those countries will be in the future, in a position to seek admission through family reunification and other regular immigration programs.

It is likely, however, that the allocated places no longer required for the former Soviet Union and Vietnam will be needed for people fleeing persecution in other parts of the world – the Bosnias, northern Iraqs, and future trouble spots yet to emerge. New agents and forms of persecution are arising, and more national governments are either unwilling or unable to protect their own people.

To assume that the Soviet and Indochinese resettlement places can be jettisoned permanently echoes an "end of history" argument that for some time has been discredited in relation to other aspects of post-cold war thinking. The history of refugee flows has always been one of ebb and flow in the movements of particular groups. Refugee flows, and the proportion of people within them who might need resettlement, are notoriously difficult to predict.

This is the reason that the legislative proposals to establish a numerical cap on refugee admissions was so ill-advised. A fixed number, whatever that number was, would rob the U.S. refugee program of its flexibility in responding to humanitarian needs and U.S. foreign policy interests. The cap of 50,000 that was in the House and Senate bills was based on the concept of a "normal flow" of refugees, which appeared in the 1980 Refugee Act but was never implemented.[2] A "normal flow" of refugees is a contradiction in terms. Since 1980, for example, the number of refugees admitted has fluctuated from a high of 200,000 in 1980 at the peak of the first Indochinese boat people crisis to a low of 52,000 in FY 1986. Whatever fixed number is chosen may be too high in some years and too low in others – but inevitably advocates or opponents of admissions will see it as either a floor or a ceiling. Responding to real-world refugee needs demands flexibility.

A continuous, substantive, analytical effort will be required to generate a defensible basis for judging how large a resettlement program is needed from year to year. The executive and legislative branches of the U.S. government should work closely with international and nongovernmental organizations in this effort, using the widest range of sources of information on conditions in countries of origin. The Bureau of Population, Refugees, and Migration in the Department of State should convene a series of broadly based national consultations on resettlement needs and capacities to provide a forum for information-sharing and assessment as well as to give the bureau a stronger basis for making decisions on admissions. The consultations might be linked to an annual international conference on resettlement under UNHCR auspices, at which the United States and other countries of resettlement would "pledge" places to meet internationally identified resettlement needs as part of their national programs. Countries other than the ten that have regular resettlement programs also should be encouraged to take part and offer resettlement places.[3]

Turning more specifically to the trends that are reflected in this wave of legislative activism, it is important to ask what objectives are sought by those who are leading it. I have mentioned the desire to radically reduce the number of admissions; but why? I see at least three elements at work here. One is simply a part of the effort to reduce over-all immigration to the United States, and to slice into refugee admissions for that purpose, regardless of the real needs for this kind of protection that exist in the real world.

Another is a determination to regain – or exert – congressional control over the refugee program, and especially over admissions. The third is a desire to introduce some consistency into the refugee program, and particularly to rationalize cold war vintage programs that have now lost their geopolitical rationale but have become entrenched – and I am speaking particularly of the large direct-departure programs that dominate U.S. admissions – from Indochina and the former Soviet Union. Direct departure programs account for nearly 80 percent of our refugee admissions. Part of the purpose of lowering the refugee admissions level is to put pressure on these large special programs. The logic is that if we were to have only 50,000 as a "normal flow," the refugee program would have had to be more selective about the numbers it takes in from countries where it is now difficult to demonstrate that there is state-sponsored persecution of large numbers of people and a lack of national protection. This logic ignores several realities, in particular the historical roots of these programs and the resulting political dynamic that sustains them.

At the time when the U.S. refugee program began to evolve, in the immediate aftermath of World War II, resettlement was the mainstay of national and international refugee programs. For the United States, the program was closely bound to evolving cold war tactics. It provided a concrete illustration of the U.S. conviction that persecution was the standard practice of communist governments – a conviction reflected in the then-prevailing definition of a refugee as someone fleeing persecution in a communist or communist-dominated country or the Middle East. It has proven difficult to recast the resettlement program in a post-cold war mold. Decades of engagement with the victims and foes of communist governments, whether in the former Soviet Union, Cuba, or Indochina, have resulted in resettlement patterns that persist in the refugee program despite the weakening of their original, political rationale.

The Refugee Act of 1980 formally replaced the political rationale for the U.S. resettlement program with a legal and humanitarian rationale. By incorporating the refugee definition of the 1951 Refugee Convention and its 1967 Protocol, it established the fear of persecution and the need for protection as the criteria for refugee status, and an ill-defined "humanitarian concern" as the basis for selecting refugees for permanent admission to the United States. Yet, fifteen years later, the resettlement program still bears a strong resemblance to the cold war program.

The protection-centered rationale opened by the 1980 Act has not been elaborated, leaving the major portion of the resettlement program hanging on the increasingly frayed threads of the cold war rationale. The failure to articulate new arguments in favor of resettlement has left the program vulnerable to calls for radical downsizing, driven by considerations other than the assurance that the need for this form of lasting protection has waned.

The resettlement program is additionally vulnerable because of the prominence in it of exceptional programs for specific countries or groups: the Cuban Adjustment Act, the Lautenberg Amendment, in-country processing programs, the use of parole authority, and so forth. Such programs are no longer of interest only to their advocates as immigration and refugee policy move up on the political agenda. In an atmosphere in which all federal spending – and particularly any that smacks of "foreign" or "welfare" – is subject to scrutiny, advocates must be prepared to make the case for specific programs in the context of a coherent refugee policy that serves the national purpose.

Of course, the desire to move away from cold war parameters has run up against a lot of controversy in the House of Representatives, where the Foreign Operations Subcommittee of the International Affairs Committee, under Representative Chris Smith, has introduced measures that severely constrain the Administration's freedom of action, particularly with respect to the Comprehensive Plan of Action for Vietnam. The proposed provisions are at odds with the attempt to move away from the cold war criteria. Beyond their effect on these specific issues, they place a severe roadblock in the way of the Administration's attempt to internationalize the responsibility for Indochinese boat people, and bring to an end the long drama of mixed migration and refugee flows from that region.

We need to articulate a new rationale for the refugee resettlement program in the United States. Why does this country have a refugee resettlement program? What does it seek to accomplish? In my view, the current program needs reorientation to make it a more effective instrument of international protection both in its overseas activities and in domestic programs. The resettlement program, in particular, should focus on those refugees whose need for protection a) is likely to be long term and b) can only be resolved outside their own country. More mechanisms, and more creative ones – chiefly involving forms of temporary asylum – need to be devised for other refugees whose need for protection can be met without permanent relocation.

Resettlement also has a role in persuading other countries to keep their borders open to refugees. If such countries are confident that the responsibility for protection will be shared, they are more likely to be willing to offer first asylum. Thus, resettlement protects more people than actually participate in it directly.

We have had a close call on the refugee resettlement program with the legislation introduced in the 104th Congress. The defeat of the refugee cap is a real tribute to the people who worked so hard to defend a generous and flexible program. But this fight is far from over. In the next legislative session, a renewed process of critical self-examination must start again. It will be much better – not only for advocates and organizations that work with refugees, but for refugees themselves – if reforms of the refugee resettlement program come from its friends rather than from its less constructive critics.

NOTES

[1] For a fuller discussion of the U.S. refugee resettlement program, *see* Newland, 1995.

[2] The "normal flow" level of 50,000 designated in the 1980 Refugee Act was chosen because it was the average number of refugees admitted to the United States each year during the 1970s. *See* Frelick, 1995.

[3] The ten countries that have regular resettlement programs are Australia, New Zealand, Canada, the United States, the Netherlands, Switzerland, Denmark, Sweden, Norway, and Finland.

REFERENCES

Frelick, W.
1995   "Testimony Regarding H.R. 1915." U.S. Committee for Refugees before House Subcommittee on Immigration and Claims. June 29.

Newland, K.
1995   *U.S. Refugee Policy: Dilemmas and Directions.* Washington, DC: Carnegie Endowment for International Peace.

U.S. Committee for Refugees
1996   "Funding for Refugee Admissions Reduced," *Refugee Reports,* 17(10).

16

Changing Public Policies toward Refugees: The Implications for Voluntary Resettlement Agencies

MARK FRANKEN
Migration & Refugee Services, U.S. Catholic Conference

The refugee resettlement community is certainly being challenged in this environment of anti-immigration and dwindling public support for current immigration policies. We are faced not only with the specter of our nation pulling back from its historical commitment to refugee protection, but are also faced with a very different resettlement environment for those fortunate, yet fewer, future refugees.

To understand the implications of the changing refugee resettlement program, this paper will 1) identify some of the changing trends in the refugee program that represent the most significant challenges for the resettlement community, particularly for the voluntary agencies; 2) from the perspective of at least one agency, explore some of the steps being taken to respond and adapt to the new realities; and 3) offer a few ideas for how the public and private agencies concerned with refugees can work together to maintain U.S. commitment to refugees.

First, though, a word of explanation about the U.S. Catholic Conference, commonly referred to as USCC. The USCC is the corporation established by the bishops to engage in public policy discussions and social action at the national level. One of the bishops' many concerns is with immigrants and refugees, so one of the offices within USCC is called Migration & Refugee Services, which is the arm of the bishops that operates the refugee resettlement program. At the present time, there are 120 local Catholic resettlement offices around the country. This network has resettled 800,000 refugees and nearly 200,000 Cuban and Haitian entrants and parolees over the past 20 years, making it one of the largest in the country.

ENVIRONMENTAL TRENDS AND CHALLENGES POSED

Reduced Refugee Admissions

Seemingly irrespective of the worldwide refugee population in need of third country resettlement, which is at historically high levels, current U.S. policies appear intent on "managing down" admissions levels. The refugee admissions ceiling in FY 1996 is 90,000, and in FY 1997, according to the Administration's budget submission, will likely be set at 75,000 (Department of State, 1996). Conventional wisdom suggests that refugee admissions in FY 1998 will fall even further.

One gets the impression that in setting refugee admissions levels for the next year and beyond, U.S. policymakers have determined that with the end of the cold war and the winding down of the two major refugee programs (the former Soviet Union and Southeast Asia), refugee admissions levels should automatically drop. Consideration of other refugee groups who may need resettlement seems not to be high on anyone's agenda (evidence of which is readily available but one of the most striking examples can be found in Africa, where there is only one U.S. refugee processing post for the entire continent).

It was interesting to observe the House floor debate on March 19, 1996, concerning the pending immigration reform bill. One of the arguments used in support of the defeated "refugee cap" provision in the bill, made by the bill's sponsors, was that if there was not a legislated level of refugee admissions, within a couple of years the United States would not be admitting even 50,000 refugees. The current trends suggest that there may be some truth to that argument.

Greater Ethnic Diversity

As the refugee flows from Southeast Asia and the former Soviet Union diminish, the composition of U.S.-bound refugees is changing. For an agency like USCC these changes are dramatic. Consider that for the past 20 years more than 80 percent of USCC's caseload comprised refugees from

Southeast Asia. Within a year or so, it is very likely that only a few, if any, refugees from that region will be admitted.

Interestingly, the other 20 percent of USCC's caseload has comprised nearly 50 different ethnicities. The resettlement community clearly has the experience responding to ethnic diversity, but what we are likely to see in future arrival patterns is new and diverse groups. They will arrive in communities where these ethnicities do not now exist, at least not in any substantial numbers.

Refugees with No Relatives Already in the United States

A rather large proportion of the refugees arriving in recent years have been joining family members in the United States. As the arrival of traditional refugee groups drops off, an increasing number of refugees admitted will not have family ties here. Again, using the USCC experience, its caseload for the past decade comprised roughly 75 percent family reunification cases. The implications of this shift in the profile of future refugees are clear when considering that of the 120 local Catholic resettlement offices, about half are currently working exclusively with refugees reuniting with relatives.

More Emergent Arrival Patterns

Increasingly, refugees found to be eligible for U.S. admission will be in situations that require their expeditious movement. The refugee processing centers that existed in Southeast Asia, for example, where refugees spent six months and more preparing for U.S. entry will not likely exist in the future. In the future, providing resettlement opportunities quickly may well mean the difference between life and death.

Other consequences inherent in more emergent arrival patterns include the fact that refugees will not be as oriented nor have had opportunities for medical treatment as did many of the earlier refugees. We will also likely see less in the way of biographical information, so important to resettlement planning, on refugees before they arrive.

Welfare Reform and Block Grants

The welfare reform and block grant bills pending before Congress would alter the public assistance programs currently available to refugees. Major responsibility for determining the type of assistance available to refugees will be transferred from the federal level to the states. We have already seen, even before federal legislation is enacted, states revamping their public assistance programs through the use of federal waivers.

Although the full implications of welfare reform are not yet understood, it is clear that there will be less public assistance available for shorter periods of time to assist refugees in their resettlement. For most refugees, these changes will not likely create hardships because refugees, by and large, seek employment opportunities as soon as possible after arrival. But, there will likely be greater competition for the types of jobs refugees typically pursue and the "safety net," as we now know it, will no longer exist for those refugees not readily employable.

Anti-immigrant Attitudes

We seem to be in one of those periods in our country's history when people's anxieties and fears about the economy and their perceived insecurity are inexplicably directed toward immigrants. The negative attitudes toward immigrants in general often have a direct effect on the public's receptivity toward refugees.

RESPONSES TO THE CHANGING REFUGEE PROGRAM ENVIRONMENT

There are many things that the voluntary agencies need to do and are doing to adapt to the changes in the U.S. refugee program. Below are just a few of the steps USCC is taking.

Advocacy/Public Education

At no time in recent memory is the advocacy role of the voluntary agencies more needed and urgent. The refugees languishing in refugee camps or fleeing for their lives do not have a voice in U.S. public policy unless we and others of good will speak up on their behalf.

Effective advocacy requires educating the public and policymakers about the plight of refugees, while also demonstrating through our resettlement programs that refugees can be efficiently resettled and become contributing members of their communities soon after arrival.

These efforts, though, will still not be enough. We must also bring to the public policy debate the voices of the local community. The axiom that "all politics is local . . ." certainly holds true for the refugee program. The voluntary agencies are uniquely positioned to help mobilize grassroots input to the shaping of policies affecting refugees. So, too, the previously resettled refugees have an important role in mobilizing their communities to participate in the public policy arena. Coalition-building in a way that brings a wide range of community groups together in a common voice on behalf of refugees is an approach to advocacy in which we need to be even more involved.

In the case of USCC, the Catholic bishops have seen the need to become more actively engaged in education and advocacy on behalf of immigrants and refugees. A growing number of Catholic schools are including immigration studies as part of their curricula (U.S. Catholic Conference, 1996). The bishops have issued public statements and teaching documents recently, designed to positively influence the immigration debate and, so as to help shape state welfare policies affecting immigrants and refugees, local Catholic structures are mobilizing at the state and county levels.

Community Volunteers and Private Resources

The voluntary resettlement agencies have a responsibility in bringing private resources to bear in the resettlement effort. More can and must be done in this area. As public funds to support transitional assistance to refugees shrink, the voluntary agencies must redouble their efforts to generate private resources and involve community volunteers, churches, civic groups, and mutual assistance associations in the task of resettling refugees.

The financial and in-kind resources that the voluntary agencies generate do much more than supplement public dollars. Each volunteer, each member of a church congregation who contributes financial support, every person who donates furniture or clothing or household goods to newly arriving refugees, represents a visible welcoming and reception into the community. No dollar value can be set for this kind of community involvement. By the way, these same volunteers who become involved in resettling refugees are also some of the best advocates for refugees and have the greatest potential for shaping local community attitudes toward immigrants.

USCC, as are some other voluntary resettlement agencies, is investing more resources for volunteer programming and the development of private resources. There are many exciting volunteer activities taking place around the country, but the potential for doing more is much greater. At a meeting last week of about 30 of USCC's smaller resettlement offices, it was amazing to hear how actively involved volunteers are with refugees in communities throughout the country. Thousands of volunteers are opening their homes, their pocketbooks, and their hearts to help refugees. Those who would have us believe that compassion fatigue dominates our society and, thus, prevents a continued generous refugee program could not be more wrong.

Managing Programmatic Changes in Refugee Resettlement

For the past couple of years we have been engaged in a rather comprehensive planning process in USCC, trying to help our resettlement network adapt to the changing trends. Our objectives are to:

- downsize, while maintaining a national resettlement capacity;

- strengthen our service capacity and performance outcomes (*i.e.*, do the best job possible helping refugees achieve rapid self-sufficiency);
- bring more community volunteers and private resources into the program;
- strengthen our advocacy capacity, particularly at the local levels;
- build local coalitions, both for designing service delivery systems and for advocacy purposes; and
- pursue creative program solutions to the changing welfare landscape.

Through aggressive pursuit of these objectives, USCC and its diocesan resettlement partners intend to maintain a viable response to future refugees in need of resettlement opportunities.

POLICY CONSIDERATIONS IN THE CHANGING ENVIRONMENT

Strengthening the Public-Private Partnership

Historically, the refugee program has been a model of public-private partnership. Few other such partnerships can be found that have accomplished as much. And, while there are many examples of excellent collaboration and successes resulting from the joint efforts of the public and private agencies concerned with refugees, improvements can be made. Now more than ever the partnership needs to be strong and mutually supportive. The public and private agencies comprising the refugee resettlement community need to be in close dialogue on the changes taking place. We need to understand each others' strengths and bring them to bear in the resettlement effort.

Some have been calling for regular meetings between the public and private agencies (State Department, the Office of Refugee Resettlement, the voluntary agencies, the states, and others) to review arrival trends, develop placement strategies, and to collectively understand and anticipate changes in local public assistance programs for refugees. This is a good idea whose time has come. We need strong, visionary leadership to make this happen.

Maintain the Resources Necessary to Successfully Resettle Refugees

Easier said than done! However, we must be creative and find ways to use the scarce resources to maximum effect. In the current political climate we cannot afford to bring refugees here and not meet their short-term transitional needs nor quickly move them toward self-sufficiency. We have seen in some areas of the country what happens when the system encourages refugees to remain on public assistance for extended periods.

The reality is that fewer public resources are going to be available to do the job. What can be done to ensure that the necessary resources are there? And how do we ensure an aggressive effort to move newly arriving refugees toward self-sufficiency without unnecessary reliance on public welfare?

Take the Refugee Program Out of the Welfare System. The Refugee Act of 1980 was well-intentioned in recognizing that refugees inherently have transitional needs that must be met in order for them to successfully integrate into this society and become contributing members of their new communities. Unfortunately, in some states the welfare system has become the primary service provider, rather than a safety net used only as a last resort. Among other things, this has stymied private resources that would have otherwise been available. In this era of welfare reform, why don't we seize the opportunity to establish a transitional assistance program for refugees outside the welfare system?

USCC and its network of Catholic diocesan resettlement offices have quite a bit of experience administering successful welfare alternatives for newly arriving refugees. A current project, jointly administered by USCC and Catholic Charities of San Diego, provides comprehensive transitional assistance to newly arriving refugees without recourse to welfare. This project has proven successful in moving refugees toward early self-sufficiency and has been cost effective compared to the public welfare system.

There are many other examples of voluntary agencies' ability to more effectively and efficiently than the welfare system move refugees toward self-sufficiency. In a demonstration project conducted in Chicago in the early to mid-1980s, for instance, the participating voluntary agencies were provided a larger "per capita" grant from the Department of State, which allowed the agencies to work with refugees without relying on public cash assistance for up to six months, as opposed to only one month, after arrival. Under this project the voluntary agencies were able to move nearly 80 percent of the employable refugees into jobs within six months of their arrival. This compares to only 20 percent of the refugees having gotten jobs within one year prior to the project (USCC, 1984). Another, current initiative that for the USCC network is producing 80 percent employment outcomes for refugees within four months of their arrival is the Match Grant program.

To varying degrees, a couple of states – Massachusetts and New York – have moved in this direction. Pennsylvania is also poised to remove the refugee assistance program from the state's welfare system. Maryland is considering alternatives to welfare for its refugees. These initiatives should be encouraged and supported.

I am afraid, though, that in some of the other resettlement locations we cannot leave it entirely to the states to fashion and maintain a refugee-specific transitional assistance program. When the federal resources to support public assistance are block granted and there are fewer dollars than at the present time, are the states going to direct those limited resources to a transitional assistance program specifically for refugees? I do not believe so.

Also, the experience of states working collaboratively with the private agencies to develop resettlement partnerships that allow a pooling and maximizing of public and private resources is, at best, spotty.

Do Not Block Grant Refugee Assistance Programs and Funds. It is essential that the refugee program remain national in scope and that the federal government ensures that the resources and effective public-private partnerships are in place to meet refugees' transitional needs. The congressional proposal to block grant some of the social services funds administered by ORR must not succeed. Those resources are critical to transitioning refugees during their initial resettlement period. And, as I mentioned, it is not likely that states will extract from the block grant the resources necessary to administer a program specifically targeted to refugees. Moreover, refugee admissions is a federal responsibility. It follows, therefore, that the federal government should provide the resources and administer the resettlement program for newly arriving refugees. To do otherwise amounts to imposing an "unfunded mandate on state and local governments."

Government Contractors Must Demonstrate Private Contributions. Another thought would be to direct the increasingly scarce public funds to entities that can demonstrate the ability to substantially supplement government resources with private contributions. In other words, although the public sector should continue to shoulder a significant portion of the costs associated with resettling refugees, groups receiving government funds should not be totally dependent on those resources to do their work. These groups must demonstrate that they bring to the table significant resources of their own to supplement the government's contribution.

Maintain a National Resettlement Capacity

Even though the refugee arrival numbers are down, we need to maintain placement opportunities throughout the country so as to avoid unnecessarily concentrating refugees in just a few communities. Not only is it important that we not create adverse impact due to restricted placement capacity, but we need to ensure that the base of public support for refugees is broad.

Recent policy shifts and administrative changes by the State Department are having the effect, unintentionally I believe, of restricting the national placement capacity. For example, beginning in FY 1996, voluntary resettlement agencies can no longer receive waivers for conducting on-site program reviews for small affiliates, even when within a year only one refugee reunites with a relative in that area. Also, beginning in FY 1996, the State Department discontinued issuing "placement exceptions" to agencies with local capacity but without a

State Department approved "affiliate." If the voluntary agencies and the concerned government agencies could engage in a more collaborative planning process, we could achieve a more efficient program, a more effective program, and one that continues to enjoy public support.

CONCLUSION

These are volatile times for refugees. The continued leadership of the United States in pursuing durable solutions for refugees, including those in need of resettlement opportunities, is critical. As we consider what our future policies and attitudes toward refugees should be, let us be mindful of our traditions and the principles that we as a people hold as fundamental.

In his homily at Giants Stadium in 1995, Pope John Paul II very eloquently and so poignantly observed,

> Is present-day America becoming less sensitive, less caring toward the poor, the weak, the stranger, the needy? It must not! Today, as before, the United States is called to be a hospitable society, a welcoming culture. If America were to turn in on itself, would this not be the beginning of the end of what constitutes the very essence of the American experience?

REFERENCES

Department of State, U.S.
1996   "FY 1997 Emergency and Migration Assistance Budget Proposal." Washington, DC:
            Migration and Refugee Assistance, U.S. Department of State.

U.S. Catholic Conference (USCC)
1996   "Who Are My Sisters and Brothers: A Catholic Educational Guide for Understanding
            and Welcoming Immigrants and Refugees." School curriculum guide for grades
            K-12. Washington, DC: Office of Pastoral Care for Migrants and Refugee Services,
            U.S. Catholic Conference.

_____
1984   "The Chicago Project: A Study by Refugee Policy Group." Washington, DC:
            Migration and Refugee Services, U.S. Catholic Conference.

17

The Mischaracterized Asylum Crisis

DEBORAH ANKER
Harvard Law School

In January 1995, the Clinton Administration began implementation of regulatory reform of the United States asylum process. These reforms maintain the basic structure of the current system, *i.e.*: 1) an informal Immigration and Naturalization Service (INS) 'screening' adjudication before an asylum officer for applicants who are not in removal proceedings; and 2) a formal Executive Office of Immigration Review (EOIR) evidentiary hearing before an immigration judge for applicants who are not granted asylum after the INS adjudication, or who apply after INS initiates removal proceedings (*see* Butterfield, 1995). Although the reforms retain this basic structure, they modify the role of asylum officers who will only grant cases, immediately referring all others to immigration judges for a full evidentiary hearing. Asylum applicants also will be unable to receive permission to work until 180 days after filing, which in most cases will be after they are interviewed.

In addition to these regulatory changes, there have been more radical legislative proposals for restructuring of the asylum process which call into question fundamental principles of asylum protection. For example, in 1993, then Congressman Mazzoli introduced a bill that would have eliminated immigration judges altogether and instead provided asylum applicants with a single interview before an asylum officer, without a right to an evidentiary hearing or a decision by an independent adjudicator.[1] Other proposals have suggested the creation of a new type of hearing officer and a change in the standard of proof for asylum.[2] There also have been several legislative proposals for "summary exclusion." These proposals would create expedited preliminary informal interviews for certain asylum applicants using a legal standard different from the asylum standard. They provide minimal if any administrative review and severe limitations on most forms of judicial review. Applicants who did not pass this screening stage would be forced to leave and return to the country of feared persecution, without having access to the regular asylum process.[3]

All of these reforms are justified by an argument that the existing asylum system is too generous and that fraudulent claims discredit and overwhelm it. Anti-immigrant and anti-refugee lobbies have conducted successful media campaigns which have had a significant impact in mobilizing public opinion in favor of these legislative initiatives.[4] The INS responded to these contentions with the 1995 regulations which institute significant restrictions such as expedited procedures at the first INS asylum officer level with no written decision or review, and denial of work authorization to applicants until the time of interview and determination of claim validity (Butterfield, 1995). INS and EOIR practice continues to reflect major procedural limitations including lack of guaranteed legal representation, noncertified and even untrained interpreters; denial rates continue to be high. Notwithstanding these restrictive practices and the clear difficulties in obtaining asylum, the perception remains strong that asylum is an easy vehicle for admission to the United States and that asylum applicants have too many rights and are abusing the system.

I briefly want to address the realities behind these perceptions, based on data from studies conducted by the Immigration and Refugee program at Harvard Law School. The results of one of these studies are contained in a report by my colleague, Sarah Ignatius, released in 1993. The two-year report of the National Asylum Study Project was the first comprehensive nongovernmental study of the implementation of the 1990 asylum reforms. Among other changes, the 1990 reforms replaced INS examiners, working under the jurisdiction of the local district directors, with full-time trained asylum officers who are responsible to the Central INS Asylum Office. The study analyzed 1,331 cases that a total of 151 asylum officers adjudicated in all (then) seven asylum regions; these cases included asylum applicants from 60 countries. The study contained analyses of 880 notices of intent to deny or preliminary assessments to grant asylum, including 477 received from attorneys and 403 that the INS provided for review. The study concluded that the asylum officer corps was a significant improvement over the past system of INS adjudication, where there was no specialized training, and, according to a report by the Government Accounting Office, adjudicators routinely avoided adjudicatory responsibility by adopting the recommendations of State Department officials. The study did find substantial management and related problems attributable, in large part, to a failure to fund and otherwise resource the program at an appropriate level. Overall, the assessment and recommendations on management and administration were similar to those of a Department of Justice report, released contemporaneously (Department of Justice, 1993).

I want to discuss some of the study's findings that relate to the possible existence of an asylum crisis, as it has been promoted and described in the media. First – and this is based on publicly available statistics – asylum applicants arriving in the United States primarily come from refugee-producing countries. The study compiled statistics after the first eleven months of 1993, and out of approximately 133,000 asylum applicants, 70 percent came from ten countries: Bangladesh, China, El Salvador, Guatemala, Haiti, India, Mexico, Nicaragua, Pakistan and the Philippines. In each of these except Mexico, human rights organizations have documented widespread human rights abuses that produced refugee flows. As the National Asylum Study Project report notes, in Mexico, these same human rights organizations have documented targeted persecution (Ignatius, 1993).

Second, there was a relatively low no-show rate – only 16 percent – for applicants at INS asylum interviews. As the final report notes, what is quite remarkable is that this appearance rate of 84 percent existed despite computer problems that in many cases resulted in "no notice at all of asylum interviews, notice only to the applicant and not his or her attorney, or notice only two or three days before the interview" (Ignatius, 1993:4–5). For example, the then Newark asylum office, "the office with the highest no-show rate was also the office with the allegations of the most computer errors in the INS database" (Ignatius, 1993:5).

Third, many of the present problems in the asylum process result from inefficiency, mismanagement, unfairness, and discrimination attributable to the INS. Thus, of the over 318,000 cases in the backlog at the end of the study period, the previous system left 114,000 undecided. Another 50,000 were Salvadoran and Guatemalan claims which the Bush Administration, under a settlement agreement in *American Baptist Churches v. Thornburgh* (760 F. Supp. 796, N. D. Cal, 1991), agreed had to be re-adjudicated because of discrimination against those groups under the pre-1990 INS district director asylum system (*see* Blum, 1991).

Fourth, as noted above, the overall assessment of the asylum officer corps was of a "substantially more professional, informed, and impartial body of asylum decisionmakers than the pre-1990 INS examiners" (Ignatius, 1993). Asylum officers generally were successful at eliciting the applicant's claim and

in conducting the interviews in a nonadversarial manner. The study did
identify serious legal errors and substantial unevenness in the quality of
decisionmaking. Despite these and other problems, however, the study found
that the asylum officer corps was moving in the direction of improved adjudication. Most of our recommendations related to better management, improved
resources, training and hiring criteria. Although there are several important
matters with which the study disagreed,[5] many of the recommendations were
consistent with the regulatory reforms instituted by the Administration in
January of 1995, which, as noted, maintain the present structure of asylum
officer and immigration judge adjudication with additional resources for
improved management and quality of decisionmaking. The study strongly
recommended the implementation of these changes rather than "a drastic
overhaul of the process or the design of another new administrative structure,
which would create additional expense and delay in case adjudication" (Ignatius, 1993:2).

Fifth, many of the problems the National Asylum Study identified are
systemic and are inherent to the nature of the asylum officer corps program.
The asylum officer interview is an informal adjudication. Applicants are not
afforded basic due process protections guaranteed in the immigration court.
This includes the right to present and cross-examine witnesses and the right to
a court-appointed interpreter (Anker, 1992). There is no meaningful role allowed for the asylum applicant's counsel and no record of the proceedings.
Therefore, there is no possibility for accountability in the form of administrative
or judicial review (Anker, 1991). The study concluded that this type of process
cannot be the sole means of determining asylum claims. It recommended,
therefore, maintaining the right to a hearing before an immigration judge
allowed under the current system.

Accountability must continue to be built into asylum adjudication. The
asylum and immigration administrative systems have suffered – and this is
critical – from both the perspective of fairness and efficiency, from a lack of
accountability. For those who care about improving the administration of our
immigration laws, it is essential that immigration officials be given less, not
more, unreviewable power and discretion. Moreover, the asylum system must
be not only be expeditious, but also must be perceived as credible. Studies of
the current and prior systems reveal decisionmaking processes that often have
not produced consistent and substantively fair outcomes. As noted, the National Asylum Study Project found problems in the quality and independence
of decisionmaking among the current asylum officer corps.[6] A 1987 Government Accounting Office study, which included cases decided by the INS under
the pre-1990 system as well as those decided by immigration judges, found that
adjudicators evaluated the claims alleging the most serious forms of persecu-

tion differently and that the outcomes varied according to the applicant's nationality (GAO, 1987:22, 23).

Another case study of an immigration court conducted by our program at Harvard in 1988 found that the court only granted 10 percent of the apparently strongest cases (Anker, 1992:452-454) and that the immigration court system was seriously compromised by lack of formal procedures, the ad hoc determinations, lack of independence of judgment, overreliance on the State Department, lack of criteria for establishing precedents at the Board of Immigration Appeals, and other significant inefficiencies. The immigration court study found that these inefficiencies largely were the responsibility of the agencies. They were the result, for example, of INS trial attorneys refusing to concede meritorious cases and of immigration judges making inappropriate scheduling decisions, routinely allowing only an hour or two for a hearing which led to continuances for a complete hearing on a claim. The EOIR's difficulty in producing transcripts for appeals was the most significant cause of delay in the process. The unavailability of these transcripts resulted in delays averaging 22 months after the immigration judge rendered a decision. In addition, the Board of Immigration Appeals required, in most cases, two to three years, and sometimes longer, to issue decisions after applicants' attorneys submitted briefs. Clearly, if hearings by immigration judges are to continue, that system itself needs substantial improvement such as training of judges and issuance of rules that require the Board of Immigration Appeals to make its decision-making processes open and principled.

It is particularly significant that both the Harvard asylum officer corps and immigration court studies found that many, indeed most, delays are attributable not to the applicant but to the agency, either because of poor, unmonitored judgments or insufficient resources. If we embark on a course – one that I fear is implicit in many of the legislative proposals – of giving INS more unreviewable power and discretion, we will exacerbate these management problems as well as create an alarming precedent for arbitrary governmental conduct. The positive changes in the asylum system over the last fifteen years – beginning with the advocacy for the Refugee Act of 1980 – are the results of outside voices and scrutiny by the public, the nongovernmental and academic community, as well as by the federal judiciary (*see* Martin, 1982; Anker and Posner, 1981). Many of the best features of the current INS process – indeed, the very endeavor to create a quasi-independent and professional asylum officer corps – are the results of this independent examination and advocacy.[7] The establishment of the Resource Information Center (*see* Martin, 1990), the provision in the regulations permitting proof based on the treatment of similarly situated persons (8 C.F.R. § 208.13(b)(2)(I)),[8] and the instructions on evaluating credibility in light of information on human rights conditions in the country of origin (8 C.F.R. § 208.13)[9] are attributable to advocacy efforts or judicial review.

We have a choice to respond to a mischaracterized crisis and turn back the clock, or continue the process begun over the last fifteen years of the "transformation" of immigration law – that is, making the practice of immigration agencies consonant with salient norms of administrative law and constitutional due process (see Schuck, 1984), and making agency adjudicatory and decision-making processes, accessible, principled, and accountable.

NOTES

[1]H.R. 3363, 103d Cong., 1st Sess, 1993.

[2]H.R. 1679, 103d Cong., 1st Sess, 1993.

[3]See e.g., S1333, 103d Cong., 1st Sess, 1993.

[4]See e.g., "60 Minutes: How Did He Get Here" (CBS television broadcast, March 14, 1993), reprinted in Asylum and Inspections Reform: Hearings on H.R. 1153, H.R. 1355, and H.R. 1679 before Subcommittee on Immigration Refugees and International Law of House Committee on the Judiciary, 103 Cong. 1st Sess, 1993.

[5]For example, the National Asylum Study disagreed with the elimination of notices of intent to deny (NOIDS). It found that rebuttals to NOIDS served an important corrective role, particularly given the significant incidence of fundamental legal errors in decisions. In addition, the study recommended interviews and adjudications of applications for work authorization within 90 days of filing.

[6]Asylum officers are instructed to reach decisions on individual cases independent from foreign policy considerations (INS, 1991). Further INS regulations acknowledge the usefulness of nongovernmental sources in evaluating conditions in the country of origin (8 C.F.R. 208.12(a), 1995). INS developed these guidelines in response to criticisms from many quarters that asylum adjudicators were inappropriately influenced by foreign policy and ideological considerations. The National Asylum Study found that asylum officers continued to rely on State Department materials in assessing a well-founded fear of persecution in 80% of the cases studied; credible nongovernmental sources were used only on a limited basis. In both these respects, however, asylum officers' decisions demonstrated an improvement over time (Ignatius, 1993).

[7]INS proposed regulations in 1987 that would have created asylum officers not as a separate corps but as part of the normal INS district director structure. These regulations would have eliminated immigration judges from any role in asylum adjudication. The regulations were defeated by a coalition of advocacy organizations which protested that immigration judge hearings were necessary to ensure protection of basic due process rights. (See "Asylum Plan is Under Attack," The New York Times, October 27, 1987, A.18.) Many of these same groups worked closely with the Justice Department in establishing a consensus for the 1990 reforms, that, as noted, retained the immigration judges and established a professional and quasi-independent corps of asylum officers.

[8]Before the reforms, numerous courts had suggested that evidence of persecution of those similarly situated constituted proof of the seriousness of the risk to the applicant. See e.g., Bolanos-Hernandez v. INS (767 F.2d 1277, 9th Cir. 1984), citing evidence of persecution of applicant's friends, who, like he, had refused to join guerrillas, and newspaper articles showing violent consequences for those who refuse to join political guerrilla groups.

[9]This regulation (8 C.F.R. § 208.13) is based on principles first articulated by the Ninth Circuit. See Bolanos-Hernandez v. INS (767 F.2d 9th Cir. 1984 at 1284-1285) overruling the Board of Immigration Appeals and noting the relevance of the applicant's "general evidence, newspaper articles that demonstrate the political and social turmoil in El Salvador . . ."; see also Blum (1986), providing a comprehensive discussion of the role of the Federal Court of Appeals for the Ninth Circuit in reviewing Board of Immigration Appeals asylum decisions.

REFERENCES

Anker, D.
1992   "Determining Asylum Claims in the United States: A Case Study on the Implementation of Legal Norms in an Unstructured Environment," *New York University Review of Law and Social Change*, 19:433, 442.

———
1991   "In re ——— (BIA March 7, 1991)," *Law Asylum in the United States: Administrative Decisions and Analysis*, 3:102. American Law Foundation.

Blum, C. P.
1991   "The Settlement of *ABC v. Thornburgh*: Landmark Victory for Central American Asylum Seekers," *International Journal of Refugee Law*, 3:347.

———
1986   "The Ninth Circuit and the Protection of Asylum Seekers Since the Passage of the Refugee Act of 1980," *San Diego Law Review*, 23:327.

Butterfield, J. A.
1995   "The New Asylum Regulations: A Practitioner's Guide," *Immigration Briefings*, 95-01.

Department of Justice
1993   *Management Review of the INS Affirmative Asylum Processing System*. Justice Management Division, Management and Planning Staff. Washington, DC: Department of Justice.

Government Accounting Office (GAO)
1987   *Asylum: Uniform Application of Standards Uncertain - Few Denied Applicants Deported*. Washington, DC: Government Accounting Office.

Ignatius, S.
1993   *An Assessment of the Asylum Process of the Immigrant and Naturalization Service*. National Asylum Study Project. Cambridge, MA: Harvard Law School Immigration and Refugee Program.

Immigration and Naturalization Service (INS)
1991   *Immigration and Naturalization Service Basic Law Manual: Asylum A Training Manual for Immigration and Naturalization Officers, Refugee Law and Practice, a Reference of Perspectives and Parameters on Selected Legal Issues 8*. Washington, DC: Asylum Branch & Office of the General Counsel.

Martin, D. A.
1990   "Reforming Asylum Adjudication: On Navigating the Coast of Bohemia," *University of Pennsylvania Law Review*, 138:1207.

———
1982   "The Refugee Act of 1980: Its Past and Future," *Michigan Year Book of International Legal Studies*, 91.

18

In Re Fauziya Kassindja: The BIA Grants Asylum to Woman Threatened with Female Genital Mutilation

ELIZABETH HULL
Rutgers University

When the Board of Immigration Appeals (BIA) – the highest administrative tribunal in the United States immigration system – granted asylum on June 13, 1996, to a woman fleeing female genital mutilation (FGM), it became the first appellate court in the country to acknowledge that violence directed specifically at women as a class can constitute persecution.

The Bia ruling in *In Re Fauziya Kassindja* (BIA Interim Decision 3278, 1996 WL 379826), which is binding on the nation's 179 immigration judges, thus bears enormous symbolic importance. The case is important, as well, for its documentary value, providing as it does a stark record of the travails facing anyone seeking asylum in this country. As in Kassindja's case, these travails include prolonged detention under harsh conditions; insensitive and biased hearing officers; and an administrative system that is unconscionably difficult to maneuver for anyone without experienced and dedicated legal representation.

The case involved Fauziya Kassindja, who was raised in Togo under circumstances notably different from those of other females in the Tchamba-Kunsuntu tribe. She grew up in an affluent family headed by a father who, unlike virtually every other patriarch in the region, opposed both polygamy and FGM (he had witnessed his own sister being tied up and circumcised, and was at her side shortly thereafter when she died from tetanus infection); by virtue of his wealth, Kassindja's father was able to defy community tradition. He sent his daughter to a boarding school in neighboring Kenya and made sure that none of her four older sisters was either mutilated or forced into an arranged marriage (BIA Interim Decision 3278 at 2; Dugger, 1996a; Rosenthal, 1996).

Life as Kassindja knew it came to an abrupt halt in 1993 when she was sixteen. That year her father died and, as mandated by custom, her mother was banished from the household and her paternal aunt moved in. Within weeks, the aunt ordered Kassindja to drop out of school (education being wasted on a woman), enter into an arranged marriage with a prosperous middle-aged man who already had three wives, and, after the wedding ceremony, submit to a procedure in which, as Kassindja described it, a tribal elder would "scrape my women parts off" (BIA Interim Decision 3278 at 2–3; Dugger, 1996a).

Just before the "scraping" was to occur, however, in a clandestine escapade worthy of a LeCarre thriller, Kassindja's sister managed to smuggle her out of the family home and onto the first flight departing from a nearby airport. Kassindja landed in Dusseldorf, Germany, where she stayed until a Nigerian acquaintance offered to sell her a passport. In December 1994 she flew to the United States, where a cousin awaited her.

When the seventeen year old arrived at Newark Airport she immediately requested asylum, on the ground that if she were returned to Togo, her husband would inevitably find her and compel her to undergo FGM. Her request was denied at the time, and eight months later it was again denied by Donald V. Ferlise, a Philadelphia-based immigration judge who explained that having " . . . taken into account the lack of rationality, the lack of internal consistency, and the lack of inherent persuasiveness in her testimony," he could only conclude that "this alien is not credible" (Tr. at 24; BIA Interim Decision 3278 at 7).

After Judge Ferlise announced his decision, Kassindja was handcuffed, her feet were shackled, and she was led back to jail. She ultimately spent sixteen months in detention, under conditions that were unrelievedly grim. Much of this time was spent at the Esmor Detention Center in Elizabeth, New Jersey (a privately-run jail under contract with the INS). There she was stripped in the presence of male guards, occasionally put in chains, and at one point thrown into solitary confinement because she washed her hands before sunrise in preparation for her morning prayers – unwittingly violating a rule forbidding anyone from using the showers before six A.M.

In June 1995, Kassindja was teargassed and beaten during a riot staged by Esmor detainees angered by onerous living conditions and their prolonged incarcerations (INS later conceded that guards had treated inmates with "capricious cruelty") (Dugger, 1996b). After the uprising, Kassindja was transferred to another privately-

run and equally harsh facility in Pennsylvania, which in addition was remote
from attorneys, family, and friends. While there, she was often strip-searched
and shackled and, apparently because of inadequate space, kept in a maximum
security ward with hard-core American felons. (Kassindja was moved to
different quarters only after an investigative commission issued a public report
in September 1995, revealing the prison's abysmal conditions.) She was not
released from jail until April 24, 1996 – only a week before her scheduled appeal,
and, notably, only a week after another public disclosure, this an article in *The
New York Times* detailing her plight (Dugger, 1996a).

When Kassindja appeared before Immigration Judge Ferlise in August 1995, she
was represented by Eric Bowman, an attorney retained by her cousin. Unfamiliar
with the intricacies of asylum procedures, he inadvertently handicapped his new
client by failing to provide the court with a narrative of her experiences. Moreover,
the cross-examination at this hearing – which in the absence of a narrative is the
sole means of establishing an applicant's credibility – was conducted by Bowman's
23-year-old research assistant, who had never before questioned a witness in court
(nor even met Kassindja until the day of the proceeding).

Layli Miller Bashir, the research assistant, was devastated by the outcome of
the hearing. When she returned in the fall to American University's Law
School, she persuaded Karen Musalo, the head of its international human
rights clinic, to take the case on appeal, pro bono. Ms. Musalo and several law
students became absorbed in their new assignment, spoke by phone with
Kassindja at least once a day for six months and, upon her eventual release,
were there to meet Kassindja at Pennsylvania's York County Prison. Then, after
mutual tears and embraces, they drove her to suburban Washington, where
she lived with a Bahai family during the appeals process.

Musalo and her team prepared Kassindja's case with a sense of urgency: there
was scant case law to guide them, a young woman's future was at stake and, as
they were well aware, to date claims of persecution based on gender-specific
grounds had rarely succeeded. Their first challenge was to determine upon what
grounds Kassindja qualified for asylum. The 1980 Refugee Act stipulates that
eligible aliens must possess a well-founded fear of persecution based upon either
race, religion, nationality, political opinion or membership in a particular social
group. They chose the last ground, arguing that Kassindja belonged to a group
comprised of young women of the Tchamba-Kunsuntu tribe who resist FGM. This,
they calculated, was an appropriately nuanced position, one narrow enough to
benefit Kassindja without simultaneously disadvantaging prospective applicants
whose circumstances might be somewhat different.

Kassindja's legal team benefited from the testimony of Merrick Polansky, a
retired anthropology professor from UCLA who since 1979 had conducted
research in Togo. He asserted that Kassindja's fear was rational and her story
believable: women in Kassindja's tribe were often compelled to enter into

polygamous marriages and forced to endure FGM; and if she were returned to Togo she certainly would be seized by the police who, assured a bribe from her husband, would deliver her to him.

The INS mounted a similarly-nuanced argument: it agreed that "female genital mutilation is a deeply objectionable cultural practice increasingly subject to condemnation on an international plane," and accordingly that the fear of this practice should justify asylum in some cases; INS insisted, however, that the BIA should deny relief to women who had already experienced the operation, or who would face nothing more serious than ostracism if they refused to submit – in other words, that "[a] woman must literally face being forced into it" (*The New York Times*, 1996). The agency also urged the BIA to schedule another hearing to determine Kassindja's credibility before it awarded her asylum.

The BIA found it unnecessary to hold a second hearing, notwithstanding the INS admonition, and on May 2, 1996, it granted Kassindja the relief she sought. In an opinion written by Chairman Paul W. Schmidt, and supported by ten of the tribunal's eleven other judges, the BIA concluded that Kassindja's story was "plausible, detailed, and internally consistent" (BIA Interim Decision 3278 at 7). It quoted from a report prepared by the INS: "It remains particularly true that [*re* FGM in Africa] women have little legal recourse and may face threats to their freedom, threats or acts of physical violence, or social ostracism for refusing to undergo this harmful traditional practice, or attempting to protect their female children" (BIA Interim Decision 3278 at 5).

The Board of Immigration Appeals held that FGM, as practiced by Kassindja's tribe, constituted persecution, that her fear was well founded, and that, notably, she was targeted on the basis of her membership in a particular social group. Finally, in response to the Immigration and Naturalization Service recommendation that only women as yet uncircumcised be considered for asylum, the BIA responded: "We decline to speculate on, or establish rules for, cases that are not before us" (BIA Interim Decision 3278 at 2). As a jubilant Karen Musalo pointed out, the BIA thereby rejected the narrow framework proposed by the INS, and "clearly left open the door to women who have been mutilated in the past" (Dugger, 1996a).

ANTI-TERRORISM ACT OF 1996 AS RESTRAINT ON KASSINDJA'S IMPACT

The BIA's ruling in *Matter of Kassindja* will not spur the female inundation that its detractors predict; in fact, as Colorado Congresswoman Patricia Schroeder observed, "[i]t is going to be very rare that anybody can use this" (*The New York Times*, 1996). Indeed, how many girls or young women have either the physical means or the psychological wherewithal to flee their home and family for an alien land? How many, once here, will have access to a legal team as resourceful and skilled as Kassindja's (let alone one willing to provide pro bono services) and thus have even a "fighting chance" of winning asylum?

The ruling may have limited practical impact for yet another reason. Congress recently passed, and President Clinton signed, the so-called Anti-Terrorism Act of 1996, which prohibits most future asylum seekers, including those with claims as compelling as Kassindja's, from even appealing negative rulings to the BIA. The Act applies to any alien who arrives at one of this country's 300 ports of entry with fraudulent documents or none at all – as many asylum seekers do since they can seldom procure traveling papers from the very authorities they are fleeing. (By the terms of this statute, Fidel Castro's daughter would have been turned away at the border since she landed in the United States with a false passport (A. Lewis, 1996b).) Those like Kassindja who arrive without adequate documentation will be subjected to expedited processing, under which an immigration judge may exclude them without a hearing unless they request asylum, in which case they will be referred to an immigration officer, who will determine whether they have a "credible fear" (a phrase nowhere found in immigration law) (*Immigration Law Report*, 1996).

A "credible fear" is found, in turn, only if it is more likely than not that the alien's statements are true and if a "significant possibility" exists that he or she can establish eligibility for asylum. Applicants establishing a credible fear will be detained pending a full hearing; everyone else will be ordered excluded without further appeal, subject only to "an immediate review by a supervisory office at the port" (*Immigration Law Report*, 1996).

Expedited exclusion orders are not ordinarily subject to administrative or judicial review, since according to the Act "no court shall have jurisdiction" either to hear summary denials "or any challenge to the new process" (except for a habeas corpus proceeding, and even then courts are only authorized to determine an alien's immigration status) (*Immigration Law Report*, 1996).

Columnist Anthony Lewis maintains that the Anti-Terrorism Act is misnamed since its real victims are not bomb throwers but aspiring asylees – a fact prompting him to ask: "Why should a bill supposedly aimed at terrorists be used as a vehicle to keep victims of official terrorism from finding refuge?" (1996b).

FGM: A POLARIZING RITUAL

What to its opponents is genital mutilation, pure-and-simple, is to its practitioners the traditional and hallowed rite of female "circumcision." As a consequence those intent upon eradication of FGM should proceed with sensitivity.

FGM is widespread, occurring in 26 African nations and parts of the Middle East, Arabian Peninsula, India, and East Asia. The World Health Organization estimates that anywhere from 85-to-114 million females – mainly prepubescent and adolescent girls, but occasionally infants and even pregnant women – have undergone the operation, and that every year another 2 million girls – some 6,000 a day – experience it. (Americans may be shocked to learn that at least 40,000 females have been subjected to mutilation while living in this country (H. Lewis, 1995; Setareh, 1995).

The procedure is typically carried out by tribal women, some of whom restrain the young girl, who is rarely anesthetized, while someone else, usually a village elder, uses a knife, razor, or perhaps a glass shard to perform the excision. Usually the girl receives either a cliterodectomy or an "infibulation," which involves the removal of both the clitoris and the labia minora and the cutting of the labia majora so they can be stitched together across the vagina, with a small opening left for the passage of body fluids (H. Lewis, 1995). Nahid Toubia, a Sudanese surgeon, has drawn this analogy: in a man it would range from amputation of the penis to "removal of all the penis, its roots or short tissue and parts of the scrotal skin" (Rosenthal, 1996).

Some victims of FGM experience devastating and lifelong psychological traumas. Virtually all experience chronic and potentially life-threatening physical reactions: extensive bleeding and hemorrhaging; both urine retention and incontinence; shock, fistula formations, chronic uterine infection; tetanus, septicemia, vulval abscesses, and the loss of sexual sensation. Scar tissue renders intercourse painful and childbirth agonizing, and often makes the simple act of walking awkward for a woman the rest of her life. Health officials now fear the practice will accelerate the spread of AIDS since the same knife or razor is often used to perform several operations (Setareh, 1995).

Given the grim consequences, why is FGM performed? Some authorities believe the practice dates to an era when girls, then considered chattel, were sold to men who would pay extra money for virgins. The practice persists for a variety of reasons among which are: it increases the husband's sexual desire and assures him that any child borne by his wife is indisputably his; it ensures a woman's virginity and later her marital fidelity. The scar tissue serves as a chastity belt, making intercourse so painful that few women apart from fulfilling their marital obligations, would voluntarily engage in the practice. Women believe the procedure signifies their purity and enhances their desirability (and convincing them otherwise is as difficult as convincing adolescent girls in the United States that razor-thin bodies are neither healthy nor attractive).

In practicing societies, women not only submit to FGM, organize and carry out the procedure, but also retaliate against anyone who avoids or opposes it. They do so for the same reason women (and men) in every society conform – they either feel powerless to oppose community dictates or, more likely, are so successfully indoctrinated that they rarely question these dictates. Besides, what fate awaits the occasional dissident? In the Sudan a woman cannot marry if her genitals are intact, and any adult female without a husband is a virtual pariah; in many other societies she cannot inherit money or property, and in some places she and her children can even be killed (H. Lewis, 1995).

For whatever practical good it may do her, the rare nonconformist now has the moral support of the international human rights community. FGM has become a major issue on its agenda, due in large part to the efforts of both Western and African nongovernmental organizations. The United Nations and regional bodies, moreover, have recently adopted resolutions explicitly condemning the practice; for instance, the U.N. Population Conference, held in Cairo in 1994, issued a Final Declaration in which it urged governments "to prohibit female genital mutilation wherever it exists, and to give vigorous support to efforts among nongovernmental and community organizations and religious institutions to eliminate such practices" (Rosenthal, 1994).

In September 1995, representatives from 189 countries met in Beijing at the U.N.'s Fourth World Conference on Women. Those in attendance, who disagreed on many issues, concurred on one – female genital mutilation (the term officially adopted) must be eradicated. To this end, participating women, including those from countries where the practice is deeply entrenched, issued a detailed Platform for Action (Nathan, 1995; Warren, 1994).

GENDER BIAS IN INTERNATIONAL LAW

Four months before the BIA ruling in *Kassindja*, an immigration judge in Baltimore denied asylum to a woman from Sierra Leone who had been abducted, gagged, bound, and mutilated with a knife. The judge maintained that for asylum purposes, anyone claiming membership in a particular social group "must share some common characteristic that is beyond the respondent's power to change, or is so fundamental to the individual identity or conscience that he or she ought not be required to change." The respondent does not meet these requirements because, the judge explained, while she could not change her sex, "she could choose whether to submit to her tribe's customary practice of genital mutilation," which he felt was important "for maintaining tribal unity" (Interpreter Releases, 1995).

His concluding statement illustrates, if in particularly stark fashion, the gender bias that still permeates the international legal system. (Imagine a judge denying relief to a Cuban dissident, for instance, on the ground that he should simply adjust to life under Castro and curb his divisive activities lest he weaken the regime.)

This bias is evidenced by the callous disregard with which international law tribunals have treated the victims of FGM, say, or sexual assault. Among the few tribunals that have been willing even to address claims arising from gender-specific violence, most have minimized its gravity by characterizing it as sex discrimination rather than a human rights violation.

This dismissive attitude, in turn, springs from an assumption, firm as bedrock, that underlies domestic as well as international law – *i.e.*, that human life is divided into two distinct spheres, one that is male-dominated and public, subject to external regulation; the other that is female-dominated and private, generally exempt from international and sometimes even domestic law (Copelon, 1994; Warren, 1994).

This paradigm, fundamental to Western liberal thought, is salutary in its intent, which is to insulate intimate relationships from the heavy hand of the state. In operation, however, it serves to perpetuate the subjugation of women by reinforcing the arbitrary notion that whereas abuses typically affecting males, such as torture or prolonged detention, occur in the public realm and accordingly should be avenged by civil authorities, abuses associated with women as a class, such as FGM or sexual assault, are "private" matters that, *pro bono publico*, should be ignored by these same authorities. The *Kassindja* ruling is noteworthy in part because it identifies violence for what it is, regardless of the context in which it occurs.

This public/private distinction is sanctified in the U.N. Charter itself, which explicitly insulates activities occurring within a state's "domestic jurisdiction" from outside interference. Article 2(7) of the Charter specifies that "[n]othing contained in the present Charter shall authorize the United Nations to intervene in matters which are essentially within the domestic jurisdiction of any state or shall require the Members to submit such domestic matters to settlement under the present Charter" (Walker, 1994).

Article 2(7) was included at the behest of developing nations, still reeling from the effects of colonization and intent upon averting further super-power interference in their "internal affairs." Now, some 50 years later, the "sphere" insulated from outside interference has shrunk considerably, but these nations still invoke Article 2(7) whenever Western states or international bodies threaten to condition investment and much-needed economic aid on improvements in their human rights record.

So-called "first world" nations, for their part, blazon the flag of noninterference when doing so excuses their failure to provide adequate assistance for "internal" problems (problems often created in the first place by their earlier imperial ventures) (Walker, 1994).

The principle of "domestic jurisdiction," then, while historically justified and a necessary deterrent still, nevertheless has served to exempt gender-specific abuses from outside redress. In states where the human rights of women are most egregiously violated, even today the principle is ardently intoned. China's Premier Li Peng, for instance, delivered a speech to the U.N. Security Council on January 31, 1992, proclaiming that "[t]he people and governments of the various countries are entitled to adopt the social system and ideology of their own choice in light of their national conditions" (U.N., 1992).

The public/private dichotomy is also inscribed in asylum law. According to the 1980 Refugee Act, as well as the 1951 Refugee Convention on which this Act is based, anyone eligible for asylum must have a "well-founded fear of persecution" based on action perpetuated or tolerated by the state (*INS v. Cardoza-Fonseca*, 480 U.S. 421, 1987). A woman seeking protection from FGM, then, is at a disadvantage. The practice is rarely condoned and may even be formally outlawed by the state; it is conducted by a family member, or perhaps a village midwife and with the "consent" of the parents. Domestic abuse, bride burning and sexual assault are similarly performed by nonstate actors and usually in contravention of official (if rarely enforced) injunctions.

Yet the distinction between state-sanctioned and so-called private action is bogus. The government is always involved when systematic abuse goes unredressed, even if the executor is a nominally private actor. Nor can a state disclaim responsibility for FGM or other abusive acts simply by labeling them "cultural" or "private" rites of passage, or even religious dictates. Whatever the label, practices become political whenever they serve to maintain and reinforce power disparities. Genital mutilation, so considered, is a profoundly political act because it denies women control over their sexuality, reproductive systems, indeed their very physical autonomy.

In adjudicating asylum claims, immigration judges should abandon their strained attempts to distinguish between "public" and "private" activities and concentrate instead on determining the extent to which persecutory actions are effectively redressed by the state (thereby honoring the principle, enshrined in the Universal Declaration of Human Rights, that individuals who suffer human rights violations and have no effective legal recourse in their own countries are entitled to seek and enjoy asylum elsewhere) (U.N., 1948).

In the United States, prospective asylees must also convince the presiding judge that he or she either suffered or has a well-founded fear of suffering persecution. Judges have defined persecution as "harm or suffering inflicted on a person in order to punish that individual for possessing a belief or characteristic the persecutor seeks to overcome" (*Guevara-Flores v. INS*, 786 F.2d 1242, 1249, 5th Cir. 1986); or as "the infliction of suffering or harm upon those who differ in a manner regarded as offensive" (*Kovac v. INS*, 777 F.2d 509, 516, 9th Cir. 1985). Under either definition, women victimized by FGM, or sexual assault, are at a disadvantage because they are punished simply for being women, not because of their particular beliefs or purportedly offensive characteristics.

Assuming a female applicant has thus far established state responsibility and a well-founded fear, she still has another hurdle to vault. She must show that her persecution is based on one of the five enumerated grounds mentioned above – race, religion, nationality, political opinion, or membership in a particular social group. Gender is not among the enumerated grounds, so women who have been mutilated or sexually abused must attempt to wedge their experiences into one of these five ill-fitting categories. Some immigration judges have recently facilitated these efforts by concluding either that in defying her country's discriminatory norms a woman risks persecution for her political opinions, or, as the BIA held in *Kassindja*, that in fleeing FGM (and by implication, other forms of gender abuse), she becomes a member of a particular social group (Hull, 1995; Warren, 1994).

HUMAN RIGHTS STANDARDS: UNIVERSAL OR CULTURALLY-BASED?

Even a generous asylum policy, of course, is no substitute for the broad-based political reform that alone can minimize institutionalized violence against women. In the short run, such a policy can even impede change. When the BIA concluded that FGM can constitute persecution, it was in effect condemning a deeply embedded cultural rite, perhaps encouraging those practicing this rite to embrace it with renewed fervor.

Regardless of the consequences, immigration tribunals are entitled and even obliged to make value judgments, which are at any rate unavoidable whenever hard choices must be made. Because of its misplaced deference to the "sensibilities" of patriarchal elites, in fact, the BIA condemnation of FGM was inexcusably overdue. In contexts that are not immigration-related, however, human rights activists are responding appropriately when they ponder the degree to which outside intervention is either justified or productive.

Some activists, so-called "universalists," maintain that the international community must at least intervene when fundamental human rights are imperiled. Unless these rights are considered absolute and identifiable, moreover, the danger is inherent, as Chaloka Beyani warns, "that the general process of modifying custom will largely depend on power relations that disadvantage women" (Beyani, 1994: 299).

Universalists agree that outsiders must be sensitive to cultural traditions – except when these traditions serve to victimize women or other vulnerable classes of people. For a variety of reasons they regard FGM as fundamentally wrong, but above all because it subjects children and young women, whose welfare is the particular responsibility of the human rights community, to acute physical pain and chronic, life-threatening illnesses.

Cultural "traditions" are often self-serving male constructs, devised without female input and invoked talisman-like by elites who distort complex religious law and custom to justify oppressive behavior and immunize it from outside criticism (H. Lewis, 1995; Walker, 1994). Besides, if in the name of "local custom" a society is justified in mutilating millions of girls and young women, why can't it also practice slavery or infanticide?

How can rights be absolute, cultural "relativists" respond, when they so often conflict? And if rights are absolute, why has the West been so notoriously selective in passing judgment – much quicker to condemn oppressive practices in Cuba, say, than in countries considered strategic allies. Moreover, how is it that these "absolute" standards bear such an uncanny resemblance to the ones embraced at any given time by the West?

Relativists fault human rights activists for elevating the importance of civil and political rights, market capitalism, and unrestrained individualism over non-Western principles that place greater emphasis on economic and social rights, for instance, or collective and cooperative endeavors. They point out, moreover, that members of traditional societies might understandably recoil at the notion, espoused by some feminists, that untrammeled sexual freedom is a woman's birthright, and with some justification ask themselves whether the "liberated" Western woman, perhaps twice-divorced and conflict-ridden, indeed occupies an enviable status.

Relativists are ever-conscious of the West's long and sad history of cultural expansionism and, as a consequence so fearful of reviving this legacy that, as Hope Lewis suggests, they may regard any human rights activity initiated by Westerners as inherently imperialistic (1995). They accordingly maintain that traditions should be judged primarily by culturally specific values and, moreover, that even practices such as FGM (which they might personally abhor) should be countered only by people native to the countries where they are observed.

Finally, relativists argue, if Western human rights activists genuinely want to eradicate genital mutilation, why don't they focus on the conditions that sustain it? Why aren't they similarly outraged by poverty, illiteracy, the dearth of basic health care?

PRACTICAL (IF HUMBLE) WAYS TO DISCOURAGE FGM

Surely activists can militate against poverty and other social ills and still work unobtrusively to discourage FGM. Surely they can find a position, however uneasy, between the extremes of self-righteous intervention and timid withdrawal. Doing so, however, requires that they eschew any notion that indigenous people are hapless victims in need yet again of outside deliverance, or that mothers are cruel or uncaring because they subject their daughters to FGM, or that members of practicing societies are somehow less civilized.

Feminists have learned the hard way that arrogance is both misplaced and counterproductive. Now, in discussing FGM with non-Westerners, they are quick to draw parallels with the foolish or even dangerous practices that entrap American and European women – liposuctions, for instance, or breast implants, face lifts, even radical hysterectomies. They add that until the 1930s surgeons in the West also performed clitoridectomies and infibulations, in these instances on women who masturbated or were considered "promiscuous" or "aggressive."

Would-be reformers must apprehend how deeply-entrenched FGM remains despite both the organized and grassroots opposition that has emerged during the last twenty years. The likelihood of eradicating the ritual anytime soon remains about what it was 70 years ago when Scottish missionaries undertook the effort, warning families in Kenya that unless they renounced the practice their children would be expelled from school. (Lieblich and Rios (1995) point out, "the classrooms were soon emptied".)

The U.N. campaign in the 1950s to publicize the dangers of FGM yielded scant (if any) results. Several countries, including Nigeria, Ethiopia, Ghana, Egypt, and the Sudan, have formally outlawed the ritual, but their actions, like those of the United Nations, have left behavior unaffected. The Sudanese experience is illustrative. As far back as 1946, leaders there forbade the most radical forms of genital mutilation (while still allowing for removal of the free and projecting part of the clitoris). Dr. Nahid Toubia estimates that, notwithstanding the prohibition, at least 89 percent of girls and women in Northern Sudan still have their vaginas sewn (Lieblish and Rios, 1995).

Eradication efforts have failed, in part, because those encouraging them have underestimated the extent to which the ritual serves as a cultural and political linchpin, crucial to a society's identity and the maintenance of its power relations. As Jomo Kenyatta, the former president of Kenya, explained:

> . . . [FGM] is still regarded as the very essence of an institution which has enormous educational, social, moral and religious implications, quite apart from the operation itself. . . . Therefore the abolition of the surgical element in this custom means to the Gikuvu [a practicing tribe] the abolition of the whole institution. . . .The real anthropological study, therefore, is to show that cliterodectomy, like Jewish circumcision, is a merely bodily mutilation which, however, is regarded as the *condition sine qua non* of the whole teaching of tribal law, religion and morality. (H. Lewis, 1995)

Up against so entrenched a practice, the human rights community is not powerless to effect change, but it must content itself with measures that are incremental and even humble. To begin with, as Mertus and Goldberg (1994) suggest, members of the community "can invite more people to the table," including the oppressed themselves whose voices are seldom heard.

Members of the human rights community can learn to be followers, acceding leadership roles to people from practicing societies (and, to a lesser extent, to African Americans, such as the influential author Alice Walker, who through her writings has been singularly successful in kindling opposition to FGM) (H. Lewis, 1995).

Activists can adopt a multifaceted approach: collect and disseminate information on the hazards of FGM, such as that gathered by the U.N. Special Rapporteur on Violence Against Women, or the U.S. Department of State for its annual human rights report; support both the organizations that nurture the development of human rights norms and all manner of grassroots educational, health, and leadership programs. The World Health Organization encourages those opposing genital mutilation to focus on its health risks, a strategy some opponents of the practice find ethically problematic. While such an approach is not as imperialistic as some other ones, it suggests that FGM would be less offensive from a human rights standpoint if it were performed by professionals or under antiseptic conditions.

Countries can also take concrete steps on the domestic front, still important if largely symbolic. A. M. Rosenthal, writing in *The New York Times*, urges the United States to apply one percent of its foreign aid, roughly $100 million, to fund African-led educational and training projects designed to fight FGM. "That won't end the horror," he says, "but it will speed the day, and certainly is better than edging daintily away or obeisance to local customs that bring agony and lifelong deprivation" (1996).

Sweden and the United Kingdom have outlawed FGM, and France punishes its practitioners for child abuse. Congresswoman Patricia Schroeder has introduced a bill that, if enacted into law, would similarly penalize anyone in this country who facilitates the rite (H. Lewis, 1995). The United States could also withhold foreign aid from countries which tolerate the practice, although this approach might backfire. By withholding money, even the meager sum it currently provides, the government might succeed only in exacerbating the poverty that sustains FGM.

The United States should offer asylum to any female applicant who succeeds in escaping conditions that are seriously abusive. To this end, Congress should include "persecution on account of gender" among the grounds for asylum enumerated in the Refugee Act; or, alternately, the INS should adopt a policy explicitly equating gender-based violence with persecution based either on the victim's political opinions or her membership in a particular social group. Immigration judges in this country, as indeed throughout the world, must also expand the definition of the "public" sphere to embrace serious depredations against women that occur in the context of their homes or communities.

Ultimately, not only FGM, but every other travesty visited upon women as a class, will continue unabated unless and until the international community commits itself to a proposition that is still not self-evident – *i.e.*, that women's rights are human rights.

REFERENCES

Beyani, C.
1994   In *Human Rights of Women: National and International Perspectives.* Ed. R. J. Cook.
           Philadelphia: University of Pennsylvania Press.

Cook, R. J., ed.
1994   *Human Rights of Women: National and International Perspectives.* Philadelphia:
           University of Pennsylvania Press.

Copelon, R.
1994   "Surfacing Gender: Re-Engraving Crimes against Women in Humanitarian Law,"
           Hastings Women's Law Journal, 5:243.

Dugger, C. W.
1996a   "Asylum for African Fearing Mutilation Hailed as 'Global' Victory for Women," *The
           New York Times,* June 15.

1996b "U.S. Frees an African Fleeing from Mutilation," *The New York Times*, April 25.

1996c "Women's Plea to U.S. for Asylum Puts Ancient Tribal Ritual on Trial," *The New York Times*, April 15.

Hull, E.
1996 "At Long Last: Asylum Law is Beginning to Address Violence Against Women." In *In Defense of the Alien*: Volume XVII. New York: Center for Migration Studies. Pp. 186–202.

Immigration Law Report
1996 "New Antiterrorism Contains Sufficient Immigration Provisions." May 15.

Interpreter Releases
1995 *Interpreter Releases*, 72:1265.

Lewis, A.
1996a "How Terrorism Wins," *The New York Times*, March 11.

1996b "Slamming the Door," *The New York Times*, April 19.

Lewis, H.
1995 "Between *Irua* and 'Female Genital Mutilation': Feminist Human Rights Discourse and the Cultural Divide," *Harvard Human Rights Journal*, 8:1:55.

Lieblich, J. and M. Rios
1995 "A Ritual of Oppression," *The Sunday Oregonian*, September 17.

Mertus, J. and R. Goldberg
1994 "A Perspective on Women and International Human Rights after the Vienna Declaration: The Inside/Outside Construct," *New York University Journal of International Law and Politics*, 26:201.

Nathan, T.
1995 "Perspectives on the NGO Forum on Women," *UCLA Women's Law Journal*, 6:177–187.

Rosenthal, A.
1996 "Fighting Female Mutilation," *The New York Times*, April 12.

1994 "A Victory in Cairo," *The New York Times*, September 6.

Schmitt, E.
1996 "Immigration Overhaul Moves toward Vote," *The New York Times*, August 2.

Setareh, D.
1995 "Women Escaping Genital Mutilation Seeking 1995 Asylum in the United States," *UCLA Women's Law Journal*, 6:123:159.

The New York Times
1996 "The Asylum System Needs Work," *The New York Times*. June 22.

United Nations (U.N.)
1992 Security Council Session, January 31, Address by Premier Li Peng of China. New York: United Nations.

1948 General Assembly Resolution 217. New York: United Nations.

Walker, K.
1994 "An Exploration of Article 2(7) of the United Nations Charter as an Embodiment of the Public/Private Distinction in International Law," *New York University Journal of International Law and Politics*, 26:173.

Warren, P.
1994 "Women Are Human: Gender-Based Persecution Is a Human Rights Violation against Women," *Hastings Women's Law Journal*, 5:281.

19

The Divorce Between Refugee Determinations and Pursuit of Human Rights Objectives Through the Conduct of U.S. Foreign Policy: The Case of Female Genital Mutilation

MARK GIBNEY
Purdue University

By now, the saga of Fauziya Kassindja is well known. In an attempt to flee an arranged marriage and with that the tribal practice of female genital mutilation, Ms. Kassindja fled her native Togo and eventually made her way to the United States in December 1994. At Newark airport, Ms. Kassindja informed customs officials that the passport she was using was fraudulent, whereupon she requested asylum in the United States. The events that followed were nearly as cruel as the fate from which she had escaped.

Kassindja was immediately transported to a prison where, for the first time in her life, she was stripped and forced to appear naked in front of a group of strangers. Similar humiliations followed, including shackles, sharing cell space with a convicted felon, and being placed in solitary confinement for violating a prison rule for washing her hands before 6 A.M. On August 23, 1995, Ms. Kassindja's case went before an immigration judge who denied her asylum claim based on what he perceived to be Kassindja's lack of credibility. Ms. Kassindja then remained imprisoned during nearly the entire time that her appeal was pending. In June 1996, the Board of Immigration Appeals (BIA) overturned the decision of the immigration judge and granted Fauziya Kassindja asylum in the United States.

The *Kassindja* case has been heralded as a great victory, and on one level at least this is true. Certainly Fauziya Kassindja herself will be spared female genital mutilation, a cultural practice where parts of a female's clitoris are cut off, oftentimes in a very crude and extraordinarily painful manner.[1] In addition, other women who are able to make their way to the United States will now be able to rely on the *Kassindja* precedent when making their own asylum claims based upon a similar set of facts. It also seems hopeful that female asylum claims quite generally will now be given more serious consideration than they have been in the past (Kelly, 1993; Goldberg, 1993; Love, 1994; Warren, 1994).

Having said this, it is important to underscore what the granting of refugee status to Fauziya Kassindja will not do – namely, assist and protect the tens or hundreds of millions of women in the world who will still be subjected to female genital mutilation. There are at least two reasons for this. One is that despite the claim that our borders will now become flooded with women fleeing female genital mutilation, in reality only a very tiny portion of those who would be forced to undergo this practice will ever leave their country of origin, and a considerably smaller subset will ever be able to journey to a country like the United States. In short, the idea that overwhelming numbers of women from countries where female genital mutilation is practiced will now descend upon American borders to claim refugee status is simply ludicrous.

Logistical considerations aside, the second reason why the *Kassindja* decision will ultimately prove to be little more than a hollow victory for those who will face this brutal treatment – and the one that I wish to focus on in this paper – is the isolated and narrow manner in which asylum decisions are made. To explore this, consider two models of refugee decisionmaking. In one, the granting of refugee status is essentially a means of providing a safe haven to a particular person because of specific human rights violations suffered by that individual. Under this model, the primary focus of the receiving country's efforts is on offering protection to the fleeing individual who is now within its borders. Changing the conditions that gave rise to the asylum claim is secondary at best, and irrelevant at worst. I would suggest that this first model describes asylum decisionmaking in the United States and elsewhere. In contrast to the model outlined above would be one where the granting of refugee status to an individual would take place within a much broader foreign policy framework. Under this model, while providing a safe haven to a persecuted individual within the receiving country's borders is commendable and important enough, it is by no means the only action that is taken by the receiving country in response to the human rights violations that gave rise to the grant of asylum in the first place. In fact, under this model, the granting of refugee status is merely a precipitating event that prompts a wide array of responses by the receiving country. Some of these actions will be directed at the offending country itself: diplomatic initiatives, economic and trade sanctions, and complaints lodged in regional and international fora. Other responses, such as working towards the creation of international covenants and mechanisms to enforce them, will be directed more at eliminating the egregious practice itself, wherever it occurs.

It is important to note that these foreign policy responses are intended not so much to punish the nation where the human rights violation took place, but simply to change that country's behavior. Moreover, these actions are taken with the understanding that those who have been granted asylum, much more often than not, will represent only a very small fraction of those (in the offending country and elsewhere) who suffer from the same brutal treatment on which the grant of asylum was based. The *Kassindja* case is an excellent example of this. Certainly we know (or should know) that granting refugee status to Fauziya Kassindja will, by itself, do little to change the widespread practice of female genital mutilation. Why is it, then, that this will comprise a very large part of the U.S. government's response to a practice that it has recognized as a serious act of persecution?

I will consider several reasons why we respond (or perhaps more accurately, don't respond) the way that we do. One is simply the fear of being swamped by the needs of countless millions. The granting of refugee status, then, becomes a compromise position where we can show abhorrence to a practice, while at the same time attending to a relatively small and manageable number of people. The problem, however, lies in thinking that our only course of action is in granting refugee status. The argument that I will set forth here is that a much sounder way of proceeding is by bringing together a nation's refugee policy and its foreign policy. What is important to note, however, is that rather than having foreign policy drive U.S. refugee policy as it has in the past (Loescher and Scanlan, 1986; Zucker and Zucker, 1987), the converse should be true. That is, U.S. refugee policy should be based on meeting the basic needs of desperate individuals (at our borders or otherwise), while U.S. foreign policy (or a substantial part of it) should be geared towards removing the causes of human suffering that give rise to refugee populations.

Given the power and the prestige of the United States government, there is no question that substantial headway could be made. To use a hypothetical situation, if the U.S. government were truly serious about working towards the elimination of female genital mutilation, there are a host of means by which it could pursue these objectives. There are, however, at least two problems. The first is that, despite motions toward human rights considerations, U.S. foreign policy has never been focused in the direction of this goal (Donnelly, 1984; Forsythe, 1988). Rather, national security goals dominate U.S. foreign policy interests; this is just as true in the post-cold war period as it was previously. Secondly, this lack of resolve by the "leader of the free world" has all too frequently been mirrored by the international community as well. The end result of all this has been a world where human rights practices in the world have seriously deteriorated (Gibney, Apodaca and McCann, 1996) and where refugee and displaced person populations have grown almost exponentially, but where the interest, the political willpower, and the institutional mechanism to halt egregious practices simply do not exist.

The argument that I make here is that a country (or countries, plural) would do much better by employing the second model of refugee decisionmaking. The example that I use is female genital mutilation, although there obviously are a host of other human rights practices that could (and should) be targeted as well. The primary reason why I do this is my belief that it would be useful for refugee scholars to focus on concrete political phenomena. The refugee literature is replete with calls to examine "root causes," but all too often there is very little illumination of exactly what this phrase means, never mind how one would go about achieving this in a particular case (Thornburn, 1996). Although it is certainly important to view the various causes of refugee flows in a "holistic" manner, it would be most unfortunate if an endless search for these root causes was thereby interpreted by policymakers as exoneration from taking any meaningful action.

What is needed at times, instead, is a very strong and comprehensive message that certain behavior is morally and legally unacceptable. Notwithstanding the fact that this issue is fraught with charges of Western imperialism (Steele, 1995), female genital mutilation is such an issue. The West is generally (perhaps universally) of the mind that this is a barbaric practice that violates the human rights of women in those societies where it is practiced. Since this is the case, the West ought to act in a manner to eliminate it. This will not be actualized by providing refugee status to the relatively small number of women who are somehow able to arrive in the West. Nor will it occur by banning the practice domestically, as Britain, France, and most recently the United States have done. Rather, this will only be accomplished when Western countries begin to have their foreign policies informed by their refugee determinations.

HOW WE CONCEPTUALIZE REFUGEES VERSUS HOW WE CONCEPTUALIZE OTHER HUMAN SUFFERING

As a general rule, we respond to refugees who arrive at our borders in a much different manner than we do to the needs – sometimes the same exact needs – of those who do not come to our shores. To state the proposition baldly, we (eventually) are much more concerned with the prospects facing Fauziya Kassindja than those of millions of unknown women who will face the same cruelties – but who will never come before us. Why is this? For one thing, there is an immediacy – and a reality – to the claims of those who arrive, as it were, in our living rooms that is somehow missing when the suffering is more distant. Perhaps reflecting this, Western countries continue to spend far more attending to the refugee claims before them than they contribute to international refugee relief efforts.

The immediacy of refugee claims, however, only explains a small part of why there is this separation between refugee determinations, on the one hand, and the conduct of foreign policy. What is just as important – perhaps far more so – is the fear of getting on any kind of "slippery slope," and thereby somehow becoming responsible for many more people than we think we are capable of dealing with.

Granting refugee status to a relatively small number of people, then, becomes a symbolic compromise. By providing refugee status to Fauziya Kassindja, we are able to show a certain abhorrence of female genital mutilation. Yet, we quickly balk at the prospect of attending to the protection of all who will encounter this same practice. Better to stake out a moral position through the granting of refugee status to a few select individuals than to attempt to address the phenomenon head on.

This, of course, is not the language that nation-states employ. Instead, they rely on the sovereignty principle to justify their inattention to nearly all of the egregious practices taking place in other countries. We hold ourselves out as being against torture, for example, but we otherwise act as if we are powerless to interfere in the domestic policies of countries where such practices routinely take place – including Israel and Egypt, the two major recipients of U.S. foreign aid (U.S. State Department, 1996).

What this completely ignores are the principles of international law that emerged at Nuremberg and in the post-World War II period, and recently reaffirmed by actions such as Operation Safe Comfort: sovereignty does not protect a country when it is engaged in committing serious human rights abuses (Reisman, 1990; Chopra and Weiss, 1992). Still, except in rare instances, the nation-states of the world continue to operate in this manner. This not only includes those countries that are responsible for committing human rights abuses, but other countries as well, including those who receive refugees fleeing these intolerable conditions.

PROVIDING OURSELVES WITH TOO FEW OPTIONS

One of the major shortcomings in the refugee literature is the inability to articulate meaningful options that could be pursued. Instead, notwithstanding all of the verbiage of "root causes," and despite "early warning" initiatives, we are still left with little to show except burgeoning refugee populations and, concomitant with that, the need to somehow accommodate these overwhelming flows. The problem, I would suggest, is that we have not thought broadly enough, and we oftentimes have limited ourselves to false, dichotomous choices.

A prime example of how we have limited our options is the continued reliance on granting refugee status as a "solution" to human rights abuses. Admittedly, this option has provided safety to literally millions of individuals. Yet, what we never bother to calculate are the individuals who, for one reason or another, have not been protected in this manner – the failures of the current refugee system. These people (and there are very many of them) either suffer persecution and/or are killed, but they do not appear in our data regarding refugee populations; in fact, for us they figure very little.

An example of this limiting of options can be found in Jim Hathaway's (1991) widely received article "Reconceiving Refugee Law as Human Rights Protection." As the title indicates, Hathaway argues for a much closer connection between refugee and international human rights law. The problem, however, is that the "solution" he offers is for persecuted individuals to "vote with their feet" (if they can) by leaving oppressive countries. Hathaway writes:

> As the wheels of international scrutiny of human rights slowly turn, people continue to suffer. Refugee law can be a means of beginning to address this inadequacy of international human rights law. Its essential premise would be the affirmation of an autonomous right of individuals and communities to access an interim remedy when continued residence in their own state ceases to be viable. Refugee law would therefore facilitate and complement the implementation of international human rights law, but would retain a distinctly palliative orientation. (1991:121)

As an empirical matter, Hathaway is indeed correct: the human rights "machinery" that presently exists is slow, politically biased, and more often than not completely ineffectual (Guest, 1990; Donoho, 1993; Byrnes, 1994). What is by no means clear, however, is how the admission of refugees "can be a means of beginning to address this inadequacy of international human rights law," as Hathaway suggests. In fact, one could well make the opposite argument: that one of the unintended consequences of the admission of refugees has been to sharply inhibit any reformulation of the implementation of human rights. One reason this might be the case is that admitting refugees allows us to think that we are "doing" something. In point of fact we are doing something; the question is whether we are accomplishing anywhere near all that we could.

This is not to say that refugee relief should not be an integral means of assisting individuals in great need. What is being suggested, however, is that we have failed to take a comprehensive approach to refugee flows and, more importantly, to fully grasp what refugee flows represent – the existence of serious human rights abuses in other lands. We have failed to strengthen the means of enforcing human rights;

and we have failed to push our governments to adopt foreign policies that would address larger human rights phenomena, in large part prompting these flows. Ultimately, we have failed those who have had to become refugees to avoid this violence. But more than this, we have utterly failed to protect so many who have not been able to leave their country of origin or who have not been able to find a place of refuge for, as Shacknove (1985) reminds us, in some strange way refugees are oftentimes the "lucky" ones.

Unfortunately, when other options are discussed, the choices provided are often dichotomous. Thus, "intervention" to prevent human rights abuses or to halt refugee flows is almost always taken to mean military intervention (Walzer, 1977, 1980; Freedman, 1995), although, as should be obvious, there are a whole host of ways that a country can – and does – intervene in the affairs of other countries well short of the military option.

The problem is that military intervention is an extreme measure, and because of this should only be employed under particularly egregious circumstances. A more useful approach has been suggested by Jack Donnelly's (1984) notion of "positive nonintervention," which entails a concentrated effort by the international community of noninvolvement with regimes guilty of massive violations of human rights. However, there still remains the need to address lower levels of human rights abuses that, sadly enough, are the norm in so many parts of the world. To finally begin to address these practices, we will need to employ a battery of foreign policy initiatives.

HAVING REFUGEE DETERMINATIONS INFORM THE CONDUCT OF FOREIGN POLICY

In an important article written over a decade ago, Jack Garvey (1985) called for a "reformulation of international refugee law." Garvey argued that rather than continuing to rely upon humanitarian premises (which in turn has led to never-ending refugee flows), international refugee protection should instead be treated as a matter of interstate rights and obligations and guided by the traditional resources of international law.

The position taken here differs slightly from that taken by Garvey, who was writing in the context of mass expulsions, but it too is premised on the idea that refugee matters should be governed by principles of international law and international relations. If the human rights machinery is too slow to respond to the needs of refugees, as Hathaway (1991) correctly points out, then it is vital to address this shortcoming. To attempt to continue to rely almost exclusively on the refugee option is to ignore two things. One is the ugly political mood against refugee populations in general. Second, and perhaps more importantly, this also ignores how few who suffer persecution have ever – or will ever – receive assistance in the form of refugee relief.

What, then, is to be done? Returning to the example with which we started out, female genital mutilation, the position taken here is that granting refugee status to Fauziya Kassindja, and to a relatively small number of women like her, ultimately achieves very little. The World Health Organization estimates that between 80 and 100 million women have already had to endure female genital mutilation, and an additional 2 million women face this cruelty each year. The question is: Why don't these egregious practices prompt some form of concerted international effort?

One place to begin would be in international fora. Unfortunately, international law, at least as it stands at present, offers remarkably little protection to women. As Joan Fitzpatrick (1994:542) has pointed out, the only codified prohibition on female genital mutilation in international human rights law apparently is Article 24(3) of the Convention on the Rights of the Child, which rather mildly requires state parties to take "all effective and appropriate measures with a view of abolishing traditional practices prejudicial to the health of children." In addition, the Committee on the Elimination of Discrimination Against Women (CEDAW) in General Recommendation 14 also linked genital mutilation to the guarantee on health in Article 12 of the Women's Convention. Finally, the Sub-Commission, responding to a report of its Working Group on Traditional Practices, labeled female genital mutilation as a violation of the rights of women, but without offering a specific textual basis for this position.

In addition to shortcomings in the law itself, enforcement of women's rights has been virtually nonexistent (Byrnes, 1994). For starters, there is no individual complaint procedure under CEDAW (Bayefsky, 1994). And while the U.N. Commission on the Status of Women does have the power to receive communications, the procedure is little known and seldom used (Byrnes, 1994).

Notwithstanding these severe defects (perhaps because of them), it is important that the United Nations human rights "machinery" be reformulated and reformed. Summarizing his excellent study of the role of human rights in global security issues, Douglas Donoho (1993) writes:

> Ultimately, the central underlying issue is defining the role of international human rights and human rights institutions in the world governing process. Expanding the role of human rights in the peacekeeping process would require that international human rights institutions move dynamically from the overtly political, weak supervisory capacity they now serve to a much more authoritative role in which their interpretations of the specific content and meaning of rights would be implemented by the UN's political organs to promote peace and security. (1993:869)

Still, Donoho is not particularly optimistic: "As currently situated however, it is clear that most of the international community strongly favors vaguely worded norms and the extremely weak international supervisory role of the UN's human rights institutions" (1993:869).

It is important to note that the United Nations human rights apparatus is merely one mechanism – and with only rare exceptions, a very small one at that – for addressing human rights violations throughout the world. Just as important are diplomatic initiatives that nation-states might take, by themselves or in concert with other countries. Here there are a myriad of ways that countries attempt to influence the behavior of other countries, employing both the carrot and the stick. Using the latter, in the face of gross levels of human rights abuse (such as female genital mutilation), a country could engage in diplomatic protests, recall its ambassador to the offending country, halt foreign aid, employ trade sanctions, conduct economic boycotts, and so forth. Obviously, these efforts will have more chance of success in countries where the United States has more influence. One such country would be Egypt, one of the largest recipients of U.S. foreign aid, where it is estimated that between 80 and 97 percent of the women in the country undergo female genital mutilation (MacFarquhar, 1996).

Rather than responding in such a manner, Western countries have instead viewed female genital mutilation as a matter of "local concern." Thomas G. Hart, U.S. Ambassador to the Ivory Coast, describes female genital mutilation in this manner: "It's a matter principally for local society to determine the extent to which these practices are tolerated" (Dugger, 1996a:5). A spokesperson for the French Embassy in the Ivory Coast similarly states: "This is a marginal problem. It's important, but to feed people is probably more important. I don't think it can be an issue when negotiations take place on aid provided to African countries" (Dugger, 1996a:5).

Given the cultural sensitivity inherent in the issue at hand, the proper course – at least initially – is for the West to support educational efforts in countries where female genital mutilation is practiced (Slack, 1988:485). In addition, there must be every effort to downplay the role of outsiders and instead aim at creating what Abdullahi Ahmed An-Na`im (1994) describes as an "internal discourse" on this issue. Still, in the final analysis, the penultimate issue is whether female genital mutilation persists or not, and I am suggesting that the West has a duty to assist those who face this kind of persecution – beyond the granting of refugee status to a few, or applying criminal penalties to those who engage in the practice within the domestic bounds of the United States. What needs to happen is that countries have to begin to conceive of refugee determinations in a much different manner than they have to date. Rather than viewing the granting of refugee status as an endpoint, countries should instead view this as the beginning of an attempt to eliminate much larger human rights violations.

CONCLUSION

This article has been loosely centered around the case of Fauziya Kassindja, a native of Togo, who in 1996 was granted political asylum in the United States on the basis of her fear of returning to her homeland where she faced female genital mutilation. The argument presented here is that as commendable as this ruling was, and as noteworthy as the legislative proposals that followed in its wake, these things offer scant protection to the millions and millions of women who will face this cruel practice.

The problem, as I have suggested here, is that there is a divorce between our refugee determinations and the conduct of U.S. foreign policy. Granting refugee status to Fauziya Kassindja indicates that the United States government believes that female genital mutilation constitutes a serious human rights violation. Yet, with the exception of providing asylum to Kassindja and a few similarly situated women, and in addition to modest legislative actions, the U.S. government will itself apparently commit few resources to eliminating this practice, ambassadorial officers will continue to view female genital mutilation as a "local" cultural phenomenon that is beyond their purview.

One major problem in all this is that, notwithstanding a lot of noise in this direction, human rights concerns have played a very minor role in the conduct of U.S. foreign policy. Instead, American foreign policy has been based on certain ideological, security and economic interests that have, at best, done little to promote human rights and, at worst, have served to contribute to the stagnation or deterioration of human rights conditions abroad (Donnelly, 1984).

The ironic thing about all this is that unlike so much of U.S. refugee and asylum policy, political considerations (of the ideological kind) seemed to have played only a very minor role in the decision to grant refugee status to Fauziya Kassindja. Instead, it could legitimately be argued that human rights considerations were paramount. What is being asked for here is that these same human rights concerns be incorporated into – and coordinated with – the conduct of American foreign policy (Loescher, 1993:169). Only in this manner do we stand a chance of reducing refugee populations. Of equal or even greater importance, only in this way, will we begin to eliminate persecution, whether it leads to refugee flows or not.

NOTE

[1]There are several methods of female genital mutilation, ranging in severity from the ceremonial cutting of the prepuce (thus analogous in some respects to male circumcision), to excision which involves removal of the clitoris and the labia minor, to infibulation which involves removal of all the outer female genitalia and sewing the remnants of the labia majora together so as to leave only a small opening for the passage of urine and menstrual blood (Slack, 1988). The female genital mutilation feared by Ms. Kassindja was infibulation. In this essay I use the term "female genital mutilation" to encompass all methods, although the most severe forms are the most objectionable and constitute the most serious human rights violation.

REFERENCES

An-Na`im, A. A.
1994   "State Responsibility under International Human Rights Law to Change Religious and Customary Laws." In *Human Rights of Women: National and International Perspectives*. Ed. R. Cook. Philadelphia: University of Pennsylvania Press.

Bayefsky, A.
1994   "General Approaches to Domestic Application of Women's International Human
         Rights Law." In *Human Rights of Women: National and International Perspectives*. Ed. R.
         Cook. Philadelphia: University of Pennsylvania Press.

Byrnes, A.
1994   "Toward More Effective Enforcement of Women's Human Rights through the Use
         of International Human Rights Law and Procedures." In *Human Rights of Women:
         National and International Perspectives*. Ed. R. Cook. Philadelphia: University of
         Pennsylvania Press.

Chopra, J. and T. G. Weiss
1992   "Sovereignty Is No Longer Sacrosanct," *Ethics & International Affairs*, 6:95–117.

Cook, R. ed.
1994   *Human Rights of Women: National and International Perspectives*. Philadelphia:
         University of Pennsylvania Press.

Donnelly, J.
1984   "Humanitarian Intervention and American Foreign Policy: Law, Morality and
         Politics," *Journal of International Affairs*, 37:311–328.

Donoho, D. L.
1993   "The Role of Human Rights in Global Security Issues: A Normative and Institutional
         Critique," *Michigan Journal of International Law*, 14:827–869.

Dugger, C. W.
1996a   "African Ritual Pain: Genital Cutting," *The New York Times*, October 5. A1.

_____

1996b   "New Law Bans Genital Cutting in the United States," *The New York Times*, October
         12. A1.

Fitzpatrick, J.
1994   "The Use of International Human Rights Norms to Combat Violence against
         Women." In *Human Rights of Women: National and International Perspectives*. Ed. R.
         Cook. Philadelphia: University of Pennsylvania Press.

Forsythe, D.
1988   *Human Rights and U.S. Foreign Policy: Congress Reconsidered*. Gainesville: University
         of Florida Press.

Freedman, P.
1995   "International Intervention to Combat the Explosion of Refugees and Internally
         Displaced Persons," *Georgetown Immigration Law Journal*, 9:565–601.

Garvey, J.
1985   "Toward a Reformulation of International Refugee Law," *Harvard International Law
         Journal*, 26:483–500.

Gibney, M., C. Apodaca and J. McCann
1996   "Refugee Flows, the Internally Displaced and Political Violence (1980–1993): An
         Exploratory Analysis." In *Whither Refugee? The Refugee Crisis: Problems and Solutions*.
         Ed. A. Schmid. Leiden, the Netherlands: PIOOM.

Goldberg, P.
1993   "Anyplace But Home: Asylum in the United States for Women Fleeing Intimate
         Violence," *Cornell International Law Journal*, 26:565–604.

Guest, I.
1990   *Behind the Disappearances: Argentina's Dirty War against Human Rights and the United
         Nations*. Philadelphia: University of Pennsylvania Press.

Hathaway, J.
1991 "Reconceiving Refugee Law as Human Rights Protection," *Journal of Refugee Studies,* 4:113–131.

Kelly, N.
1993 "Gender-Related Persecution: Assessing the Asylum Claims of Women," *Cornell International Law Journal,* 26:625–674.

Loescher, G.
1993 *Beyond Charity: International Cooperation and the Global Refugee Crisis.* New York: Oxford University Press.

Loescher, G. and J. Scanlan
1986 *Calculated Kindness: Refugees and America's Half-Open Door, 1945 to the Present.* New York: The Free Press.

Love, E.
1994 "Equality in Political Asylum Law: For a Legislative Recognition of Gender-Based Persecution," *Harvard Women's Law Journal,* 17:133–155.

MacFarquhar, N.
1996 "Mutilation of Egyptian Girls: Despite Ban, It Goes On," *The New York Times,* August 8. A3.

Reisman, W. M.
1990 "Sovereignty and Human Rights in Contemporary International Law," *The American Journal of International Law,* 84:866–876.

Schmid, A., ed.
1996 *Whither Refugee? The Refugee Crisis: Problems and Solutions.* Leiden, the Netherlands: LISWO.

Shacknove, A.
1985 "Who is a Refugee?" *Ethics,* 95:274–284.

Slack, A.
1988 "Female Circumcision: A Critical Appraisal," *Human Rights Quarterly,* 10:437–486.

Steele, R.
1995 "Silencing the Deadly Ritual: Efforts to End Female Genital Mutilation," *Georgetown Immigration Law Journal,* 9:105–135.

Thornburn, J.
1996 "Root Cause Approaches to Forced Migration: A European Perspective," *Journal of Refugee Studies,* 9:119–135.

U.S. State Department
1996 *Country Reports on Human Rights Practices for 1995.* Washington, DC: GPO.

Walzer, M
1980 "The Moral Standing of States: A Reply to Four Critics," *Philosophy and Public Affairs,* 9:209–229.

——
1977 *Just and Unjust Wars.* New York: Basic Books.

Warren, P.
1994 "Women are Human: Gender-Based Persecution Is a Human Rights Violation against Women," *Hastings Women's Law Journal,* 5:281–315.

Zucker, N. and N. Zucker
1987 *The Guarded Gate: The Reality of American Refugee Policy.* San Diego, CA: Harcourt Brace Jovanovich.

20

Operational Plan for Durable Solutions within the Framework of Annex 7 of the General Framework Agreement for Peace in Bosnia and Herzegovina and Related Regional Return and Repatriation Movements[1]

PRESENTED BY ANNE WILLEN BIJLEVELD
Representative, UNHCR, Washington, D.C.

On January 16, 1996, the United Nations High Commissioner for Refugees (UNHCR) chaired a meeting in Geneva of the Humanitarian Issues Working Group (HIWG) of the International Conference on Former Yugoslavia (ICFY), which was the last such meeting within the ICFY framework. At that HIWG meeting, UNHCR presented a document entitled "Post Conflict Solutions: UNHCR Program in Bosnia and Herzegovina and Other Countries in the Region" (HIWG/96/2), which contained the initial strategic planning for return and repatriation, formulated in close consultation with the parties, and examined the phasing out of temporary protection arrangements in the context of the implementation of the General Framework Agreement for Peace in Bosnia and Herzegovina (Peace Agreement).

This initial strategic planning document, including its provisions relating to the phasing out of temporary protection, was widely endorsed by the participants at the HIWG meeting. UNHCR was encouraged, however, to make progress in formulating a detailed plan of operations for implementation of Annex 7, to be discussed at a high-level working meeting which the Government of Norway kindly offered to host in Oslo, Norway, on March 8, 1996.

The plan of operations described below takes as its starting point the document entitled "Post Conflict Solutions: UNHCR Program in Bosnia and Herzegovina and Other Countries in the Region" (HIWG/96/2) and builds upon the foundations laid by it. This plan should therefore be read in conjunction with the latter document, as well as with the "United Nations Revised Consolidated Inter-Agency Appeal for Bosnia and Herzegovina, Croatia, the Federal Republic of Yugoslavia, the former Yugoslav Republic of Macedonia and Slovenia (Consolidated Inter-Agency Appeal)" issued jointly by UNHCR and the Department of Humanitarian Affairs (DHA) on March 1, 1996.

It is the conviction of UNHCR and the parties that a large proportion of displaced persons and refugees will return and repatriate voluntarily if, in practice, a secure and safe environment exists, and if adequate shelter and essential services are available. For return and repatriation to be viable however, the phases of planned movements must imperatively be linked closely to the creation of absorption capacity in returnee areas within Bosnia and Herzegovina.

The overall primary objective of the return and repatriation operation is to ensure that lasting solutions are found for displaced persons and refugees through a process of early, peaceful, orderly and phased return to a place of their choice in Bosnia and Herzegovina. All efforts will be made to promote the reintegration of individuals and families into stable communities where their fundamental human rights will be protected and where their basic needs are met. Humanitarian assistance, targeted in scope and designed to encourage local production of relief items, will continue in parallel with the return and repatriation program, owing to the likely continued dependence of populations on assistance from the international community, at least in the short term. Over time, a second objective is gradually to phase out the provision of humanitarian assistance to refugees, displaced persons, and the war-affected, as a function of the consolidation of peace and stability, and progress in rehabilitation and reconstruction.

LIFTING OF TEMPORARY PROTECTION

Temporary Protection Following the Peace Agreement

The document presented to the HIWG meeting of January 16, 1996, identified certain benchmarks which will play a critical role in the lifting of temporary protection. Pending the fulfillment of those benchmarks,

UNHCR is facilitating spontaneous repatriation and is planning for the start of the UNHCR-organized voluntary repatriation operation. Current conditions within Bosnia and Herzegovina are such that returns must, at this initial stage, be voluntary. The manner in which repatriation takes place, and its success and durability, will be important indicators of progress towards the benchmarks.

The fulfillment of the benchmarks will confirm that there is no longer a presumption that persons from Bosnia and Herzegovina require international protection. The lifting of temporary protection should be followed by action to determine and implement a solution for every Bosnian refugee who has sought protection from persecution and human rights abuses as well as from the more general effects of the conflict, including those cases for whom repatriation is not possible. This process will take into account individual circumstances and should, ideally, parallel progress towards shelter, rehabilitation, and reconstruction. In light of the preceding considerations and until the benchmarks have been fulfilled, the standard of treatment accorded to beneficiaries of temporary protection will need to be maintained.

The transition from temporary protection to a durable solution has already taken place for many of the refugees from Bosnia and Herzegovina. UNHCR has noted with appreciation that a great many Bosnians who were initially allowed to remain under temporary protection arrangements were subsequently provided with a more durable status.

Voluntary Repatriation and Temporary Protection

UNHCR has long been charged with pursuing the promotion of voluntary repatriation for all or part of a group when the office deems that the prevailing circumstances are appropriate. Organized promotion of voluntary repatriation is often preceded by the facilitation of spontaneous return; in other words, providing support, as appropriate, to refugees who return voluntarily under conditions which are not yet conducive to organized repatriation. Core elements of the promotion of voluntary repatriation include: establishment, and the subsequent monitoring, of guarantees pertaining to the refugees' repatriation; the ability of UNHCR to have direct and unhindered access to returnees; voluntariness of return; and the choice of location.

UNHCR wishes also to draw attention to citizenship issues, as any refugees who have lost or are unable to establish their nationality might be impeded from repatriating. Within UNHCR's mandate under the 1961 Convention on the Reduction of Statelessness, and with regard to the problem of statelessness generally, UNHCR will monitor citizenship aspects particularly as relevant to repatriation to Bosnia and Herzegovina and to other countries in the neighboring region.

Both facilitation of spontaneous repatriation and the organized promotion of voluntary repatriation can take place in advance of the lifting of temporary protection, in view of their voluntary nature. Following the lifting of temporary protection, persons who do not require international protection may be returned, unless their status in the host country has been regularized. The identification of continued international protection needs has been addressed in Annex II of the document presented by UNHCR to the January 16, 1996, HIWG Meeting, "Temporary Protection Following the General Framework Agreement for Peace in Bosnia and Herzegovina."

Benchmarks for the Lifting of Temporary Protection

The three benchmarks identified as conditions precedent to the lifting of temporary protection for Bosnian refugees are the implementation of the military provisions of the Peace Agreement; the proclamation of an amnesty for crimes other than serious violations of international humanitarian law as defined in the Statute of the International Tribunal for the former Yugoslavia and other than common crimes unrelated to the conflict; and the establishment and functioning of mechanisms for the protection of human rights. The attainment of these benchmarks will indicate, with reference to objective factors, that it is safe for most refugees to return and that such returns have good prospects of being lasting. The parties have agreed, as part of the Peace Agreement, to adhere to recognized principles of international law and, in particular, have recognized the importance of the observance of human rights and the protection of refugees and displaced persons. UNHCR's observations regarding progress on the benchmarks are as follows:

Implementation of the Military Provisions of the Peace Agreement (Annex 1-A). While there are certain delays in the implementation of some aspects, notably concerning the release of detainees and in respect to missing persons, overall implementation continues according to schedule. UNHCR remains in close contact with the NATO-led Implmentation Force (IFOR), which is responsible for ascertaining and assessing compliance.

Amnesty. The parties to the Peace Agreement have agreed to grant amnesties to returning refugees and displaced persons for crimes related to the armed conflict, "other than a serious violation of international humanitarian law as defined in the Statute of the International Tribunal for the former Yugoslavia." According to Article VI, Annex 7, charges for crimes shall in no case be imposed for political or other inappropriate reasons or to circumvent the application of the amnesty. In an important step, the Bosnian Parliament agreed to an amnesty law on February 12, 1996. The law will enter into force when published in the official gazette. At the time of writing, there was no information regarding the enactment of analogous provisions in the "Republika Srpska." Together with the entities, UNHCR will examine the implementation of amnesties throughout the territory of Bosnia and Herzegovina.

Security and Human Rights: Functioning of Mechanisms of Human Rights Protection. The safety of returnees depends, above all, on the security of the person and the principle of nondiscrimination. Returnee protection is not intended to privilege the returning refugees or to elevate their standard above that of the resident population. Returnees must, however, enjoy adequate safety, and they should not be targeted for harassment, intimidation, punishment, violence, or denial of fair access to public institutions or services, or discriminated against in the enjoyment of any basic rights. In this connection, the parties have agreed, as part of the Peace Agreement, to adopt a number of confidence-building measures "to prevent activities within their territories which would hinder or impede the safe and voluntary return of refugees and displaced persons." Successful returnee monitoring will itself depend on functioning human rights mechanisms. UNHCR has welcomed the appointment as Ombudsperson of Ambassador G. Haller, who is expected to assume her functions effective early March. The High Representative has set up a Task Force on Human Rights and has also established a Human Rights Evaluation Unit in Sarajevo to monitor progress. UNHCR is represented on both bodies. UNHCR emphasizes the importance of establishing the additional human rights mechanisms as soon as possible and regrets the delays in the deployment of the International Police Task Force.

The planned elections in Bosnia and Herzegovina, while not a benchmark for return, are obviously of direct relevance to it, through the establishment of democratic political institutions. The fulfillment of commitments associated with free and fair elections will demonstrate progress towards democratic processes and respect for human rights. In this connection, it may be noted that the reference in the Peace Agreement to voting by absentee ballot as an indication of intention to return is an expression of a political commitment and not a legal obligation. The Organization for Security and Cooperation in Europe (OSCE) recognizes the desirability for all citizens to participate in the election and acknowledges that the number of absentee ballots is likely to be high.

Conclusion

Making repatriation possible depends on confidence building, which is necessarily a gradual process, especially following civil conflict. UNHCR will continue to place considerable emphasis on its responsibility for monitoring the fulfillment of guarantees in respect to returnees, and for providing comprehensive information for the benefit of refugees and host countries. UNHCR is committed to promoting the voluntary repatriation of as many refugees as possible, to the lifting of temporary protection through close collaboration with host countries and the country of origin, and through continued multilateral consultations. Conditions in the country of origin including absorption capacity, will determine the safety and viability of repatriation. In due course, residual issues will need to be addressed jointly, as has been done with considerable success in major repatriation operations elsewhere in the world.

PLAN OF OPERATIONS

Basic Prerequisites for Implementation of the Plan

This plan has been elaborated in close consultation with the parties to Annex 7, especially with the Ministry for Refugees and the Diaspora of the Republic of Bosnia and Herzegovina, the Ministry for Social Welfare, Displaced Persons and Refugees of the Federation of Bosnia and Herzegovina, and the Ministry for Refugees and Displaced Persons of the "Republika Srpska." UNHCR will implement this plan within the framework of the principles laid down in Annex 7, entitled the "Agreement on Refugees and Displaced Persons," both through direct implementation and with the assistance of various operational partners, whether governmental, intergovernmental, or nongovernmental. To do so, UNHCR requires the continued invaluable support of the European Community Humanitarian Office (ECHO) and the European Commission, other generous donors, as well as its many important governmental, intergovernmental, and nongovernmental partners, whose concerted efforts have helped to save countless lives throughout the conflict.

At the very outset, it must be recognized that just as humanitarian action alone could not bring an end to the conflict, neither can implementation of this plan of operations in itself undo the damage of the war. This plan simply cannot be implemented unless rehabilitation and reconstruction efforts effectively go hand in hand with the return and repatriation process. The International Management Group (IMG) can play a significant role in bridging the gap between the modest, immediate shelter assistance provided within the framework of this plan and more ambitious rehabilitation and reconstruction efforts.

The success of the plan ultimately depends on the following factors, many of which are beyond UNHCR's control:

1. the sustained commitment of the parties, interested states and organizations to full implementation of all provisions of the Peace Agreement, including provisions relating to freedom of movement and choice of residence, human rights observance, elections and amnesties, as well as to a multilateral approach to return and rehabilitation;

2. speedy and coordinated responses by the international community to the needs of returning displaced persons and refugees inserted in a long-term rehabilitation perspective, in order to make a significant contribution to building confidence in the peace process and thereby building momentum for voluntary return;

3. in view of the extent of destruction of housing, which has been total in many areas of Bosnia and Herzegovina, an urgent response to the need for accommodation – both to eliminate gradually collective-center and host-family arrangements and to rapidly restore a measure of normalcy and stability to lives shattered by years of conflict;

4. the provision of timely and detailed statistical information by countries providing temporary protection, or other forms of protection to Bosnians, to assist and further refine planning, particularly owing to the long-recognized complexities of the situation in Bosnia and Herzegovina; and

5. the provision of timely and detailed information to prospective returnees and returning displaced persons on the situation prevailing in their former home areas or desired area of return or relocation, security and material conditions such as the availability of housing and other basic services.

Another formidable constraint should also be highlighted. As elsewhere in the world, landmines have emerged as a pervasive problem in many parts of Bosnia. According to a recent World Bank report, they are known to be present in particular around Sarajevo, Banja Luka, Zenica, Vitez, Mostar, Srebrenica, Tuzla, Medugorje, Bihac, Zepa, Gorni Vakuf and Gorazde, as well as in innumerable other locations. The NATO-led Implementation Force (IFOR), in cooperation with the parties, has begun to assess the extent of this problem, particularly along former front-line areas, and has begun to demine. Eradication of the problem, however, will take many years and requires a long-term program. While many of the war-affected and displaced persons may have had the opportunity to familiarize themselves with the locations of these risks, refugees repatriating from farther afield will need to be made aware of the risks and need to receive information on mine awareness. **Recommendation 1: The international community should encourage the parties and experienced agencies to expand demining activities within Bosnia and Herzegovina, particularly in areas where threats to life and safety could diminish the momentum of return.** A related concern is the presence of vicious boobytraps in damaged and deserted houses and other buildings. The extent of this problem is yet unknown.

Finally, it must be recognized that the problems of refugees and displaced persons affect not only Bosnia and Herzegovina, but also the Federal Republic of Yugoslavia, the former Yugoslav Republic of Macedonia, Croatia, and Slovenia. A regional and even-handed approach to assistance will continue to be necessary.

Planning Assumptions

In view of the many statistical and related planning assumptions which can only be built up over time, this plan of operations is necessarily limited in scope and is designed to meet the immediate and short-term needs of returning displaced persons and returnees. This limitation is inherent in the level of financing likely to be made available to carry out the operation.

Planning Figures. According to the 1991 census, 4.3 million people were living in Bosnia and Herzegovina at that time. It is currently estimated that there are about 3 million people now living in Bosnia and Herzegovina. The conflict has rendered about 80 percent of the population – some 2.4 million people – dependent, at least in part, on international assistance. Preliminary surveys suggest that there are well over 2 million Bosnian refugees and internally displaced (*i.e.,* half of the country's total population) scattered across a large number of locations in Bosnia and Herzegovina as well as in some 25 host states.

Planning for repatriation is a process which is initially based on working assumptions, until verifiable statistical data become available. Whereas the initial assumption was that up to 500,000 displaced persons would return and 370,000 refugees would repatriate (170,000 from the immediate region and 200,000 from other countries) during 1996, it is clear today that these are maximum figures contingent on security, funding, immediate large-scale re-construction and demining keeping pace with the actual rhythm of return and repatriation. This planning figure will be revised over time, not only as a function of the actual momentum of movements, but also of concrete information to be provided by asylum countries, as well as through surveys and predeparture registration.

It is assumed that the majority of those returning or repatriating will do so between April and November. At the time of writing, some 12,000 to 13,000 Bosnian Serb displaced persons had returned to the area known as the "anvil" (Mrkonic Grad, Sipovo, and parts of Kluj). Some 10,000 Bosnian Muslims repatriated from Croatia to Velika Kladusa in Bosnia and Herzegovina. It will be difficult to generate firm figures on spontaneous return and repatriation movements until an accurate and verifiable data-collection system at the municipal level is effectively set in place.

Priority Movements. The plan of operations envisages two major groups: inter-nally displaced persons and refugees.

Internally displaced persons. During 1996, priority will be placed on identifying durable solutions for persons accommodated in difficult living conditions in collective centers and to close the highest possible number of them. To do so, municipal authorities, working closely with UNHCR, are reviewing a number of options, including the temporary use of vacant housing to be rehabilitated for this purpose; accommodation of the displaced with friends or relatives; and initiatives for their local integration in the entity within which they are presently located. The return or relocation of displaced persons in majority ethnic groups to majority areas is conditioned upon the availability of housing and sufficient infrastructure. The return of minority groups to majority areas is even more complex. The extent of the problem of internally displaced who lack adequate, long-term shelter will clearly require the construction of new housing. It has been estimated that more than 60 percent of all housing units have sustained some damage, while some 18 percent have been completely destroyed. Such construction obviously goes beyond the mandate and capacity of UNHCR.

The relocation of displaced persons, both spontaneously and as part of assisted movements, has illustrated the daunting challenge to be met. On November 2, 1995, Bosnian President Izetbegovic and Federation President Zubak signed an agreement in Dayton for the return of 600 families to Travnik, Jajce, Stolac, and Bugojno. The agreement envisaged the return of 100 displaced Bosnian Croat families to Muslim-controlled Travnik; 200 Muslim families to Croat-controlled Jajce; 100 Muslim families to Croat-controlled Stolac; and 200 Croat families to Muslim-controlled Bugojno. UNHCR has been actively involved in the negotiations on the implementation and has agreed to assist with transport, as well as with the provision of basic materials for small-scale repairs and food for up to six months, subject to UNHCR confirming that the movements are voluntary.

These "pilot projects" for the return of the displaced have proved to be highly labor-intensive and have highlighted the complexity of return movements. They have also demonstrated that return of the displaced will be heavily conditioned by the availability of housing and the scrupulous observance of and commitment to the basic principles of Annex 7 by individual municipalities.

At the time of writing, the planned return of 100 Bosnian Croat families to Muslim-controlled Travnik had been almost completed. Several families have visited Travnik and are planning to return when the weather is milder and the school year has ended. Many have returned to homes requiring minor repairs, which they are in the process of carrying out with UNHCR assistance. Others, whose homes require more extensive repairs, are staying with friends or relatives until their homes are made more liveable. Many have reported their satisfaction with return and have urged other Bosnian Croats to do the same.

UNHCR has also been able to confirm substantial progress in return to Croat-controlled Jajce. Out of the planned 200, 83 families had returned at the time of writing. Twelve others have returned and are staying with neighbors while waiting for displaced Croats, temporarily occupying their houses, to depart. Some 80 persons have been visiting Jajce to check on their houses or do repair work daily on them and are planning to return in the near future.

After six weeks of intensive negotiations, facilitated by UNHCR, the Office of the High Representative, and representatives of Germany and the United States of America, 100 houses were agreed upon to which Bosnian Muslim families from Stolac, currently displaced in East Mostar, could return. A signing ceremony held on February 4, 1996, formalized the agreement. At the time of writing, not one family had returned. All of the houses require substantial reconstruction or repairs. UNHCR will supply basic repair kits and domestic items such as blankets, stoves, kitchen sets, beds, etc. The IMG will coordinate more extensive reconstruction. In addition to the need for reconstruction, most of the Bosnian Muslims cite lack of adequate security guarantees as another obstacle to return.

Finally, there has been no progress on returns to Bugojno, whose local authorities condition the arrival of Bosnian Croats on the departure of displaced persons presently there to other locations, notably to Jajce.

Refugees. The suggested phases for planned movements from neighboring and other host countries are the following. First, movements of refugees to their own home areas where they constitute the majority today. These would, in principle, be the easiest movements to carry out provided that adequate accommodation is available or can rapidly be made available and that absorption capacity is quickly improved. Second, the repatriation of refugees who do not wish to return to their former home areas, where they would now be in the minority, and who wish to relocate to new areas within the entity in which they would constitute the majority. The third phase, which would be the most difficult one, is the repatriation of refugees to their areas of origin where the ethnic group of the returnees now constitutes the minority. For the implementation of these phases, it is imperative to have adequate information on the refugees, their places of origin, ethnic origin, and wishes regarding return.

Revised Assumptions. It is believed that the majority of movements, particularly initial spontaneous movements, will take place in private vehicles or through readily available public overland transport (buses and trains). Where other modalities are required for organized movement (by air, road, or rail), the International Organization for Migration (IOM) will facilitate them, in cooperation with UNHCR, as an integral part of phased repatriation movements.

In principle, the decision of a refugee to repatriate voluntarily, either spontaneously or with UNHCR assistance, will be taken as a function of the specific situation of the individual or family (end of school term, availability of housing, ability to return to home areas or areas close to them, employment or business opportunities, etc.).

Time Frame

For the purpose of this plan of operations, the tentative time frame for the return of the displaced and repatriation of refugees is two years from the signing of the Peace Agreement.

Information and Monitoring Relating to Return and Repatriation

Recognizing the importance of clearly delineating roles and responsibilities with respect to civil activities relevant to returnees, in November 1995, UNHCR submitted a proposal to donors which outlined the monitoring and information activities to be undertaken by the Office. The proposal included the minimum resources necessary to ensure that repatriation and return takes place in conditions of safety and dignity. UNHCR activities encompass three main areas: monitoring and reporting on trends and developments affecting returnees; promoting the equal treatment of re-turnees; and intervening with national or local authorities when the return or reintegration process may be threatened. A crucial component of UNHCR's repatriation monitoring activities which was identified is the gathering and dissemination of information on conditions of return. At the end of February 1996, eight Information and Training Officers had been deployed throughout its offices in Bosnia and Herzegovina.

Participants at the January 16, 1996, HIWG meeting recognized that an important aspect of promoting durable solutions is equal access for all refugees and internally displaced persons to accurate and up-to-date information on conditions in the intended areas of return or relocation. Article I, paragraph 4 of Annex 7 of the Peace Agreement provides that the parties "shall facilitate the flow of information necessary for refugees and displaced persons to make informed judgements about local conditions for return." UNHCR is committed to ensuring that refugees and displaced persons have equal access to objective and up-to-date information on conditions in their intended areas of return or relocation. To do so, the Office, in cooperation with the parties, has already begun to produce and disseminate reports which include information on security and pertinent legal developments.

These Repatriation Information Reports (RIRs) cover the following topics: political and security conditions, housing, registration procedures, routes and means of transportation, documents required, pertinent legal developments, infrastructure, public utilities, public services (such as hospitals and schools), economic activity, as well as available UNHCR and other assistance programs. The principal duties of the Information and Training Officers are to: 1) using a standard reporting template, collect, analyze, and process information on conditions in Bosnia and Herzegovina; 2) prepare and update, on a regular basis, the RIRs, based upon the cumulative field monitoring assessments of the respective field office teams; 3) monitor closely legislative developments and local practices pertaining to returnees with a view to continuous update of the RIRs; and 4) facilitate interagency repatriation information exchange.

UNHCR is seeking the active support of host governments and nongovernmental organizations (NGOs) operating in asylum countries for translation of the reports. UNHCR has completed the first six reports, and the objective is to complete reports on well over 50 percent of all municipalities in Bosnia and Herzegovina by the end of June. A central unit in Sarajevo collates and edits field reports and forwards them to Geneva and elsewhere for dissemination. UNHCR will make the RIRs available through the respective authorities in Bosnia and Herzegovina and to governments and NGOs in refugee-hosting countries for further dissemination to individual refugees. Arrangements to disseminate return-and repatriation-related information through the media (radio) in Bosnia and Herzegovina and major refugee-hosting countries are being explored, as is the possibility of producing short video tapes on the situation prevailing in major returnee areas. The RIRs are transferred to UNHCR's Branch and Regional Offices in host countries via electronic mail. Newly posted Liaison Officers stationed within UNHCR Branch and Regional Offices in Western Europe will facilitate effective distribution of the reports to governments, NGOs, and other interested parties.

UNHCR is also exploring the possibilities of posting the RIRs on its World Wide Web Internet page. Among other possibilities which states may wish to explore, bearing in mind existing priorities and funding constraints, is the establishment of a toll-free number which prospective returnees could call to obtain up-to-date information in the local language. Such an arrangement could also assist to generate information to facilitate the placing process, since information could be gathered anonymously on issues such as the intention to return, the timeframe, and any incentives which could influence the decision to return or repatriate voluntarily.

Furthermore, information campaigns may be organized in asylum countries, through which essential information on the parameters of the return program (beneficiary eligibility criteria, entitlements and logistics, host authority support of the program, registration procedures, etc.) could be disseminated. **Recommendation 2: It is suggested that information campaigns be organized by host-country governments and/or NGOs with the support of UNHCR.**

Just as prospective returning displaced and returnees require objective, accurate and up-to-date information on the situation prevailing in their places of return or relocation, so do governments and policymakers. Beyond the RIRs described above, UNHCR remains ready to facilitate field visits for government officials for a first-hand assessment of the situation. UNHCR will also readily provide detailed briefings in capitals and in intergovernmental fora. Briefing and/or strategic planning missions are scheduled to occur, with UNHCR assistance, before the March 8, 1996, meeting in Oslo, and thereafter, for officials of the Federal and a number of Länder Ministries of the Interior of Germany and other interested states, as well as of ECHO and the European Commission.

To facilitate liaison in capitals hosting multilateral institutions formally charged with implementing different aspects of the Peace Agreement or hosting UNHCR offices with regional or national coverage in areas/countries with large numbers of Bosnians, by mid-January 1996 UNHCR temporarily deployed six Liaison Officers in the following locations: Bonn, Brussels, Geneva (2), Stockholm, and Vienna. The two Liaison Officers posted in Geneva will help to facilitate the timely flow of information among Field Offices, particularly those in major host countries, and also to Permanent Liaisons in Geneva and major intergovernmental fora. This arrangement is being reviewed, with a view to providing cost-effective support to implementation of the plan of operations and limiting related administrative expenditure.

UNHCR, recognizing the importance of close cooperation with IFOR, has created five Liaison Officer posts with the IFOR Headquarters, with the ACE Rapid Reaction Corps (ARRC) Headquarters at Ilidza in Sarajevo, and with each of the three IFOR Multi-National Division Headquarters. Close cooperation with IFOR on security issues will continue to be a prerequisite for organized movements within Bosnia and Herzegovina and for repatriation from neighboring and other host countries.

To reinforce the public-information dimension of the operation, and to improve coverage on the evolution of events on the ground, by the end of February 1996 three new Public Information Officers had been deployed in the following locations: Banja Luka, Mostar, and Tuzla. Working under the coordination of the Special Envoy, these officers will augment UNHCR's ability to generate information suitable for the mass media, both local and international, on the evolution of the operation and implementation of Annex 7. They will also play an important role in mass information campaigns within Bosnia and Herzegovina.

Procedural Aspects of Voluntary Repatriation

Registration of Applications for Repatriation in Host Countries. Registration procedures and focal points will vary host country by host country, as a function of already established governmental administrative structures. **Recommendation 3: UNHCR recommends, particularly in countries with large numbers of Bosnians, the establishment of national/regional coordinating bodies responsible for voluntary repatriation.** UNHCR will keep these organizations/authorities informed on developments in Bosnia and Herzegovina, particularly through its Repatriation Information Reports.

UNHCR has requested IOM to assist in the operational and logistical aspects of repatriation in host countries outside the former Yugoslavia. Further, in discussions with certain host governments, UNHCR may, in a limited number of countries, be responsible for these tasks. It is anticipated that a majority of Bosnians returning from host countries will travel by land and will organize their own travel, at least in the initial spontaneous movements in the spring and summer of 1996. For those who are not in a position to arrange for their own travel, transport will be provided. This will be the responsibility of the government of the host country in question, in cooperation with IOM. IOM may, as far as contributions allow, also offer assistance through the resources of its General Return Fund. Detailed coordination arrangements between UNHCR, IOM, and respective governments of host countries are being elaborated and are the subject of an agreement between UNHCR and IOM. UNHCR will support IOM's activities by providing the latter with information regarding any requirements which may be established concerning individual confirmation by the government of Bosnia and Herzegovina of the possibility to return, as well as on required identification and travel documents, transit visas, as well as customs or other requirements.

In light of the importance of channeling information regarding the numbers and locations of Bosnian nationals living abroad to the Provisional Electoral Commission, UNHCR or the relevant governmental authority competent for the registration of Bosnians will, to the extent possible, keep the commission informed of repatriation movements. **Recommendation 4: States are encouraged to provide to the commission the information at their disposal or which may be gathered.** UNHCR is cooperating actively with the Organization on Security and Cooperation in Europe (OSCE) with respect to the election-related role conferred upon OSCE in the Peace Agreement.

Clearance Procedures. The government of Bosnia and Herzegovina has, in view of the widespread destruction of houses and the need to use vacant housing for accommodation of displaced persons, informed UNHCR that the local authority in the municipality of destination will have to confirm the availability of accommodation prior to assisted repatriation movement. UNHCR agrees with the authorities of Bosnia and Herzegovina that such a procedure of clearance, based on absorption capacity, is fully within the principle of phased return as expressed in Annex 7 of the Peace Agreement, at least until reconstruction is well under way. It is, however, of utmost importance that such a procedure does not work to delay unnecessarily, owing to administrative bottlenecks, the departure of candidates for organized repatriation. This is an issue which will be followed closely by UNHCR.

Travel Documents. It is expected that refugees will travel with a national passport. There will be a number of situations, however, where this is not possible, for different practical reasons, and where other travel documents (*e.g.*, host country documents or International Committee of the Red Cross travel documents) will be used. **Recommendation 5: UNHCR would recommend that host states consider issuing to returnees a document (which could be standardized in agreement among host states and the government of Bosnia and Herzegovina) which would assist them in registration at the municipal level upon return and entitle them to a number of benefits during travel (*e.g.*, exemption from highway tolls and facilitation of border crossings).** Such a document would be of particular importance for those repatriating spontaneously, assuming that all Bosnians in host countries can be informed effectively of its availability.

Transit Arrangements. Practically all European countries have imposed visa requirements on Bosnian nationals. It should be recognized that these will constitute an impediment for spontaneous and organized repatriation movements. A number of consultations are currently taking place among "transit countries" regarding facilities for repatriation movements. UNHCR welcomes the offer of Hungary to host a consultation in Budapest on the facilitation of voluntary repatriation movements. **Recommendation 6: UNHCR would recommend that states include the Office in their consultations and rapidly seek to identify appropriate solutions to facilitate transit. Recommendation 7: UNHCR recommends that these include a waiver or abolition of transit visas and fees, as well as customs formalities and related levies.** UNHCR wishes to commend those governments who are already taking practical initiatives to facilitate transit through, *inter alia*, the waiver of highway toll fees.

Border Registration. The government of Bosnia and Herzegovina has indicated that there will be no requirement of registration at the border for repatriating refugees. Registration will take place at the municipal level following arrival.

Right of Reentry to Asylum Countries. At the HIWG meeting of January 16, 1996, several countries announced their intention to enable refugees to retain a right of reentry following visits to areas of potential return in Bosnia and Herzegovina. **Recommendation 8: UNHCR would encourage other states to adopt similar measures as a means to facilitate as well as promote voluntary repatriation.**

Organized Visits. UNHCR believes that "look-and-see" visits could usefully be organized as a means of facilitating informed decisionmaking. Caution must be exercised, however, in view of the complexities of the situation on the ground. UNHCR will determine when, and under which circumstances and conditions, it wishes to be associated with or facilitate such visits.

Assistance

Prior to Departure and During Movement. Considerations for assistance prior to departure and during movement of repatriating displaced refugees will encompass provision for travel and pocket finances, and the return of critical skills and talent.

Travel and pocket money. All repatriates who wish to benefit from international transport assistance to be organized by IOM at the request of UNHCR may apply to the nearest IOM "Contact Point," which may be a designated government office or NGO. IOM structures and return programs already in place (*e.g.*, the REAG program in Germany or analogous programs in Belgium and the Netherlands) will be used as far as possible in the implementation of this plan of operations.

Refugees repatriating from abroad should not be made a privileged group in their local communities through substantial individual assistance from their asylum or host country. On the other hand, lack of individual financial means should in no way constitute an impediment to return. The major criterion for assistance in this phase should therefore be that it facilitates return, without creating undesirable imbalances at the destination. In addition, any movement of persons between host countries which might be driven by differing levels of predeparture assistance provided by host countries should be avoided. In principle, no cash allowances should be provided, with the exception of limited pocket money. **Recommendation 9: UNHCR would recommend that all states hosting Bosnian refugees and displaced persons agree upon comparatively uniform levels of predeparture assistance (taking into consideration relevant pre-agreed variables such as travel distance).**

Pending further discussions between UNHCR, the government of Bosnia and Herzegovina, and IOM, UNHCR/IOM assistance will be limited to transport from countries outside the immediate region. In addition to transportation, assistance for organized voluntary repatriation will cover a limited amount for pocket money for travel and transit assistance, if required. **Recommendation 10: UNHCR would strongly urge states to provide installation grants or similar incentives which are linked to community-based programs within Bosnia and Herzegovina within the country of asylum. UNHCR is prepared to develop a proposal for a common fund for this purpose.**

Detailed coordination arrangements between UNHCR, IOM, and respective governments of host countries will be elaborated in the coming weeks and will be the subject of an agreement between UNHCR and IOM. It has already been agreed that IOM will be responsible for all operational and logistical aspects of organized international repatriation movements, within the limits described above, including receiving applications from prospective beneficiaries and maintaining a database of applications. UNHCR will support IOM's activities by providing the latter with information regarding any requirements which may be established concerning individual confirmation by the government of Bosnia and Herzegovina, as well as on required identification and travel documents, transit visas, and customs or other requirements. Detailed procedures on the organization of travel (by land or air) will be established. Likewise, policies on luggage restrictions, no-shows, etc., will soon be established. Any response to subsequent travel needs (*i.e.*, local onward travel beyond the designated arrival points to the final destination) will be established in consultation between UNHCR, IOM, and the authorities in Bosnia and Herzegovina.

Return of talent. Any return of qualified nationals program should ideally target persons with skills critical for the reconstruction of the country, particularly in view of the severely destroyed housing stock, while at the same time encourage the return of professionals with skills critical to longer-term rehabilitation and reconstruction.

Following Arrival. All returnees, both those arriving spontaneously or in organized movements, are requested to contact the municipal authorities immediately upon arrival with a dual purpose in mind: for registration and for entitlement to any local/UNHCR registration assistance, based on an assessment of actual need. Transit centers will be established within Bosnia and Herzegovina to accommodate returnees who cannot travel back to their home areas within a one-day period. Stays in these centers will be of minimal duration, prior to onward travel.

Installation. The basic focus of returnee assistance should be the community in which returnees will attempt to (re-) integrate This community-based approach will afford the best guarantee of evenhanded assistance to all categories of the needy, war-affected local population. **Recommendation 11: UNHCR would urge the international community, particularly hosting states, to establish a fund for community support, which would provide the Bosnian authorities with funds needed rapidly to improve absorption capacity in major areas of return and repatriation, while longer-term rehabilitation and reconstruction programs get off the ground.** The fund, to make rapid investments at the municipal level, could help to meet immediate needs for the repair and rehabilitation of community infrastructure and to provide short-term soft loans for microenterprises, housing rehabilitation, and agricultural rehabilitation and, possibly, education. Such a mechanism would ensure that all the war-affected are put on an equal footing with repatriating refugees and that return and repatriation work to benefit the entire community.

Other forms of assistance. During the past years, UNHCR and its many partners have implemented a humanitarian assistance program on behalf of refugees, internally displaced, and war affected individuals in Bosnia and Herzegovina. This program will continue, simultaneously with the implementation of the return and repatriation operation, but will be gradually phased down over time. In view of the ongoing implementation of a humanitarian relief operation and the expected return or relocation of displaced persons and repatriation of refugees from abroad, a temporary increase in the number of beneficiaries of food aid and relief items distribution may be foreseen and planned for. For additional details, please refer to the Consolidated Inter-Agency Appeal. Among elements designed to support the Peace Agreement, pending investments in longer-term rehabilitation and reconstruction, are those contained in the shelter sector.

UNHCR TRUST FUND FOR SHELTER MATERIALS IN BOSNIA AND HERZEGOVINA. The World Bank estimates that, of the housing available before 1991, some 60 percent were houses and some 40 percent were apartments. Between 30 percent and 40 percent of homes and apartments were not owned by the occupants themselves, but by factories, the army, state, and para-statal agencies and instrumentalities. This situation will raise thorny questions to be resolved within the framework of the Commission on Displaced Persons and Refugees envisaged in the Peace Agreement. The rehabilitation of the country's housing stock will require a long-term program and enormous financial resources, far beyond UNHCR's mandate, means, and capacity. Yet it is essential to provide immediate support to the displaced and returnees, to enable them to undertake at least the most urgent repairs to their accommodation. Other immediate construction and repair, as well as a linkage with a sustained, longer-term program for the rehabilitation of the country's housing stock, to be undertaken by other institutions, is a priority to which the IMG can make a significant contribution.

The UNHCR appeal entitled "Trust Fund for Shelter Materials in Bosnia and Herzegovina," issued on February 6, 1996, aims at expanding UNHCR's established shelter material support program to include repair of housing, with a view to meeting urgent needs. Of the total amount requested for the housing sector, the trust fund amounts to $30 million and has two basic components: procurement and distribution of basic shelter materials throughout Bosnia and Herzegovina ($25 million) and a glazing project for Sarajevo ($5 million). The trust fund has been incorporated within UNHCR's component of the Consolidated Inter-Agency Appeal. An agreement relating to implementation of the first subcomponent of the trust fund was signed by UNHCR on February 8, 1996, in Sarajevo. UNHCR will also cooperate closely with the IMG regarding the subcomponent.

Based on observation in the field, damage to houses and apartments may be classified in the following categories:

1) "Serious structural damage," meaning damage which undermines the integrity of the structure itself. Examples are serious damage to roofs or to the basic structure of the dwellings.

2) "Combination of structural and nonstructural damage," meaning damage both to the integrity of the structure as well as to non-structural elements such as plumbing, windows, electricity, etc.

3) "Nonstructural damage," meaning damage which does not affect the soundness of the structure (plumbing, windows, door-frames, sashes, etc.).

The shelter material component will support large-scale, local production and distribution of a few selected shelter materials throughout Bosnia and Herzegovina, for immediate and urgent self-help home repairs for persons in need who are returning or repatriating in the first six to nine months of 1996. Most of the materials (roof tiles – both clay and concrete – concrete blocks/bricks, cement, structural timber, lime) will be produced locally, to the extent possible, thereby enhancing employment opportunities and generating new income at the local level. Following initial procurement of the required materials, the identification of beneficiaries will be the responsibility of local authorities but will be carried out in close consultation with respective UNHCR offices and with the support of implementing partners. Both operational partners and UNHCR offices in Bosnia and Herzegovina will assist the authorities at the municipal level in monitoring implementation of the project.

Assistance will be targeted initially to internally displaced persons, as well as to needy spontaneous returnees, to enhance interethnic stability and relieve overcrowded conditions in public buildings which are being used for collective accommodation. Projects will be identified in both entities of the Republic and the widest possible geographical distribution will be considered. In order to begin housing rehabilitation quickly, procurement of construction materials is already underway. Implementation procedures within the territory of the "Republika Srpska" will follow the same parameters.

The basic assumption underlying this subcomponent is that, in addition to the materials provided through the project, beneficiaries will also purchase or secure other materials with their own resources or will receive support from other agencies/funding sources. On the basis of actual need, beneficiaries would be given sufficient materials to render habitable from 30 to 40 square meters of space (benefiting an average of five persons per family) while longer-term housing support is devised by financial institutions such as the World Bank. The limited amount of resources available makes it necessary to view this subcomponent as a pilot project, which can later be linked to and augmented by other partners.

The second component, the Sarajevo Glazing Project, will support the installation of glass in windows which were damaged during the war. The project will be implemented in all areas of the Sarajevo area which, under the terms of the Peace Agreement, will revert to Federation control. This includes the following eleven municipalities Centar, Grbavica, Hadjici, Ilidza, Ilijas, Nedzarici, Novi Grad, Novo Sarajevo, Rajlovac, Stari Grad, and Vogosca. The subproject will target 50,000 of the worst-affected families (some 250,000 people), *i.e.*, over 70 percent of those in need of assistance. In addition, a limited number of public buildings and social service institutions in each municipality will benefit from this project.

DOMESTIC ITEMS. Needy returning displaced and returnees will benefit from a program for the supply of a limited number of household items. Returnees will be screened by municipal authorities and, according to needs, supplied with a variety of items designed to ease their reinstallation. These items include beds and mattresses, stoves and kitchen sets, clothing, footwear, and soap. UNHCR has already initiated local procurement procedures for some of these items. In an effort to stimulate the local economy, local procurement will have priority over international purchases. UNHCR has identified small-scale and medium-scale manufacturers to produce all items required inside Bosnia and Herzegovina. In view of the current state of devastation of much of the country's manufacturing infrastructure, this program will initially be implemented through, *inter alia*, the provision of up-front cash, raw materials and machinery, in combination with appropriate bidding and monitoring procedures.

SUPPORT TO LOCAL-LEVEL INITIATIVES. Support to meet needs at the community level, begun in previous years, will be expanded and adapted to the new, post-conflict environment. UNHCR Field Offices will continue to fund local initiatives with immediate impact in improving services or local absorption capacity. In cooperation with local authorities and communities, UNHCR Field Offices will identify projects helping to improve local production, encourage capital investment, promote training and local capacity-building, and meet immediate community needs. Initiatives which will continue to be supported are basic, low-investment repairs to school or other community buildings, in-kind donations of fuel to jump-start local transport – particularly to areas long isolated during the conflict – support to the start-up of local bakeries, small income-generation for vulnerable families, the start-up of family and community vegetable and other gardening projects. Decisions on which projects to finance will be delegated to UNHCR field-level offices. Support to initiatives by local NGOs will intensify.

PILOT PROJECTS FOR THE RETURN OF DISPLACED PERSONS. In light of the experience gathered in implementing the pilot projects for return to Jajce, Travnik, Stolac, and Bugojno, other similar projects will be implemented. Given the shifts in populations produced by the war, it is essential that any person considering return has the option of choosing voluntarily his or her place of destination of return. This may be the place of origin or any other place inside Bosnia and Herzegovina. An important confidence-building measure in this regard will be the full implementation of the above-mentioned pilot projects for the return of displaced persons.

CAPACITY-BUILDING ACTIVITIES. With the further consolidation of peace and stability in the country, it is essential that the responsibility for response to humanitarian problems in Bosnia and Herzegovina, which during the past years has been assumed by the international community, be gradually transferred to local structures. Therefore, UNHCR will strengthen the capacity of central, cantonal, and municipal local authorities, as well as of nongovernmental organizations to respond to the needs of their own population through the provision of technical advice, appropriate training, and general promotion of their greater involvement in the planning and implementation of assistance activities. These activities will include support to the creation of new local NGOs and general institution-building activities

SOCIAL SERVICES. The conflict has created tens of thousands of persons who are suffering the mental and physical hardship of upheaval, loss of family members and homes, and post-traumatic stress disorders. The forthcoming return of many refugees from abroad is expected to generate increased demand on the already overstretched programs dealing with social and psychological problems. UNHCR will mobilize support for local structures through community-based social services, together with other United Nations and nongovernmental organizations active in this field. National NGOs are becoming increasingly important as UNHCR operational partners and they will expand existing mobile services to assist groups such as isolated elderly persons suffering from psychological disorders or trauma, single-parent headed families, vulnerable women, the handicapped, and children with behavioral problems. Women who have lost their menfolk in the conflict will receive particular attention through counseling and women's support groups. In Sarajevo, for example, an SOS service and telephone line is available for persons in distress.

IMPLEMENTATION OF THE PLAN OF OPERATIONS

Beyond the progress in the design and implementation of the plan of operations highlighted above, UNHCR has also taken a number of measures to enhance its readiness to proceed. Most important among these was the transfer, in January 1996, of the Office of the Special Envoy and the Chief of Mission for Bosnia and Herzegovina and their staff to Sarajevo; the deployment of Public Information Officers and Military Liaison Officers; the relocation of the Bosnia and Herzegovina desk from Belgrade to Pale; the opening of offices in five (Serb) municipalities of Sarajevo; and the deployment of six Repatriation Officers (Sweden and Norway). A thorough review of staffing needs is also under implementation.

SUPPORT FOR THE PLANNING PROCESS REQUIRED OF HOST STATES

Planning for return and repatriation, as well as for elections will hinge upon the rapid collection of basic planning data. Whereas progress has been made in the neighboring republics to collect detailed information on Bosnian refugees, an analysis of available data from other asylum countries, notably from member states of the European Union, reveals that additional data collection will be necessary. The government of Croatia has already carried out a full registration of refugees and displaced persons. The government of the Federal Republic of Yugoslavia will begin to register refugees in Serbia and Montenegro shortly, with funding from UNHCR. **Recommendation 12: Host governments are urged to support UNHCR by carrying out such a data-collection exercise and to furnish the resulting information to the Office.**

Among the data required for planned and phased repatriation movements are numbers of Bosnians broken down according to ethnic group, place of origin and previous residence, family composition, age and gender; areas of desired return; time frame for voluntary return; percentage and category of persons at risk (*i.e.*, vulnerable groups) such as single-parent heads of household, the handicapped, the elderly, and persons undergoing psychological or other medical treatment. The Bosnian authorities at both the central and local level and UNHCR Field Offices have almost completed analogous surveys of persons displaced within Bosnia and Herzegovina, but this information must be complemented by data on potential returnees from abroad.

In the Federal Republic of Yugoslavia, Croatia, and Slovenia, detailed data are being or have been collected and will provide a comprehensive overview of the presence of Bosnians in the region. In Bosnia and Herzegovina itself, comprehensive and systematic assessments of conditions in the various municipalities where major returns are expected are being completed and/or updated. Data collection includes population figures (resident population, displaced persons currently being hosted from elsewhere, and expected returnees), the level of destruction of the housing stock and of essential community infrastructure according to preestablished criteria (water supply, roads, health, and education facilities) and constraints (security and the presence of landmines).

Additional, although partial, data will also become available with the commencement of voluntary repatriation registration. Through such registration, which also has a vital protection orientation, the voluntary nature of the individual decision to return can be verified and additional information, such as that set out above, can be collected. This data will only give a partial view of the potential pool of returnees, but is indispensable for planning organized voluntary repatriation movements.

ADDITIONAL PLANNING MEASURES

The active involvement of government representatives, intergovernmental and nongovernmental partners will be pursued at the local level and in meetings such as the High-Level Working Meeting on Implementation of Annex 7 in Oslo, Norway, consultations with Permanent Missions located in Geneva, and additional ad hoc consultations.

Owing to the critical importance of augmenting absorption capacity within Bosnia and Herzegovina in the implementation and phasing of the operation, planning sessions will continue in Sarajevo and the various field offices in the country, followed by similar processes in neighboring and other host countries. A food aid survey cosponsored by the World Food Program (WFP) and UNHCR, is being conducted by CIET, throughout Bosnia and Herzegovina. Subsequently, a joint mission by WFP, the Food and Agriculture Organization (FAO) and UNHCR, with the participation of ECHO, will assess the impact of the food component of the humanitarian assistance program and seek to improve the targeting of such assistance by moving away from blanket coverage.

LINKAGE TO LONGER-TERM RELIEF AND REHABILITATION EFFORTS

As explained above, it is well understood that UNHCR cannot and should not, acting alone or in conjunction with its partners, assume sole responsibility for addressing even the immediate and urgent rehabilitation needs facing returnee communities in Bosnia and Herzegovina. To a greater extent than in any other operation undertaken by UNHCR, return and repatriation will be conditioned by full implementation of all aspects of the Peace Agreement and, hence, by the effectiveness of other institutions. To cope with the devastating effects of the war, Bosnia and Herzegovina needs urgent investments from the international community and demonstrable progress in laying the foundation for longer-term rehabilitation of damaged economic and physical infrastructure. UNHCR's plan is therefore situated in the context of a comprehensive and coordinated operation addressing the overall short-term and mid-term rehabilitation needs of the country. UNHCR will pursue close coordination with these investments and projects so as to ensure that its initial rehabilitation activities on behalf of returnees can be transferred smoothly to and continued by other, more specialized, institutions.

Likewise, close cooperation with other institutions will be pursued to encourage initiatives to foster the earliest possible achievement of self-sufficiency by returnees and local populations. This will allow the phasing out of any initial post-arrival distribution of food aid and relief items at the earliest opportunity. It is assumed that other institutions, in coordination and consultation with UNHCR, in particular the World Bank and FAO, will assume responsibility for these important activities.

In order to enable effective planning for the prospective linking of UNHCR's limited rehabilitation activities to the overall comprehensive rehabilitation efforts by others, joint needs assessments will urgently be conducted.

SUMMARY OF INITIAL FUNDING NEEDS

The United Nations Revised Consolidated Appeal was issued on March 1, 1996, and will present to the donor community the total United Nations-agency financial needs for 1996 which amount to more than $823.2 million for Bosnia and Herzegovina and the entire region. UNHCR is requesting $353.5 million for its program for the region, of which $196.8 million is for Bosnia and Herzegovina, excluding UNHCR Program Delivery and Administrative Support costs. Funds are urgently required to meet UNHCR's commitment to the peace process and implement its role under Annex 7 of the Peace Agreement.

CROATIA

The principles of Annex 7 of the Peace Agreement also offer a valid basis for approaching the problem of the return of refugees and displaced persons in Croatia, and in Eastern Slavonia in particular. UNHCR will continue its humanitarian activities in Eastern Slavonia and will exercise its mandate to assist the voluntary return of refugees and displaced persons to this area when conditions for safe return exist. As the civilian and military components of the United Nations Transitional Administration for Eastern Slavonia, Baranja, and Western Sirmium (UNTAES) make progress in establishing such conditions, UNHCR will identify villages in the area to benefit from UNHCR assistance to promote return and reintegration. Pilot projects will be established to instill confidence in the right of displaced persons to return home. With this aim in mind, UNHCR participates in meetings of the Joint Commission, within the framework of the Office for Transitional Administration, whenever the issue of internally displaced persons is discussed.

Many houses and apartments in Eastern Slavonia to which refugees and displaced persons would like to return are currently occupied by Croatian Serbs who were displaced from Western Slavonia, the Krajina, and other parts of Croatia, including areas bordering on Eastern Slavonia such as Osijek and Vinkovci. Still others are currently occupied by Serb refugees from Bosnia and

Herzegovina. These persons will have to benefit from analogous return assistance if further displacement is to be avoided.

While Security Council Resolution 1037 of January 15, 1996, on the establishment of UNTAES confirms the right of Croatian displaced persons to return to their places of residence in Eastern Slavonia, the statement by the President of the Council dated February 23, 1996, indicates that the same principles underlying these returns also apply in the case of the Croatian citizens of Serb ethnicity now displaced in Eastern Slavonia and elsewhere. For very practical reasons, solutions will need to be found for Croatian Serbs displaced in Eastern Slavonia, and their return to their places of origin promoted, if they are to make room for returning displaced Croats. UNHCR will support the return of Croat displaced persons to Eastern Slavonia with adequate reintegration projects. It has also proposed pilot projects to the Croatian authorities in support of the planned return of Croatian Serbs to their original places of residence in Croatia.

It should furthermore be noted that some 30,000 Croatian Serbs, displaced by military offensives in the Summer of 1995, who have been granted asylum in the Federal Republic of Yugoslavia, have contacted UNHCR and expressed their desire to be repatriated. The Croatian authorities have indicated that they, in principle, welcome the return of these refugees, and 2,000 have already received an entry permit. UNHCR has on various occasions been informed by the Croatian authorities that the repatriation of their citizens of Serb ethnicity (originating from Krajina and Western Slavonia) from the Federal Republic of Yugoslavia will have to await the outcome of the process of normalization of relations between the two countries. In this regard UNHCR recalls the statement of February 23, 1996, by the President of the Security Council, calling on the Croatian authorities not to link the repatriation of refugees to the process of normalization of relations between the two countries. UNHCR stands ready to assist the authorities of both Croatia and the Federal Republic of Yugoslavia in working out the practical modalities for the early voluntary repatriation of refugees to their country of origin.

NOTE

[1]High-Level Working Meeting on Implementation of Annex 7 of the General Framework Agreement for Peace in Bosnia and Herzegovina, Oslo, Norway, March 8, 1996.

APPENDIX I

Program of the CMS Nineteenth National Legal Conference on Immigration and Refugee Policy

Ramada Renaissance Hotel, Washington, D.C.
March 21–22, 1996

Thursday, March 21

7:45 a.m.–8:45 a.m.   **Final Registration**

8:45 a.m.–9:50 a.m.

Welcome: Lydio F. Tomasi, *Executive Director, Center for Migration Studies*

Opening Remarks: **Maria Echaveste**

Administrator of Wage and Hour Division
Office of Employee Standards Administration
U.S. Department of Labor

9:30 a.m.–10:45 a.m.   **Session I**   *Thursday, Auditorium*
UPDATE ON THE STATUS OF HOUSE AND SENATE BILLS

Chair: Austin T. Fragomen, Jr.
Fragomen, DelRey and Bernsen, NY

1. **Richard Day**
   Chief Counsel, Subcommittee on Immigration and Refugee Affairs,
   U.S. Senate
2. **Michael Myers**
   Subcommittee on Immigration and Refugee Affairs, U.S. Senate
3. **Andrew Schoenholtz**
   Associate Director, U.S. Commission on Immigration Reform

11:00 a.m.–12:30 p.m.　　　　**Session II**　　　　*Thursday*
　　　　　　　　　　　　　　　　　　　　　　　Auditorium

CRITICAL ANALYSIS OF PRACTICAL IMPLICATIONS OF NEWLY PROPOSED LEGISLATION

Chair:　　Hon. Romano Mazzoli
　　　　　　Stiles & Havinson, Louisville, KY

　　1.　**Family-Based Immigration**
　　　　　• Frank Sharry
　　　　　　Executive Director, National Immigration Forum

　　2.　**Employment-Related Immigration and Nonimmigrant Admission for Employment**
　　　　　• Daryl R. Buffenstein
　　　　　　AILA President

　　3.　**Due Process Concerns**
　　　　　• Lucas Guttentag
　　　　　　American Civil Liberties Union

　　4.　**Employer Sanctions and Verification System**
　　　　　• Mary E. Pivec, Esq.
　　　　　　Washington, D.C.

12:30 p.m.–2:00 p.m.　　　　**LUNCH**　　　　*Thursday*

　　Video Presentation:　"How Legal Immigrants Strengthen America"
　　　　　　　　　　　　　　American Immigration Law Foundation

2:00 p.m.–3:30 p.m.　　　　**Session III**　　　*Thursday, Auditorium*

WELFARE REFORM PROPOSALS: WHAT BENEFITS FOR IMMIGRANTS?

Chair:　　Antonio Duran
　　　　　　Director, Migrant Health Program, DHHS

　　1.　**Changes in the Scope, Participation and Costs of Social Programs**
　　　　　• Michael Fix
　　　　　　The Urban Institute

　　2.　**New Responses to Undocumented Immigrants**
　　　　　• Stephen Legomsky
　　　　　　Washington University School of Law

　　3.　**Impacts on Health Programs and Civil Rights of Migrant Farmworkers**
　　　　　• Cynthia Schneider
　　　　　　Migrant Legal Action Program, Washington, D.C.

　　4.　**Thinking Immigration Policy in the Context of Human Rights**
　　　　　• John Isbister
　　　　　　University of California, Santa Cruz

| 4:00 p.m.–5:45 p.m. | **Session IV** | *Thursday, Auditorium* |

**REDEFINING THE ROLES OF LOCAL AND
STATE GOVERNMENT IN IMMIGRATION POLICY**

Chair: Charles B. Keely
         Georgetown University

1. **Framing the Issues: States/Cities, Federalism, and
   Global Competitiveness**
   - Anne Morse
     State and Local Coalition on Immigration

2. **Impact on the State**
   - Sheri Steisel
     *Senior Committee Director, Human Services
     National Conference of State Legislatures*

3. **Impact on the County**
   - Dr. Susan Allan
     Arlington County Health Director

4. **Effects on the Relationships between State,
   Local Government and Voluntary Sector**
   - Michael Hill
     Government Liaison, NCCB/USCC

| 6:00 p.m.–8:00 p.m. | RECEPTION AT U.S. CAPITOL | *Thursday* |

Cosponsored by the American Immigration Lawyers Association (AILA)

| 9:00 a.m.–10:30 a.m. | **Session V** | *Friday, March 22* |
| | | *Auditorium* |

REFUGEE RESETTLEMENT

Chair: Elizabeth Ferris
         Director, Immigration and Reform Program, CWS

1. **Refugee Resettlement: A View from the Administration**
   - Phyllis E. Oakley
     *Assistant Secretary of Population, Refugees and Migration
     U.S. Department of State*

2. **Legislative Developments and Refugee Resettlement in the
   Post-Cold-War Era**
   - Kathleen Newland
     Carnegie Endowment for International Peace

3. **Implications for NGO Resettlement Agencies**
   - Mark Franken
     Director, Refugee Programs, MRS/USCC

4. **New Priorities in Refugee Resettlement**
   - Ralston Deffenbaugh
     Director, LIRS, New York

Reactor: Shelly Pitterman
          Chief Resettlement Section, UNHCR

10:45 a.m.–12:15 p.m.   **Session VI**   *Friday, Auditorium*
                               ASYLUM REFORM

Chair: Sandra Lief Garrett
           Associate Vice President for Planning and Development, NYANA

   1. **Legislative Changes**
       • David Martin
         General Counsel, INS

   2. **Due Process, Asylum, and Global Stability**
       • Deborah Anker
         Harvard Law School

   3. **Group Protection vs. Individual Protection:
       Lessons from the Former Yugoslavia**
       • Anne Willem Bijleveld
         UNHCR, Washington, D.C.

12:30 p.m.–2:00 p.m.   AWARDS LUNCHEON   *Friday, March 22*
                                                    Renaissance Ballroom

Presiding: Julia V. Taft
                    President and CEO, InterAction

Invocation: Rev. Fred Kammer, S.J.
                    President, Catholic Charities, USA

Silent Tribute: The Hon. Barbara Jordan
                    Chair, U.S. Commission on Immigration Reform

Keynote Speaker: **Hon. Doris M. Meissner**
                    INS Commissioner

Honoree: **Roger P. Winter**
                    Executive Director
                    Immigration and Refugee Services of America
                    Recipient of the 1996 CMS Immigration and
                    Refugee Policy Award

APPENDIX II

Program Organizing Committee

Chairman   Lydio F. Tomasi, Executive Director
                    Center for Migration Studies of New York, Inc.

Members   Austin T. Fragomen, Jr., Esq., New York
                    Anna Grace Isgro
                    CMS Washington DC Representative
                    Charles B. Keely, Department of Demography
                    Georgetown University
                    Mark J. Miller, Department of Political Science
                    University of Delaware

ADVISORY COMMITTEE

Alexander Aleinikoff	University of Michigan Law School
Deborah Anker	Harvard University Law School
Thomas J. Archdeacon	University of Wisconsin
Frank D. Bean	Department of Sociology, University of Texas
Hans-Petter Bow	International Organization for Migration Washington, DC
Vernon Briggs	NYS School of Industrial & Labor Relations Cornell University
Jorge A. Bustamante	President, El Colegio de la Frontera Norte Tijuana
David Carliner	Carliner and Remes, P.C., Washington, DC
Fernando Chang-Muy	UNHCR Branch Office, Washington, DC

Muzaffar Chishti	ILGWU, New York
Barry Chiswick	Department of Economics University of Illinois at Chicago
Ralston Deffenbaugh	Lutheran Immigration and Refugee Program, CWS
Bishop Nicholas DiMarzio	Vicar for Human Services, Archdiocese of Newark Geneva
Antonio Duran	Immigrant Health Program, HHS
Elizabeth Ferris	Immigration and Refugee Program, CWS
Lawrence H. Fuchs	American Studies Program, Brandeis University
Dennis Gallagher	Refugee Policy Group, Washington, DC
Guy Goodwin-Gill	International Journal of Refugee Law, Ottawa
Mark Handelman	New York Association for New Americans (NYANA)
Arthur C. Helton	Open Society Institute
Stephen H. Legomsky	Washington University School of Law
Arnold H. Leibowitz	Washington, DC
Michael LeMay	California State University, San Bernardino
David Martin	Immigration and Naturalization Service
Philip L. Martin	University of California at Davis
Amy R. Novick	American Immigration Lawyers Association Washington, DC
Demetriou Papademetriou	Carnegie Endowment for International Peace, Washington, DC
Richard Parkins	Episcopal Migration Ministries, New York
Gary Rubin	New York Association for New Americans (NYANA)
Peter A. Schey	Center for Human Rights and Constitutional Law Los Angeles
Paul W. Schmidt	Board of Immigration Appeals, Washington, DC
Peter H. Schuck	Yale Law School
Frank Sharry	National Immigration, Refugee & Citizenship Forum
John Swenson	USCC Migration and Refugee Services Washington, DC
Marta Tienda	Population Research Center, University of Chicago
Michael Teitelbaum	Alfred P. Sloan Foundation, New York
Martin Wennick	HIAS, New York
Aristide Zolberg	New School for Social Research, New York

INDEX

A

Agriculture
  Commission on Immigration Reform; findings/recommendations, 13
  Farmworkers, migrant (*See* Migrant farmworkers)
  Guestworker program, necessity; Clinton Administration positions, 1
  H-2A program; Clinton Administration positions, 1
  National Agricultural Workers Survey (NAWS), 83
Allan, Susan, 113
Anker, Deborah, 149
Anti-immigrant attitudes, 140
Anti-Terrorism and Effective Death Penalty Act of 1996, 59; 156
Asylum
  See also Refugees
  Decisionmaking determinants, focus, 170
  Filing time limits, restriction, 25
  Foreign policy responses, 170
  Human rights objectives, 156; 170
  Public/private distinction, judicial, 156
  System and reforms, procedural evaluation, 149

B

Bijleveld, Anne Willem, 182
Birgisson, Gunnar, 47
Board of Immigration Appeals
  Gender-specific violence as grounds for asylum, 156
Border control/restriction, ethical validity, 91
Bosnia-Herzegovina and related regions
  Post-conflict repatriation program, recommendations; UNHCR, 182

C

California
  Merced County; services to refugees, 101
  Proposition 187 exclusions, 59; 79; 101
  Public assistance/benefits to immigrants, restriction, 59; 79
  VIS pilot program, Orange County, 36
Canada
  Spouses of permanent residents, status, 47
Citizenship
  Fourteenth Amendment, 91
  Public benefits reform legislation, impact, 59
  State and local initiatives, 101

Class action challenges, restriction/elimination, 25
Commission on Immigration Reform, U.S.
  Findings and recommendations; overview, 13; 17
  Membership, 17
Criminal penalties, 36
Croatia
  Voluntary repatriation program, Bosnia-Herzegovina; UNHCR, 182

D

Decisionmaking administrative process, immigration and asylum, 149
Deffenbaugh, Ralston, 129
Diminished procedures, 25
Discretionary relief, judicial review, 25
Due process restrictions, 25

E

Employment-related immigration/entry
  Abuse sanctions, 36
  Clinton Administration positions, 1
  Commission on Immigration Reform; findings/recommendations, 13
  Document abuse legislation, 36
  Enforcement regulations/legislation (*See* Enforcement)
  Ethical/moral policy considerations, 91
  Farmworkers (*See* Agriculture; Migrant farmworkers)
  Fraud in documentation, 36
  H-1B employers, 36
  Human rights standard, 91
  Improvement in documentation, 36
  Migrant workers (*See* Agriculture; Migrant farmworkers)
  Penalties for abuse, civil/criminal, 36
  Pilot projects for eligibility verification, 36
  Sanctions against employers; 1996 legislation, 36
  Staffing increases, federal, 36
  Verification systems, 36
  Worker training fund, 1
Enforcement
  Asset forfeiture provisions, 36
  Bureaucratic entities for employer regulation, INS; proposed, 36
  Clinton Administration, positions, 1
  Commission on Immigration Reform; findings/recommendations, 13